GOING CORPORATE

A GEEK'S GUIDE

Shailendra Kadre

ISBN-13 (pbk): 978-1-4302-3701-3

ISBN-13 (electronic): 978-1-4302-3702-0

Printed and bound in the United States of America 9 8 7 6 5 4 3 2 1

Lead Editor: Jeff Olson
Technical Reviewer: Philip Alexander
Editorial Board: Steve Anglin, Mark Beckner, Ewan Buckingham, Gary Cornell, Jonathan Gennick, Jonathan Hassell, Michelle Lowman, James, Markham, Matthew Moodie, Jeff Olson, Jeffrey Pepper, Frank Pohlmann, Douglas Pundick, Ben Renow-Clarke, Dominic Shakeshaft, Matt Wade, Tom Welsh
Coordinating Editor: Jessica Belanger
Copy Editors: Sharon Wilkey and Kimberly Burton
Production Manager: Brigid Duffy
Compositor: Mary Sudul
Indexer: Dhaneesh Kumar
Cover Designer: Anna Ischenko

Distributed to the book trade worldwide by Springer-Verlag New York, Inc., 233 Spring Street, 6th Floor, New York, NY 10013. Phone 1-800-SPRINGER, fax 201-348-4505, e-mail orders-ny@springer-sbm.com, or visit http://www.springeronline.com.

For information on translations, please contact us by e-mail at info@apress.com, or visit http://www.apress.com.

Apress and friends of ED books may be purchased in bulk for academic, corporate, or promotional use. eBook versions and licenses are also available for most titles. For more information, reference our Special Bulk Sales–eBook Licensing web page at http://www.apress.com/bulk-sales.

To

My mother, Shakuntala Kadre
and
My wife, Meenakshi Kadre

Contents at a Glance

Contents

About the Author

Shailendra Kadre has more than 17 years of industry experience, including 15 years in the Information Technology domain with services and products companies such as Satyam Computers, TCS (TATA Consultancy Services), and Oracle Financial Services Software. He has handled large customer accounts with multilocation project teams. He has also handled many large IT outsourcing deals as a bid manager. As a presales manager, he was instrumental in winning a $200 million deal for Satyam Computers. Later he worked as a transition manager from Austin, Texas, on the same assignment. He specializes in IT delivery and operations management. Kadre has also worked extensively in the manufacturing and capital markets sectors. On the technology side, he has hands-on experience designing and structuring complex web applications.

Kadre holds a master's degree in Mechanical Engineering from the Indian Institute of Technology (IIT) in Delhi. He is certified as a PMP and as a lead auditor for information security. He has published in the fields of management and IT consulting, mainly focusing on improving operational efficiencies and business transformation. He is also active as a writer and reviewer in various professional forums and trade journals. Currently, Kadre resides in Bangalore with his wife Meenakshi and two children. His hobbies include playing tennis, traveling, and photography.

About the Technical Reviewer

Philip Alexander began his career in computers back in the late 1980s while serving in the U.S. military. Since then, he has worked in both the public and private sectors in positions including engineer, project manager, principal security consultant, security architect, and IT director. He currently works for Wells Fargo Bank as an information security officer.

Philip is also an author of three books: *Data Breach Disclosure Laws – A State by State Perspective, Information Security: A Manager's Guide to Thwarting Data Thieves and Hackers,* and *Home and Small Business Guide to Protecting your Computer Network, Electronic Assets, and Privacy.* He is also an avid public speaker, and he regularly presents at security conferences around the country and abroad on a wide range of topics.

Foreword

When Shailendra Kadre asked me to write this foreword, I was truly humbled and curious. My technical expertise is negligible, so why ask me? Over the course of the time that I have known Mr. Kadre, I have learned that he possesses both exemplary technical and leadership skills—a rare combination of attributes. What I have also learned about him through the course of our association is that he embraces the fact that it is leadership that makes the difference between average and excellent in any organization. While technology is exciting, it takes the human touch to turn it into something brilliant.

This brings me to the point where I am writing the foreword to the book. The thing that drives me—that I am passionate about—is assisting people and teams to be all that they can be so that they can transform organizations and communities. The fact that Mr. Kadre honored me with the opportunity to write the foreword speaks volumes about the level of importance that he places on effective leadership. Indeed, he understands that as our dependence on technology deepens, our need for skilled leaders grows exponentially.

Our society is fraught with the most rapid change ever experienced by mankind. Archeologists know that, historically, change in human society was not measured in years, but in millennia. Each improvement in "technology" took thousands of years of slow evolution to implement.

Then, around 1900, all of that changed. Up until that time a person could expect to see little or no change in their environment during their lifespan. They knew how to plan for and react to most situations. Elders could pass on a wealth of knowledge regarding the solutions to life's challenges because those challenges were predictable. Now, the emphasis is on remaining flexible and adaptable to the ever-changing environment in order to survive.

Consider that in a single life span, a person born in 1900 saw the advent of the radio, television, cars, motorcycles, airplanes, space travel, a moon landing, genetic engineering, a cloned sheep, two world wars, computers, organ transplants and other medical miracles, an ushering in of the nuclear age, and a host of other changes both good and bad.

Technology has allowed businesses of all sizes and descriptions to accomplish things that would have been considered science fiction a short time ago. Seemingly the only boundaries of what we can accomplish are those that our own imaginations impose on us. It is truly amazing when you think that the average home computer is more powerful than what major corporations would have invested millions of dollars to acquire a few decades ago.

Yet there is a dark side to the rapid changes that technology has allowed us. With change comes uncertainty and stress. Therefore, now more than ever, organizations need strong leaders. These individuals are not the paternalistic supervisors of the past who micromanaged with a heavy hand, and who were expected to have all the answers and be obeyed without question, as described in the classical management theories.

Many people who are drawn to IT Program Management as a profession may tend to think that the technology is the focus of the skill set required to be successful. This mindset has historical roots to the time when employees were not well educated and lacked the sophistication that employees now possess. What this book informs its readers is that organizations today require strong leaders with well-developed emotional intelligence competencies. These leaders are more than just technicians who have been promoted to a position of authority. They understand that the single most important resource in any company is the people.

A client of ours recently suffered through a situation that exemplifies the necessity of strong, emotionally intelligent leadership. The organization, a midsized IT company, had a site manager who ruled with a heavy hand. The owner, who spent a majority of her time in another city at the company's headquarters, relied on the manager to keep the team motivated, to answer technical questions, and to be able to work effectively to resolve any customer concerns related to the work that his team was doing. Because of poor people skills, the company endured high employee turnover, which impacted the bottom line. Additionally, productivity suffered, as did customer relationships. The manager lacked even the basic emotional intelligence competencies, and thus the team was highly dysfunctional. After this manager was dismissed, it took nearly a year to turn the culture around and to repair the damage that he had caused. The next challenge was to locate a qualified leader to fill the position. This person needed to have not only the technical skills, but, even more importantly, the attributes necessary to work well with the staff and customers. As it turned out, this was an incredibly difficult mixture to find. There were plenty of people with the necessary technical credentials, but for the most part they lacked the leadership skills. This is a prime example of the destruction that a person who is not an effective leader can cause to a company and how difficult it is to locate that rare combination of emotional intelligence and technology expertise.

Examples of the need for the ability to lead people, not just manage them, are evident in the case studies included in this book. Whether one is responsible for managing the bidding cycle for a multimillion-dollar contract opportunity, managing a global outsourcing project, or managing the complete design cycle for the development of automotive systems, many competencies are required to affect a positive outcome for all stakeholders.

Mr. Kadre has provided valuable insights that not only will assist program managers to avoid the many pitfalls waiting to derail projects, but will also inspire confidence and help to ensure successful delivery of even the most complex of programs. The combination of systems, technology, and people skills comes together in a balance that is so often absent in many program management plans. When one brings together a logical plan with the right tools for implementation, the groundwork is prepared for successful execution. However, as is so well illustrated in the book, it takes a leader to create a team able to bring the plan to fruition. If any part is lacking, it is like a three-legged stool missing a leg.

In my experience, working with organizations from midsized to very large multinational corporations and government agencies, this balance is all too often ignored. If you, the reader, can incorporate the tools and competencies laid out here, you will find that you are a rare commodity indeed.

One of the reasons that the combination is a rarity is that it is difficult to achieve. Many people who are comfortable with part of the equation are not adept at the other. So I implore you to remember that this is a journey that continues each day that we take a breath. With each step of your journey you will learn new lessons—some of which will be quite difficult and even frustrating. The important thing is to keep moving forward and to celebrate your successes.

Rebecca Lacy

President, Pinnacle Management Group, Missouri

Foreword

Shailendra Kadre and I have worked together for many years. Together, we managed many team ramp-ups for "mega" projects. When he came to me with the first draft of this book, I was not surprised. Shailendra has been publishing papers on these topics for some time now. I have read through the book, and it's a wonderful combination of concepts and case studies—some of which I took part in.

This book will be very relevant for project leaders and project managers, and those hoping to move into these and even higher positions. Many of you will have wonderful skills in one technology vertical, or category, but severely lack knowledge on issues related to the industry/domain. As Shailendra points out, clients always want team leaders who can interact with senior business leaders in their language. And some clients, like small and medium-sized enterprises, may not talk technology all the time. They always therefore value project personnel who know their business.

This book covers many topics that a new team leader, project manager, program manager, or delivery manager should know but often does not. IT delivery is a vast topic; it requires specific management knowledge such as developing project plans and schedules, costing, and scope control. A good manager also needs soft skills for things like managing people, handling clients, grooming the team, training the team adequately, and so on. There are various fields for project managers to practice in, like delivery, transition, service delivery, portfolio management, and infrastructure, among others. IT managers can work in one or many of these areas over the course of a career. And almost every organization needs to streamline its IT operations. Things like business transformation, business analytics, and ERP are of prime importance right now. Keeping IT aligned with the business goals is another area of challenge for top IT managers. Any aspirant to top IT posts must maintain an awareness on these topics right from the beginning of his or her career as a team leader or a project manager. This book will help you do that.

The world is exploding with information, and knowledge is the key to success. Managers, right from the start, should be able to appreciate all the disciplines practiced by IT executives. Large IT deals and bid management is another area that no manager can afford to ignore. Today's IT deals run into tens and hundreds of millions of dollars. I have even seen some deals running into a couple of billion dollars. Many of these deals are managed by expert third-party consultants. Enterprise mergers and acquisitions are happening now more often than before. The needs of system integration arising due to such mergers is another area in which many managers and engineers specialize. It requires both technical and managerial skills to successfully achieve enterprise application integration on such a scale.

All these topics very realistically describe today's IT landscape and the variety of skills that an enterprising IT manager may need. This book meaningfully touches all these topics with relevant case studies taken from real-world projects. Most of the case studies are unique and published here for the first time. They are based upon the author's own experience in the IT industry.

I don't know of any other book that covers such a wide spectrum of topics with relevant case studies. Many of these topics were first-time knowledge even for me. Now I feel motivated to research further in areas like business analytics and the alignment of IT with the strategic thinking of an organization. I thank and appreciate Shailendra for bringing out this book for the benefit of all IT professionals.

Prabhakar Kanagarajan

Vice President, Mahindra Satyam Computers, India

Preface

Younger technology professionals typically get very deep into small pieces of technology and tend to ignore the business and operational aspects of their projects and products. The aim of this book is to create practical awareness of business and other topics related to operations that are important to middle management. Such awareness is essential for any IT person who would like to move into team or project leadership, management, consulting, or other, higher-level positions.

After reading this book, technology professionals should be able to appreciate enterprise architecture, delivery, and IT operations management, commercial (financial and legal) concerns, and strategic management, along with their interrelationships. The goal is to give you practical awareness of these topics and touch some issues that are important in practice but get lesser attention. It's not possible to cover each and every topic in depth, due to space constraints, and that is not the aim here. I have tried to cover the challenges in practical implementation and promote thinking in the right directions. Important concepts are explained with the help of detailed case studies. These cover such topics as business transformation, enterprise application integration, legacy transformation, and strategic management.

The overall theme behind the material in this book is as follows: Ultimately, technology professionals have to appreciate and understand business to succeed.

The target audiences of this book are technology professionals aiming for leadership and management slots, fresh graduates starting their career in the corporate world, and business management students. This book will be very useful for practicing engineers and managers as a refresher course on operational challenges encountered in the day-to-day life of executives in middle management positions.

How to Use This Book

This book is divided into two parts. The purpose of the first part is to familiarize you with the operational issues concerning an IT company or department. It starts by explaining how a project fits into the larger IT landscape of an organization. It discusses interfaces among applications and introduces the user to the concept of Enterprise IT, which takes into account the crucial business aspects of a company that too many technical people ignore. Part I also covers project management and deliveries, program management, production support and SLAs, portfolio analysis, and infrastructure elements. Part I is supplemented by two appendixes that familiarize you with a cross section of the challenges faced by IT project managers and CIOs, respectively. After reading this material, you will be able to appreciate the viewpoint of your immediate bosses and CIOs and others in executive management.

Part 2 covers topics in finance, business processes, analytics, and supply chain management. These topics are included to familiarize you with the next higher level of challenges in business and functionality and to promote thinking from a business and commercial perspective. Part 2 ends with a chapter on how to streamline IT using Service-Oriented Architecture and concepts learned throughout the book. This book starts with a generalized discussion on the same topic of achieving a lean and streamlined IT organization.

The chapters are written informally and not in typical textbook style. They include my own practical experiences and case studies—most of which come out of my experience—wherever needed.

Depending upon your familiarity with the various topics, you may want to skip some chapters and come back to them later. But I suggest you go through all the material in order, as each chapter is based on practical challenges we all face, and they contain unique case studies from the real world.

Again, the idea of the book is simple: By becoming aware of what's important to your superiors, and what's current in the industry, you will do your job better. And it will prepare you for bigger, more lucrative jobs that can amplify the positive impact you have in the companies you work for.

Please feel free to write me at shailendrakadre@yahoo.com for any suggestions and criticism.

Acknowledgments

No book is complete without the hard work and dedication of a group of people. That includes this one.

I sincerely thank Jeff Olson, my editor from Apress, who helped bring the book to its present form. He is one of the best professionals I have ever worked with. I also thank Jessica Belanger and others from Apress who were instrumental in bringing out this book. Jessica has been very cooperative and helpful throughout this effort. Technical review by Philip Alexander gets a special mention. His comments helped a lot in determining the relevance of the material presented and shaping of many concepts.

I need to mention the sacrifices made by my wife, parents, and children throughout the development of this book. Thank you for your support and understanding.

My sincere thanks to Venkat Paturi and Prabhakar Kanagarajan for their continuous guidance and encouragement during my stay at Mahindra Satyam in Bangalore.

Special Thanks

Sharad Madhav Kadre: For language support and critical reviews. He had a 40-year-long career with M.P. Government's education department. He earned an M.A. and B.Ed. from Vikram University. He has received much appreciation and honor for his English poetry.

Neena Kadre: For reviews and language support. Neena is a gold medalist from Indore University in M.Sc. Microbiology. She is currently pursuing a career in the field of English language education in Pune.

Shailesh Kadre: For contributing Chapter 14, which describes IT in vehicle development programs. Shailesh earned his master's degree in Mechanical Engineering from IIT Kharagpur. He is currently pursuing a career in CAD, CAM, and CAE with Mahindra Engineering in Pune. He has many national and international research publications to his credit in this field.

Yogesh Jain: For contributing the case study on strategic management in a ferrous foundry Yogesh is a management and quality consultant to many big industrial companies in India. He is also a serial entrepreneur now running his own consulting firm from Indore. He earned his master's degree in management from Birla Institute of Technology & Science, Pilani.

Vijay Venkatachalam: For contributing the case concerning spatial analytics in Chapter 11. Vijay is the director of Omega Analytics, Bangalore, a multimillion-dollar company spread across the globe. He earned an MBA from the Indian Institute of Management, Bangalore, and an M.Sc. in Finance from University of Strathclyde, UK.

Laxmi Narayan Sahu: For co-authoring three of the case studies. Laxmi is currently working as a delivery manager with Mahindra Satyam, Bangalore. He earned his bachelor's degree in Engineering from University of Sambalpur, Orrissa.

Milind Kolhatkar: For reviewing sections of the text for technical accuracy. Milind is currently the head of the treasury products division with Infosys, Bangalore. He earned his MBA from the Indian Institute of

Management, Ahamadabad, and his bachelor's degree in Technology from the Indian Institute of Technology, Bombay.

Srinivas D.: For reviewing sections of the text for technical accuracy. Srinivas is a Senior Delivery Manager with MindTree, Bangalore. He has global exposure in the IT and telecommunications verticals. He earned his bachelor's degree in Engineering from S.V. University, Tirupati.

Radhika Unni: For initial versions of Chapter 5. Radhika is a managing consultant with IBM. She obtained her master's degree in Business Administration from GOA University.

Pradyumna Bhat: For the book's illustrations. Pradyumna is a professional artist in the textile industry. He obtained his five years diploma in Fine Arts from Central India.

Diptesh Dasgupta: For the section on ERP testing in Chapter 12. Diptesh works as an ERP Testing Leader at GE Corporate. He has 18 years of experience in supply chain management, SAP implementation, and ERP testing. He has an MBA from ISWBM, Kolkata, India.

List of Acronyms, Terms, and Abbreviations

ABAP: Advanced Business Application Programming, a programming language for SAP

ABC: Activity-Based Costing

ADMS: Application Development, Maintenance, and Support

ADR: American Depository Receipt

APAC: Asia-Pacific Countries

API: aApplication Programming Interface

ATM: Automated Teller Machine

BA: Business Analyst

BASIS: The foundation of SAP applications, working like an operating system in the SAP environment

BCA: Business Component Architecture

BEP: Break-Even Point

BI: Business Intelligence

BOM: Bill of Materials

BPR: Business Process Reengineering

BRM: Business Relationship Manager

BT: bBusiness Transformation

CAD: Computer-Aided Design

CAE: Computer-Aided Engineering

CAM: Computer-Aided Manufacturing

CAPEX: Capital Expenditure

CD: Certificate of Deposit

CEO: Chief Executive Officer

CFO: Chief Finance Officer

CIO: Chief Information Officer

CMM: Capability Maturity Model

CMS: Content Management System

COA: Chart of Accounts

CP: Commercial Paper

CPU: Central Processing Unit (of Computer)

CRM/RM: Customer Relationship Manager

CTO: Chief Technology Officer

DAO: Data Access Object

DB: Data Base

DBA: Data Base Administrator

DCF: Discounted Cash Flow

Dev: Software Development Environment

DW: Data Warehouse

EA: Enterprise Architecture

EAI: Enterprise Application Integration

EDA: Event-Driven Architecture

EDI: Event-Driven Infrastructure

EDI: Electronic Data Interchange

E-ERP: Extended ERP

EJB: Enterprise Java Beans

EQ: Emotional Quotient

ERP: Enterprise Resource Planning

EVA: Economic Value Addition

FAB: Fabrication facility for Integrated Circuits

FDI: Foreign Direct Investment

FTP: File Transfer Protocol

GDP: Gross Domestic Product

GDR: Global Depository Receipt

GIS: Geographic Information System

GOF: Gang of Four, who pioneered run-time design patterns

GUI: Graphical User Interface

HR: Human Resources

HRMS: Human Resources Management System

HTML: HyperText Markup Language

IBM: International Business Machines

IDE: Integrated development Environment

IMS: Infrastructure Management System

IP: Intellectual Property

IQ: Intellectual Quotient

ISO: International Organization for Standardization

IT: Information Technology

ITIL: Information Technology Infrastructure Library

J2EE: Java 2 Platform, Enterprise Edition

JDBC: Java Database Connectivity

JVM: Java Virtual Machine

LDAP: Lightweight Directory Access Protocol

MBA: Master of Business Administration

MIS: Management Information System

MNC: Multinational Corporation

MOM: Minutes of Meeting

MOM: Message-Oriented Middleware

MPS: Master Production Schedule

MRP: Material Requirement Planning

MRP II: Manufacturing Resource Planning

MSA: Master Service Agreement

MVC: Model View Controller Architecture

mySAP: An all-in-one SAP business suite software program

NAB: Netscape Application Builder

NAS: Netscape Application Server

NAV: Net Asset Value

NDA: Non Disclosure Agreement

.NET: Software framework for Microsoft Windows operating systems

NPV: Net Present Value

OE/OEM: Original Equipment Manufacturer

OHRATE: Overhead Rate

OPEX: Operational Expenses

O-R Mapping-Object-Relational Mapping

Oracle Apps: Oracle Applications ERP software

P-D-C-A: Plan-Do-Check-Act, a four-step problem-solving process, also known as the Deming Cycle

PL/SQL: Procedural Language/Structured Query Language, a procedural extension language for SQL by Oracle Corp.

PM: Project Manager

PMBOK: *A Guide to the Project Management Body of Knowledge* by the Project Management Institute

PMI: Project Management Institute

PMO: Project Management Office

PMP: Project Management Professional

POC: Proof of Concept

POJO: Plain Old Java Objects

PPM: Project Portfolio Management

PRINCE2: PRojects IN Controlled Environments, a project management framework

Prod: Production Environment for Software

QA: Quality Assurance

R&D: Research and Development

RFI: Request for Information

RFP: Request for Proposal

RFQ: Request for Quotation

ROI: Return on Investment

SAN: Storage Area Network

SAP/SAP R/3: ERP software from SAP AG

SCM: Supply Chain Management

SDLC: Software Development Life Cycle

SDO: Service Delivery Organization

SLA: Service-Level Agreement

SMS: Short Messaging Service (on mobile phones)

SMTP: Simple Mail Transfer Protocol

SOA: Service-Oriented Architecture

SOAP: Simple Object Access Protocol

SOBA: Service-Oriented Business Application

SODA: Service-Oriented Development of Applications

SODA: Service-Oriented Distributed Application

SOEA: Service-Oriented Enterprise Application

SOW: Statement of Work

SPOC: Single Point of Contact

SQL: Structured Query Language

SrVP/SVP: Senior Vice President

SSO: Single Sign-On

SWOT: Strength, Weakness, Opportunity, and Threat

TOWS: Threat, Opportunity, Weakness, and Strength

TQM: Total Quality Management

UAT: User Acceptance Testing

USD: United States dollar

VP: Vice President

VSS: Virtual SourceSafe (Microsoft)

Windows NT: Network operating system from Microsoft

WIP: Work in Progress (sometimes Work in Process)

WSDL: Web Services Description Language or Web Services Definition Language

WTO: World Trade Organization

XML: Extensible Markup Language

YTD: Year to Date

IT Operational Issues

Understanding Enterprise IT

The aim of this chapter—and the book—is to enlarge our thinking sphere beyond current assignments and projects. This chapter discusses IT organization in its totality and introduces concepts like Enterprise IT Architecture and Lean IT. This chapter also discusses, in brief, business patterns, which are different from the runtime patterns we use when constructing programs. I will touch upon the concepts while keeping discussions as simple as possible—my approach throughout the book. If you wish to go into detail about any specific topic, refer to the bibliography section at the end of the book or to more advanced material specific to that topic.

As you read, remember one thing: awareness is the key as you climb the corporate ladder. If you are at the component level, it's better to know about the module. If you are at module or application level, it's better to know about the whole IT organization—including all its strengths and weaknesses. The greater your awareness, the more easily you will be able to discharge your responsibilities. And your superiors will trust you and give you more responsibilities and better jobs. It's awareness of the big picture that will motivate you to get the skill set desired for getting top managerial slots.

This entire chapter, and the entire book for that matter, is all about creating broader awareness and enhancing our thinking sphere through a judicial combination of concepts and case studies. So let's get started!

In this chapter, I first discuss how our project fits into the bigger picture of the overall IT organization. Then I'll cover some concepts relating to enterprise IT and discuss challenges to a typical IT organization. Last, I will discuss business patterns and close with Lean IT concepts.

Your Current Project Is an Important Link

Development or maintenance projects are often a small part of enterprise-wide IT systems, which contain information systems like enterprise resource planning (ERP), supply chain management (SCM), human resources management systems (HRMS) and a host of other homegrown and third-party applications. Put another way, the application commissioned on a successful completion of your project might share data and processes with many other systems in the organization. This sharing, for example, can be master data from an ERP or workflows from a Lotus Notes application. At the end of a work day, your application might be uploading tons of transaction data into a corporate data warehouse that can help the business, say by generating analytical reports on customer profiles.

As a technical team member on the project, it will help you do your job better if you understand the big picture—how your project fits in the overall corporate scene. What business problem is your assignment solving in the overall organizational context? The answer to that question may lie in the project charter. You can also ask your project manager and other senior team members. You might even request an informal seminar, led by project stakeholders, that explains how the project functions within the larger perspective. Unless the project is very sensitive or confidential, these kinds of requests will usually be appreciated and show that you are eager to develop a wider perspective.

In the case of ERP and SCM projects that have an effect on the functioning of almost an entire organization, getting a big picture view is relatively easier as the project moves on. When an ERP project goes live in production, for example, you can easily judge how your work has affected the organization. Pay attention to results; they can be unique and golden opportunities to develop a business perspective. So you need to keep your eyes open—even if you are working on a small part of a big project.

How Your Project Fits into The Big Picture

As I have just discussed, getting the big picture is very important in understanding the business aspect of your project. Let's take a look at how your piece of the puzzle fits into the whole.

- *Module or subsystems*: First, understand the module, the project you are working on. You might be using some data structures, algorithms, and probably some design patterns. Maybe it's a simple three-tier architecture having a front end, a middle tier with application logic, and a database. Or maybe it's more complex, involving messaging and e-mail with a service-oriented architecture. Naturally, many more variants in terms of complexity and architecture are possible.

- *Application or system level*: Next, ask yourself some questions that reveal how your module interfaces with other subsystems to form a complete application. How are data and processes shared? How are complex transactions getting processed across modules? How is the navigation built in across different user interfaces? What types of messages are displayed by the application to users when there is an error, while in process, and on completion of transactions? Are user interfaces intuitive enough? Do they give the same look and feel across the application? What are the different workflows, database operations, or even reports and dashboards that are integrating numerous subsystems together? These are just a few of the questions you might ask. When you answer them, you will be doing yourself a big favor and making your job easier. In addition, you'll get a firm grip on the business problem being addressed by your project. And you'll get an idea of how it fits into your organization's overall business strategy. Take some time to think through these ideas.

- *Interfaces with other systems*: Having mastered the application level, now it's time to look at your application's interfaces with other systems within and outside your organization. Your application might be heavily dependent on an ERP like SAP for master data on product codes, bill of materials (BOM), product routing, cost data, and so on. In turn, your application might be uploading transaction data like customized equipment configuration, resource utilization, and resource calendar on a real-time basis or as a batch job at the end of a business day. The exact functionality of these systems is always determined by business users or the end users, as they are called more often.

Your application might also be interfaced in a similar fashion with many other applications that are homegrown for the organization's specific processes or other third-party software, like accounting and content management systems. This is a typical scenario—a newly commissioned application shares data and workflows with other ERPs and both homegrown and third-party applications. Large corporations often have multiple enterprise-wide applications along with hundreds of homegrown and third-party systems. It's not difficult to imagine the complex web of system interfaces, interconnecting these numerous applications. Many of these applications and interfaces may be critical to the business and have 99.99 percent system uptime requirements. Anything less might translate into millions of dollars lost in revenue. Add to it the financial losses due to lost business opportunities and customer goodwill.

Again, take some time to analyze how the application you contribute to interfaces with the broader, enterprise-wide systems. Imagine the costs, infrastructure, resources, and skills required for supporting this kind of IT organization. Now you're looking at the big picture!

Understanding Enterprise IT

Developing a business perspective will naturally require a thorough understanding of how an enterprise works. You may be in the engineering sector, service sector, or any other sector; the basic elements will remain the same. Broadly, you have sales and marketing to bring in customer orders; operations to efficiently execute them; and finance, accounting, and human resources to take care of resource management and support. You can have further subdivisions like distribution, customer service, materials management, production planning, research and development, shop floor control, quality control, purchasing, administration, facilities, and so on.

These functions of an enterprise have to work in a coordinated fashion to deliver desired goods or services to the marketplace. The better the coordination, the more competitive the enterprise! So it's all about coordination and the resulting operational efficiencies when that is done well. No enterprise function can work in isolation.

Now let's turn again to IT, which is our main focus here in Part I. (In Part II, I will talk more about business and other skills.) Just as with enterprise functions, no serious IT application can work in isolation. An application has to work in coordination with other systems within the organization to produce meaningful work. Since coordination and system interfaces are so important, why not develop an enterprise or business perspective for our IT systems and projects? Let's examine something called "enterprise architecture," which can help develop that business perspective.

Enterprise architecture is not specifically an IT concept. It encompasses the relationships between business strategy, business goals, and business processes, as well as the applications, data, and IT infrastructure that supports these things. It therefore includes processes, inputs, technology infrastructure, software components, services, and personnel roles. It also includes the associations between these parts, the guiding principles that govern how the structure is constructed, and ultimately how that structure delivers business value. Software components are thus only a small part of the enterprise architecture concept. Let's examine further.

According to a recent IBM white paper,[1] enterprise architecture has four major components.

1. *Strategy architecture*: This includes business objectives, strategies, and ways to implement them.

2. *Business architecture*: This includes business services and capabilities, business locations, and organizations.

3. *Information systems architecture*: Systems that implement business processes and business scenarios. It also includes data and personnel.

4. *Technology architecture*: This includes hardware and software components used to run information systems.

This visibility helps business and IT decision makers allocate funding and implement projects that can generate the most value. Strategies, tactics, and capabilities are all governed by business policies, rules, enterprise strategy, and vision. Enterprise architecture includes functional and operational aspects. However, it does not address how a solution makes use of these functions.

---

[1] Amsden, Jensen, and White, "Actionable Enterprise Architecture Management." ftp://ftp.software.ibm.com/software/emea/de/rational/neu/Actionable_Enterprise_Architecture_Management_EN_2009.pdf , June 2009.

Figure 1-1 shows these architectural layers and their interaction. The first three layers represent strategy, business, and information architectures. The last two layers belong to technology architecture.

Figure 1-1. Enterprise IT

So how does the concept of enterprise architecture bring us closer to our goal of developing a wider business vision? It brings enterprise strategy, business, information systems, and technology, all together, into our thinking or perspective. That's in sharp contrast to our earlier way of looking at information systems. Now we can see that information systems are just a tool in the hands of business.

We have two more areas to consider before we even think of designing or implementing information systems: the organization's strategy and business architectures. We must take into account business and strategy before we come to information systems. Whenever you think of a software component, first think of business objectives and strategy. So we see enterprise architecture is a broad concept, which includes everything that is required to successfully run an enterprise—something practically impossible without our mighty information systems.

The Role of Business Patterns

As an information systems designer, you should make use of your organization's strategy and business plans as inputs. When it comes to design, we often hear of design patterns called runtime patterns. Runtime patterns are used while coding applications and they can be used again in different situations. These were pioneered by the "Gang of Four" (in *Design Patterns* (Addison-Wesley, 1994) by Erich Gamma, Richard Helm, Ralph Johnson, and John Vlissides), as they are widely referred in literature. Runtime patterns are technical in nature and much different from the business patterns that we will need to identify in our journey to develop a strong business perspective. Yet they do have some similarities: both cash in on the knowledge accumulated by our designers, and both are reusable components used in the design of information systems.

A business pattern is a set of generic models and rules used by system designers to create and define business solutions at a high level. Business patterns can be used as a common language to discuss the business architecture between functional or subject matter experts and software designers. Business patterns describe solution architecture patterns at different levels of abstraction. They are a set of reusable assets that can speed up the process of developing simple, end-to-end e-business solutions. Business patterns define, at a high level, the interaction between end users, businesses, and data. They also identify the high-level participants who may be involved in a solution.

Here's an example: think of the self-service business pattern that you find in an online marketplace like eBay or Amazon, and many other e-procurement sites. These solutions enable users to access systems directly in the form of business processes and underlying data. No intermediary like an insurance agent or a broker is involved. Another example of a business pattern is a single sign-on function that provides access to multiple back-end systems. Likewise, a collection of reusable business patterns can be used to define, assemble, and communicate a business solution quickly.

A series of business patterns are likewise available as architectural and design best practices that can be reused to minimize the overall risk of our projects. And they also help us reduce the time to market. Both line managers and system architects treat business patterns as common blueprints that facilitate their working together to arrive at more agreeable business solutions.

Challenges to Your IT Organization

As we broaden our horizon, it might help to know the typical challenges faced by your own IT organization or that of your client. As you might guess, all challenges revolve around the large number of applications and interfaces that a corporation typically has. Challenges include the following:

1. A large and disparate IT system that is "silo" based (applications are in relative isolation from each other).

2. A large number of running applications on various platforms and technologies. These include multiple ERP systems and a variety of homegrown applications developed by various business groups that have little or no interaction.

3. Exact inventory and documentation is missing.

4. Non-responsive and high-inertia IT systems make it difficult to focus on core business and new initiatives.

5. Multiple external vendors result in high management and support costs.

6. Most application knowledge resides with the vendor teams who support and maintain the systems.

7. High costs in maintaining legacy applications, which runs up to 80 percent of the total IT budget.

IT people need to be aware of these challenges to appreciate the viewpoint of their managers. They need to develop skills to overcome these challenges so that they can become managers and IT directors in the future.

Figure 1-2 depicts the typical scenario at the IT department of a large manufacturing company. There are three main ERP systems represented by vertical rectangles. Smaller systems (System A, System B, System C, etc.) interact with these ERPs through interfaces and batch processes. The system of interfaces is very complex and unmaintainable sometimes. The result is large expenditure on support and maintenance of the whole IT system.

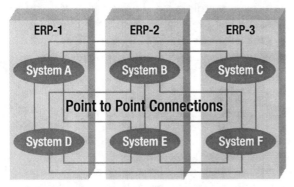

Figure 1-2. Large and complex web of applications and interfaces at ABZ

Possible Solution to Challenges: Lean IT

With all these challenges, what steps are IT organizations taking to become more responsive and business driven? Traditionally, organizations have made massive investments in IT infrastructure and incur regular expenses on maintenance, upgrades, and skilled resources. Even then systems are not responsive and agile enough to accommodate new business needs and variations in demand. Lean IT Transformation is an approach to creating agile, flexible, business-driven, and economical IT service models.

The soul of Lean IT is to minimize waste of any kind and inject small but continuous improvements into the system. It can be really rewarding for the enterprise to eliminate waste from business processes by transforming business operations and adapting to efficient and simplified functionalities. Incidentally, most of the principles in Lean IT are derived from the time-tested model of lean manufacturing and Just-in-Time manufacturing pioneered by Toyota Motor Corporation. It is also often called the Toyota Production System.

One way to create Lean IT can be to leverage the latest developments in cloud computing technology with pay-per-use and next-generation SaaS (Software as a Service)–based business models. These advances are likely to give much-wanted agility to the business and at the same time significantly reduce total cost of ownership. (However, the pay-per-use model may pose some initial difficulties for organizations with heavy investments in IT infrastructure.) A number of hosted services offered by Google and Microsoft like e-mail, Google Docs, MS-hosted Exchange, and MS-hosted SharePoint, offer much cheaper options to the corporation than hosting them in house. These services are hosted and maintained off-site by the third parties. So the cost and inconvenience of maintaining such things as infrastructure and interfaces is taken over by service providers. This allows an organization to concentrate fully on its core business, leaving the challenges of IT to competent service providers.

Current trends show corporations have already started moving towards Lean IT. Still there are challenges to realize the full benefits and to manage a smooth transition. However, with many success stories around, it's worth taking a risk and offloading some capabilities that seem to sap so much time and energy. So be a keen observer and follow the developments to lead from the front. (Note: Cloud computing is covered in-depth in Part II of this book.)

Let's compare Figure 1-3 with Figure 1-2. In Figure 1-3, the IT landscape is considerably simplified now. The number of ERPs is reduced to one from three and the legacy systems are also reduced. Now the vertical columns represent the modules or subsystems of a single ERP. This can only happen by a reorganization and business transformation in the IT department. The functionalities of many legacy applications are transferred to one ERP, and many applications are retired as a result. Interfaces are also reduced and streamlined.

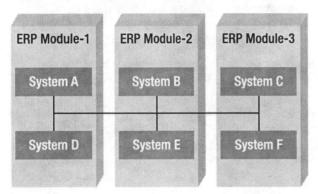

Figure 1-3. Transformed IT with only one ERP and fewer legacy systems

Short Test: Can You Answer These Questions?

Having read and thought about the contents of this chapter, you should now have an idea of how to answer the following questions as it relates to your project or assignment.

1. What is the business perspective?

2. What type of work am I doing? (Examples include development, maintenance or support, database administration, etc.)

3. What business problem am I addressing through this assignment?

4. Who are the top stakeholders in my module/project in terms of individuals and functional groups? Can I list their role in my project and how they affect me?

5. What is the monetary value of my efforts?

6. Can I list the business challenges faced by line managers in my functional area? Is the current system adequate enough to address those? If not, what changes are required?

7. Do I fully understand the enterprise architecture concept?

8. How could some of the principles of Lean IT aid my work and the organizational results?

Summary

This chapter overviewed your job efforts in the larger context of enterprise IT. The quest to develop a business perspective starts with looking at the project's connections with the business and the overall IT organization. IT needs to be seen as a tool to enable the organization to reach its goals. All IT projects and investments have to be driven by business objectives. When that happens, business executives see IT organization as a true companion that helps them in achieving objectives, and not, as is too often the case, as a stumbling block. This can happen when we, as technology experts, start appreciating the business perspective of a project.

It might be interesting for you to keep a close watch on the evolving field of enterprise architecture, which beautifully blends business with IT and involves everything that makes IT more effective in achieving business goals. There are a number of online groups that discuss and contribute positively to the emerging art of enterprise architecture. Simply being present in the discussions at CIO.com (www.cio.com) and LinkedIn (www.linkedin.com) can make a difference.

Case Study: Migration from NAB to J2EE Architectures

Over the years, there have been numerous software builds designed to upgrade older systems, but they have resulted in a patchwork of inconsistent and, at times, incompatible processes. System migrations can pose a lot of challenges to IT managers: their need may be questioned by company leaders; they need high budgets in terms of support and maintenance; and they may not be well interfaced with other systems (silos).

But systems can be replaced with newer and more efficient applications that align well with an organization's strategy and newly developed enterprise architectures. New business integration patterns are being introduced with an attempt to simplify overall IT operations.

The case that follows presents an example of what goes into a major IT overhaul—and what the $1 million price tag buys in terms of efficiency.

The Case

ABZ is a capital equipment manufacturing company headquartered in California. It has manufacturing facilities and sales offices all over the globe. The company's IT organization has an annual budget close to $30 million, with a large workforce of managers, developers, and contractors. During the late 1980s, it spent thousands of work hours developing an array of applications supporting its post-manufacturing activities. These applications were used for tracking labor availability against demand, time tracking, configuration data for tools, human resources (HR) records, skill data on engineers, facilities management, and tool warranties. The applications were developed by university students and freelancers, so they lacked a structured approach.

Many software development platforms were used for these applications, including the Netscape Application Builder (NAB), which was supported only on Windows NT. With Microsoft withdrawing support from the Windows NT operating system, it was imperative for ABZ to migrate these applications. Otherwise, it faced a huge risk in putting crucial corporate data and processes on the back of a technology no longer supported by its vendor. The applications originally developed using NAB were migrated first to J2EE (Java 2 Enterprise Edition) and ultimately to SAP in 2008. This case study deals with application portfolio migration to J2EE.

Note: There is another case study later in the book that deals with business transformation and migration to SAP.

The Need for Migration

The biggest factor governing migration was the fact that the NAB tool was restricted to Windows NT, for which Microsoft no longer provided support. Work-arounds like VMware were no longer an option and had been causing performance degradation. The organization therefore made a policy decision to move all development and production environments to Windows XP. NAB's development environment was not supported on XP, and the NAB tool had many proprietary application programming interfaces (APIs) and, further, was not based on open standards. Standard features like database connection pooling and database clustering were absent. Also missing were implicit transaction management and exception handling. The only major factor that supported the continued use of NAB was its integrated development environment and strong implicit support of Model-View-Controller (MVC) architecture. But with Windows NT support withdrawn, these features became irrelevant. With Java Server Pages (JSP) becoming a reality in J2EE, developing the presentation tier became a better option than NAB.

Migration to J2EE was thus a natural choice. It was platform independent and thousands of mission-critical applications were running on it across the globe. Given the similarities among applications, there were also opportunities to save money by reusing some code. Plus, the code and logic of applications developed using NAB were fully readable by J2EE developers. By that time, J2EE had a good pool of trained developers, a lot of knowledge base in terms of design patterns, and experience with many applications. Lots of open source applications that were compatible with J2EE were also available. Unlike NAB, working with J2EE technologies offered no possibility of getting locked in with a single vendor.

Figure 1-4 represents the application architecture prior to transformation. It is a three-tier MVC architecture that is based on a proprietary Netscape application server. The terminology specific to Netscape is explained next.

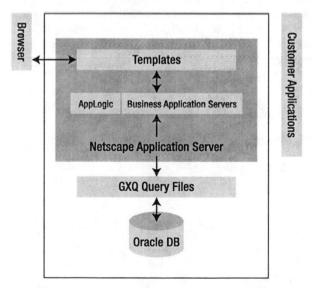

Figure 1-4. Existing customer applications with NAB architecture

HTML **templates** are used to dynamically generate the content used in the presentation tier. There is a Template Engine that can also dynamically generate templates based on the type of data. **AppLogics** are Java files that are designed in such a way to represent only one business component. AppLogic files handle input data, access the database, and do the process to generate data to populate the HTML templates. **Business objects** implement the business rules that are used by AppLogics. These business rules are defined per the application requirements. **The GXQ Query files** manage the interaction between Netscape Application Server applications and back-end data sources. These query files are called from AppLogic or business logic components.

Proposed Architecture

A simple J2EE-based three-tier architecture was found to be the best solution to the problem. This MVC-based architecture was simple, proven, and already used in thousands of applications across the globe. It was highly scalable to accommodate the growing needs of the organization. It supported application and database server clustering. Loosely coupled layered architecture helped ensure high maintainability. The business tier and Data Access Objects (DAO) could later be replaced by technologies like EJBs (Enterprise Java Beans) and object-relational (O-R) mapping tools.

The following industry standard design patterns and constructs were used in building the system. This further added to performance, standardization in construction, and maintainability.

- Value Object Pattern

- Data Access Object Pattern

- Business Delegate Pattern

- Singleton Pattern for Caches

- Façade Pattern

- Service Locator Pattern

- Front Controller Pattern

- Role-Based Security

- Database Connection Pooling

- Data Transfer Hash Map

- Data Transfer Row Sets

The legacy application was enormous but relatively simple in business logic. Huge graphical user interfaces (GUIs) interacted with databases, with very little processing in between. The application was very mature and there was very little scope for further evolution. This all indicated the need for simple but robust architecture that was fulfilled by a proposed simple, three-layered MVC-based architecture (see Figure 1-5). There was no need for distributed architecture with EJBs.

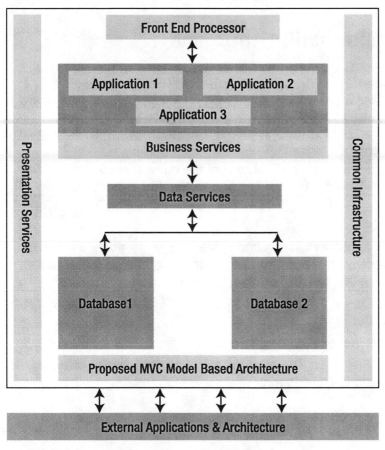

Figure 1-5. Proposed J2EE architecture: logical view

To connect to the database, the choice between using JDBC (Java Database Connectivity) or O-R mapping tools needed to be made. O-R mapping tools are known to automate the query writing and other features required to connect the business layer to the database. In this case, most of the database queries were already available in the existing legacy applicator, so the automation feature of O-R mapping tools was not desired. The queries were too complex for any O-R mapping tool to handle. So the option of DAO was chosen to work with JDBC, despite the increased length of code that needed to be written manually. The DAO layer provided a desired loose coupling between the business logic and the database. Later on it was possible to migrate to any advanced O-R mapping tool.

The Transformation Approach

The three-tier MVC architecture of NAB was replaced by a similar three-tier J2EE architecture. In the modified architecture, the front-end component of NAB was mapped to JSP, the middle tier to Java classes, and the database queries to JDBC-based Java Data Access Objects. Table 1-1 provides a mapping between NAB and J2EE components. The following list describes the exact component mappings.

- JSP-based Presentation Tier to replace current NAB Templates/PresentationGX tag support in JSP is not available

- NAB Templates to be converted to use standard JSP tags and syntax

- Using struts in the Presentation Layer to ensure adherence to MVC architecture. There are many standard design patterns that are built into its standard struts framework

- Redesign the NAB AppLogic components to Java classes of J2EE Business Tier

- NAB's Data Access logic to be migrated to J2EE's JDBC APIs

- Resource Tier (DB): The strategy to reuse the existing stored procedures and DB schema

Table 1-1. NAB to J2EE Component Mapping

Architecture Layer	Existing NAB/NAS Components	Replaced J2EE Components	Description
Presentation Logic	AppLogic	JSP/Struts	"Controls the application's interface to the user by processing requests, generating content in response, and formatting and delivering that content back to the user."[2]
Presentation Layout	HTML template	JSP	"JSP are HTML pages that contain embedded Java, and thus are much more versatile and powerful than existing HTML templates."[3] They form the User Interface component of the application.
Business Logic	BussLogic	Java Classes in the Business Tier	Controls business logic. These Java classes allow business logic to be continual across calls. They offer improved caching, and also work with JDBC for making database transactions.
Data Access Logic	JDBC (without the Connection Pooling feature)	JDBC APIs (Connection Pooling feature)	"Controls database storage and retrieval. The JDBC API is available to all Java components."[4] All database transactions are usually controlled by the Business Tier Classes.

Outcome of Transformation

This transformation exercise represents hundreds of such technology upgrade projects across the globe that are undertaken to improve business processes in an organization. With the NAB-based application, the client was at risk of running its mission-critical business processes on an obsolete technology platform. This exercise not only provided a required technology

---

[2] Oracle, "API Specifications," http://www.oracle.com/technetwork/java/api-141528.html.

[3] ibid.

[4] ibid.

upgrade but also provided a golden opportunity to upgrade the obsolete business process to global standards. Application interfaces to other systems were simplified and the overall maintainability of the application was also improved.

The following points summarize some of the benefits that were immediately realized as a result of this upgrade.

1. Moved application from obsolete NT to the higher versions of Windows

2. Adopted an open standard, robust and scalable J2EE architecture

3. Easy availability of skilled resources and easy maintainability

4. No locking with a single vendor

5. Code reuse

6. Utilized the experience and knowledge base of thousands of existing J2EE installations

The company's business leaders were very appreciative of the outcome. The huge risk of carrying critical applications on an obsolete technology platform was mitigated. The J2EE-based application introduced measurable performance improvements for end users. Due to the availability of skilled resources in J2EE, maintenance and enhancements were no longer an issue. The company expected to see monetary savings and improved business processes.

Project Management

A Different Perspective

As an IT professional, when you advance in your career you might find yourself handling modules of software projects instead of the software components that you handled at the beginning of your career. The next logical career step may be to become a team leader, where you may find yourself talking directly to senior managers and clients. Now you may need a formal plan and a schedule for your activities; simply keeping them in your head may not help any longer. You will also need good people- and client-handling skills. And of course managing stress will be even more important for you now. These all are logical acts that you may have to go through in your journey to take the next step—becoming a project manager.

To make your job easier as a project manager, a formal training in project management skills may be of immense help. This training covers topics in managing scope, planning, scheduling, budgeting, human resources, and reporting.

There are vast project management training resources available in the form of classes, online tools, and books. This chapter takes a slightly different route and covers some topics that are not readily available but are still vital to your success as a project manager. I start with the business perspective of project management and cover the importance of understanding project domain, end users, project financials, intellectual property, and regulation. Later I briefly touch upon agile methodologies, Project Management Office (PMO), and how to choose project management tools. Change management and transition are also discussed since they are skills that every project manager needs.

The chapter ends with a discussion on emotional intelligence and soft skills, and an interesting case study in which a project team finds itself in the right position after developing an understanding of a client's business.

The Project in a Larger Business Context

A project might be defined as a "temporary endeavor undertaken to create a unique product, service or result."[1] Please note that every project is defined as a temporary phenomenon that has a definite start and a definite end. The scope of a project is often specified in a contract that is dictated by business requirements. That's one reason technical team members are now expected to appreciate the business side of a project along with the technical aspects. A clear understanding of organizational goals and how projects contribute to them is necessary not only to the success of projects, but also necessary for technical team members themselves to succeed in their future endeavors. In addition, increasing organizational pressures for cost and quality improvements have also contributed to this changing environment. The message is clear, especially if you want a better job: every team member needs to think about his work in terms of the business context. Close customer relationships and quicker turnaround times, once strategic advantages, have now become norms. For project team members, all this translates into developing a thorough understanding of technology and business alike, in order to withstand the competition—and get ahead at work.

Understand Domain

Customers value professionals who understand their business. In all cases, a project will be addressing a business problem that can involve one or more functions, like manufacturing, finance, sales, distribution, or logistics. These functional areas are also called business domains. As a technical team

---

[1] PMI, *A Guide to the Project Management Body of Knowledge*, Fourth Edition. (PA: Project Management Institute, 2010).

member, if you know the domain, you can establish a meaningful dialogue with end users to understand their functional requirements on a firsthand basis. At the beginning of the project, end users are often not clear about exactly what they want. As a domain expert, you can help shape the requirements and gain control right from the beginning. Otherwise, you may completely lose control of the scope and, eventually, the project.

Gaining control of system specifications right from the beginning is handy when alterations are later suggested. In such a case, you may be in a position to optimize the changes and bring substantial cost savings to the project. In maintenance and support projects, for example, understanding the domain is particularly important as changes come only to a small portion of software but the overall impact to the business might be much larger. This is because the affected portion of the software may be a small piece of code that represents a critical part of a business process.

Understand Users

Developing applications from the point of view of the end user is a vital part of developing the business perspective of the project. It's the end users who will judge the success or failure of a project. User experience planning and developing an application prototype are very important steps in understanding the users, their business, and other, less obvious needs. As technology leaders, we need to understand our end users thoroughly. These users may be schoolchildren, teachers at various levels, corporate and government employees, job seekers, commercial artists, patients with various health issues, civil servants, taxpayers, politicians, or any other group. Like all individuals, they use our information systems in many different ways and for a variety of reasons.

Another important aspect that needs to be understood is user experience design, which is aimed at the user's satisfaction or success with applications. A good design is one that is pleasing to the overall experience of the user. Everything counts: look and feel, interface, technology, hardware, response time, and how it works. That's why details like structure, borders, labeling, icons, and buttons are so important to get right. A good design is a summation of every element used in the design, construction, and testing of an application.

The better we develop an understanding of end users and their requirements, the better we will be in a position to satisfy their needs. And we need to think ahead. With advances in technology, we are able to design applications with greater scope and functionalities. With each passing day, more and more customers use our applications in more and more ways. All of these factors must be taken into account while designing the user's experience.

Note: User experience design is a separate field in itself and, usually, specially trained professionals are required to design and develop application interfaces. This note is included here so that we all understand and appreciate this important aspect in our projects, one that is often underestimated.

Project Financials: Cost, Budgets, and Profits

As technical leaders, we often hesitate to look at the financial side of the project coin. Actually, as technical leaders deeply involved in the project, it's easier for us to appreciate the financial aspects than anybody from the outside.

We can describe project financial management as any managerial decision (or action) taken to meet or surpass budgeted revenues and earnings, or improve cash flow. It also encompasses ensuring the correctness and integrity of the financial data that goes into corporate accounting systems and compliance with laws, and other relevant standards and regulations that relate to finance, costing, and general accounts.

Project costs can be divided into direct and indirect costs. Direct costs can be attributed directly to a project, like the costs of direct labor, material, and so forth. Direct costs also include subcontract costs. Indirect costs include training and other overhead items that can't be easily assigned to a single project. They are, rather, proportionally divided among all participating projects. Projects may have multiple rates for overhead. They can be based upon a variety of factors, like infrastructure-related costs or costs pertaining to security requirements.

Another financial aspect of project management relates to pricing and the difference between forward pricing rates and billing rates. Forward rates, or bidding rates, are developed for pricing new contracts. Billing rates, on the other hand, are used for invoicing. Billing rates are usually approved by the customer for carrying out contracted work.

Project profitability is the single most important metric used by project managers to demonstrate project performance. Variations in the utilization of resources, cost allocations, and unbilled accounts receivable are some of the inputs that can cause profitability to fluctuate.

The definition of budget remains the same in all contexts, including projects. For our objectives, a broader definition of budget can be more useful. I find the definition given in Wikipedia very relevant: "A budget is a formal translation of organizational plan to monetary terms. It provides an estimate of planned revenues and expenditures. Budget enables the actual financial operation of the business that can be measured against the forecast."

Now the exercise for you is to visualize this definition in the context of the project that you are working on. Good luck!

Intellectual Property (IP) and Other Regulatory Aspects

Nowadays at the workplace, creating inventions and other intellectual property (IP) have become common phenomena. Almost every project deals with IP, and many create it, so managing IP is an integral part of a project manager's day-to-day responsibilities. In order to safeguard your company's interest, you must have an awareness of IP laws. You must ask: Can my project be patented? If yes, how? What are the advantages of a patent? How much will be lost to the competition if I don't patent or copyright the work? Getting an answer to these questions is needed for your survival and growth as a professional.

It's common for companies to have their employees sign an agreement that states that any invention created while working for the company belongs to the company. And you also need to be sure you do not misuse or appropriate another company's IP—doing so can get you and your company into a lot of trouble.

Intellectual property laws grant owners certain special rights to their intangible assets. This type of IP includes music, literary work, words and phrases, symbols, artwork, designs, discoveries, and inventions. IP is legally protected in the form of patents, trademarks, copyrights, trade secrets, and industrial design rights.

*   *Patents* are a set of exclusive rights given for an invention. These rights are given for a limited period and in turn, inventors are required to disclose their inventions to the public.

- *Trademarks* are used by individuals and businesses to distinguish their products and services from that of others. A trademark can be very important in uniquely identifying a company's products and services when used in promotional campaigns. Individuals and businesses can devise their own unique trademarks and get them legally registered so that nobody else can use them.

- *Copyrights* are a set of exclusive rights (for copy, distribution, and adaption) given to the author of an original work. Examples of original work include articles, songs, or an illustration. The copyright doesn't protect the original idea, only its expression.

- *Trade secrets* are confidential or classified pieces of information that are generated by a business and very important to its survival, competitive advantage, or business activities. This information can be business processes, technology, designs, formulas, and so on.

- *Industrial design rights* are exclusive rights over a pattern, creation of a shape, combination of colors, or multidimensional forms of artistic or industrial value.

Contract terms, detailed in a contract statement of work (SOW), are another important aspect for techies to comprehend. The SOW may include applicable government regulations. Contract terms and conditions decide the course of the project and are legally binding. They include the specifications of products and services, payment terms, and many other operational conditions. While contract terms are mutually agreed upon between a buyer and seller, regulations are the requirements imposed by a government body. Regulations often affect the characteristics of products and services. SOWs can also have administrative provisions to ensure the government-mandated compliance for these products and services.[2]

Traditional vs. Agile Project Management

In hierarchical environments, many project managers act mainly as coordinators rather than managers in a true sense. Today's project managers more often need to collaborate with teams to work on challenges

---

[2] PMI, *A Guide to the Project Management Body of Knowledge,* Fourth Edition. (PA: Project Management Institute, 2010).

posed by projects. The software development paradigm is clearly shifting towards more flexible development styles offered by agile methodologies.

Methodologies used in the manufacture of electronic hardware during the 1970s formed the basis for what are called "waterfall" models. Power and progress flow downhill to a well-defined end. Hardware manufacturing, for example, is normally done as a series of operations. Typical steps include conceptualization, feasibility study, high-level design, detailed design and drawings, manufacturing, and testing. These activities don't normally interfere with one another. An activity down the line starts only after the previous activity is finished. The waterfall model is very structured and rigid in approach. In using this model, software development was also approached in a very traditional, segmented, and bureaucratic way.

In the 1990s, agile methodologies became popular. Instead of the firm development schedules characteristic of waterfall models, these methodologies adopted multiple, iteration-based schedules. In this methodology the entire development task is divided into multiple iterations. Each iteration is equivalent to a small software development project. All iterations in an agile development go through the phases of design, construction, and testing. The emphasis is to improve outputs with every stage of iteration. The design is never frozen, and it's kept open till the last minute to incorporate any new ideas that may come up. The speed of delivering a working program is very important in agile models.

With agile project management, overhead and documentation are reduced to the bare minimum. Teams are usually cross functional, closely knit, flat in hierarchy, and self-organizing. More and more organizations are now shifting to agile methodologies for software development.

Agile models are superior to waterfall models in efficiency because they respond swiftly to the changes in design and business requirements, which are ground realities in any software development project. Already more than one third of all software development projects are based on agile models. And the number is increasing very rapidly.

Project Management Office (PMO)

According to a 1995 Standish Group Chaos Report, more than 90 percent of large IT projects miss schedules, cost, and quality goals. Only 9 percent of large, 16 percent of medium, and 28 percent of small projects could be completed within stated goals of time and budget and were measured to give desired business benefits.

There are many reasons for such failures. As a KPMG survey of 252 organizations pointed out, technology is not the most critical factor in achieving project goals. "Inadequate project management implementation constitutes 32 percent of project failures, lack of communication constitutes 20 percent and unfamiliarity with scope and complexity constitutes 17 percent. Accordingly, 69 percent of project failures are due to lack and/or improper implementation of project management methodologies."[3]

Many organizations set up a PMO to effectively address these challenges. If the same surveys were carried out today, the percentages might differ. The figures as they are presented here still show us trends that have not changed over the years.

The PMO owns the project management process in an organization. That means it defines, maintains, and standardizes procedures. It is a centralized body that keeps control over all projects and resources. PMO tasks may include the active monitoring and reporting of projects (to top management and other stakeholders), resource optimization, follow up and coordination for all active projects, help in strategic decision making, and help in decisions on closing projects.

Typically, a project manager reports the project's progress to the PMO. Thus, a PMO's function, basically, is to ensure optimized utilization, take advantage of the economies generated by repetition across projects, and act as a single point of contact for all projects within the organization. PMOs may also participate at the strategic management level. Project portfolio management is also a responsibility of the PMO at this level.

A clear understanding of PMO functioning is required because it has an effect on your day-to-day working life as a project manager or a team leader. In some companies, even resource allocation is managed by the PMO. It's likely the PMO that assigns you to your next project. Process standardization and reporting are an integral part of a PMO and they have a huge effect on you as an IT professional. PMO as an entity is important to you, it's important to your managers, and above all it's important to the whole organization.

---

[3] Wikipedia, "Project Management Office," http://en.wikipedia.org/wiki/Project_management_office.

Project Management Tools That Can Help You

The following is based upon my correspondence with my colleague from Canada, Yuri Tan, P.Eng. Yuri is a seasoned project management professional who has successfully handled many critical software projects for many companies in North America.

Note: Tan's reference to "tool" means project management software (like Microsoft Project), which prepares schedules, tracks budgets, allocates resources, and so on.

I will suggest that you review each suggestion (from your peers) on a project management tool very, very carefully to determine how it fits your processes.

Your processes are unique to your organization; no other organization anywhere has quite the same processes. So what may work for one organization may not necessarily work for you. Your organization developed its processes to suit your particular corporate culture, the particular collective character attributes of the employees (their experience, etc.), the type of projects that you execute, and the particular types customers/clients that you have (especially the regular ones).

You now have to make sure that the tools you choose work for you and your particular processes. Do NOT change your processes again to suit whatever workflow (process) is dictated by the fancy tool that the fancy salesman sold to you; you are likely to find that the tool-dictated workflows do not work that well in your organization, with the result that the employees will give up following processes and/or give up using the tool, throwing everything into chaos again.

Be careful if you are looking at tools that offer to do a number of different functions or can be made to do any function you want it to do. They seldom do the job that you bought it for particularly well. For example, I have worked with a tool that was advertised as a combination issue tracking and defect/bug tracking tool. It was used as a defect tracking tool but it was very poor; it was tremendously difficult to make it prepare useful reports. A hand-written tool set up in a spreadsheet (e.g. Microsoft Excel) or database (e.g. Microsoft Access) would have worked better.

That said, there are tools out there that are specific to one particular function but do offer flexible workflows – they may be modified to match whatever processes your organization already follows. Take a look at those.

—Yuri Tan, P.Eng.

If your organization has just started to organize the project management processes and establish a PMO, it usually means processes and other related areas are not yet explicitly defined. So there may be a huge risk trying to adopt an integrated and centralized project management system. It is more likely to offer you a very comprehensive and complex, but expensive solution—if your problems are still not defined completely. Companies often do *proof-of-concept* (POC) testing to try out a new product or application before making full deployment—a wise policy.

A more efficient approach to the selection of a project management tool should be iterative, incremental, and adaptive in nature. This means to begin with, you should use simple, less expensive tools with limited scope. These include tools with the basic functionalities of WBS (Work Breakdown Structure), scheduling, traceability (the ability to pinpoint responsibility), and custom datasheets. These tools should have the capability to exchange data with more commonly used Microsoft tools like Excel, Project, and Word. The processes are likely to mature over time and you will then know the real effectiveness of these basic tools in the context of company requirements. That may be the time to analyze and switch to more integrated solutions.

There are numerous open source and established project management tools available and, as discussed earlier, each one may need to be analyzed to determine its fit in the context of your company's requirements. The best way is to ask other professionals what tools they are using to manage projects, and their experiences while using them. Searching the web and simply picking a project management tool for use in your organization may be a little adventurous. There are places, however, to start your search. Please refer to references for this chapter in Appendix C.

Things Project Managers Need to Care About

Every project is a new challenge for any project manager. Experience helps, but a new project often brings along a new team, new clients, new bosses, and a new problem to solve. The only thing constant is change. So your ability to cope with new people and new situations becomes very important here. Let's discuss some common challenges that are inevitable for any project manager.

Project objectives. In the beginning, project objectives are not always clear. The project manager needs to determine what portions of a project are not clear to the team and other stakeholders, and note feedback and questions that come up. Project objectives and goals needs to be tightened, documented and made available to the team. Project objectives must be in line with strategic and business goals of the organization in order to get required attention from the top management.

Deadlines. Sometimes the deadlines imposed are not based upon actual time estimates or efforts, but other factors like the end of the quarter, the budget cycle, the boss's vacation, and so on. Some are more compulsory, like regulatory compliance or marketing events.

In cases where the project manager has a choice, the stress of firm project schedules and other project issues needs to be handled by managing expectations, creative planning, and finding alternative ways. In addition, the project manager needs to see that deadlines are linked to higher-level organization objectives, and that the project schedule is coordinated with the schedules of other dependent projects.

Managing risks. A project may have many risks that can be broadly categorized as technical, external, organizational, or project management risks. More specific examples are project dependencies, performance, and resource and funding risks. Once a project team qualitatively determines the potential risks, attempts can be made to determine their probability of occurrence and cost impact. And the project manager can begin to think about how best to avoid those risks or accept them as part of conducting business.

Most project plans have risk-management sections, which contain the risk data based on the analysis done before the start of the project. Beyond that, no risk analysis takes place until an issue occurs. There are many strategies to implement risk management, including mitigation, transfer, alternative analysis, and simple acceptance. Risk "transfer" means delegating risk management to a vendor through a contract. In effect, you transfer risk to a third party. In risk-mitigation strategies, we aim to reduce both the probability of occurrence and the impact.

Team skills and nonperformance. Starting with the project manager role, the core set of skills required to accomplish the expected workload needs to be documented and honestly compared to the skills of the probable team members. Using this assessment, project managers can get better performance by conducting training sessions, bringing in consultants, and adding resources. In the case of nonperformance, it may not be wise to blame an employee until you get the full story. An employee might be trying to do the right thing per his understanding, but chances are he has not received the proper training or directions to effectively perform the task.

Communicating with End Users

The effective communication of a project's progress, challenges, and issues relevant to end users and other stakeholders is very important for the smooth functioning of any project. Teams become so focused on deadlines, deliverables, and day-to-day challenges that this important aspect of communication often gets neglected. Regular meetings involving important stakeholders are required. Well-planned meetings serve as forums to exchange information and gather feedback in a timely manner. Communicating will help you avoid any surprises that may arise when the final product is being delivered.[4]

Project Communication

In a project, much of the communication and instructions are verbal. They are understood in that moment but the details get lost as the time passes. Communication might be supported by e-mails and meeting minutes that convey messages with the proper context needed to comprehend and execute them. It helps if team expectations are set from the beginning. It increases the confidence level of team members, as they will know exactly what they are expected to do. In the same context, maintain in writing any thoughts on project functionalities, use of technology, and project planning, especially those with numerous details. Otherwise, it might be impossible to recall.[5]

A project communication plan is another important tool that contains how, when, and in what form you will communicate with your team, client, and other stakeholders. It will help if the plan is presented in pictorial form and includes the names of artifacts (plans, templates, etc.) that are needed for

---

[4] Rick Cusolito, PMP, "Common Challenges Project Managers Face and Tips for Solving Them," http://www.butrain.com/project-management-training-courses/project-manager.asp.

[5] Gina Lijoi, "Effective Project Communications," http://www.projectsmart.co.uk/effective-project-communications.html.

quality communication. A table or a chart, for example, can state that the team will have weekly Monday meetings. Minutes of the last team meeting, along with an "action taken" report can be used as inputs. A client issue log and a listing of internal action items that have come up during the week are also required. If any party finds the current plan ineffective, let them suggest alternatives. This can best happen when communication strategies are formally laid out in writing.

Transition and Change Management

At the implementation phase of an IT project, you typically have new software and business processes that need to be implemented among a group of users. This implementation brings about a change over older habits and systems. And to be successful, changes must be introduced gradually rather than imposed suddenly. Plan for a transition period and transition processes. This transition and change needs to be managed effectively for every project. And it's an integral part of a project manager's portfolio of responsibilities.

End users that are affected by change may be inside or outside your company. If they are inside, a project manager might be involved directly in the implementation of change and transition plans. If the end users are customers, a project manager may indirectly assist the client's managers in successful transition. A project manager may even be stationed at the client's premises (along with key members from his team) until the project is fully implemented and transition successfully occurs.

Any change always brings with it an array of challenges. Managing it in a large corporate environment is even more challenging. Change management can be crucial, for example, in an SAP implementation, or say in a business transformation exercise. It's a very important aspect even in the outsourcing of projects. In the context of this book, it would help if we see change from a larger project perspective.

Transition and change are two very closely linked phenomena.

Change can have two physically distinct states: "as is" and "desired." From an employee point of view, transition may be more psychological than physical. Employees need to adjust to the new situation, and it may take some time. That time can be reduced with proper planning and facilitation. To successfully make a change, employees have to leave the past, something that can be done gradually at best. In the corporate context, transition starts where a project making a transformation ends.

There are three important phases in any change-management exercise:

1. Prepare vision and planning for change management.

2. Communicate the vision and implement change management.

3. Get the feedback and make a corrective action in plan and implementation.

A well-thought vision needs to drive the change. Effective communication and frequent dialogues are required with all stakeholders to overcome any possible resistance to the transformation. Management must ensure the quality of communication and see that everybody feels motivated to change.

If a change is going to succeed, the forces driving the change must overcome the forces resisting it. You must create in others the confidence that the benefits of the change outweigh the costs.

Management must also succeed in setting up a sense of urgency and motivation among all stakeholders. That's the only way you will carry out transformation successfully.

Figure 2-1 pictorially represents the three states in change management. The transition state is temporary as shown, and it leads to the future or the desired state.

Figure 2-1. Current, transition, and future states

Emotional Intelligence

Apart from technical skills, soft skills like good communication and interpersonal skills also play a vital role in the success or failure of a project. The effectiveness with which a team works, and the overall work environment can be deciding factors as well. If a project manager has an effective handle on these parameters, the chances of success increase.

Let's discuss emotional intelligence (EI)–based training practices that are emerging as a standard across the IT industry for enhancing individual and team performance.

Workplace and personal life skills like getting along with others, constructive self-confidence, motivating others, teamwork, and managing stress are categorized as emotional intelligence (EI) or emotional quotient (EQ). Categorized under intelligence quotient (IQ) are cognitive abilities like the ability to learn or understand, dealing with new situations, reason, applying knowledge, logic and analytical skills, and so forth. Anyone can learn or enhance EQ-related skills with training, but IQ is something that doesn't change significantly for an adult.

The Consortium for Research on Emotional Intelligence in Organizations is the world's leading authority and on emotional intelligence. It undertakes research projects on emotional intelligence. The existence of such an organization shows the increasing importance of emotional intelligence in the corporate world. Corporate training programs are increasingly influenced by emotional-intelligence-based models. I took the following excerpts from a Consortium technical report to substantiate how organizations are using EI-based models in executive development.

> *Developing emotional competence requires that we unlearn old habits of thought, feeling, and action that are deeply ingrained, and grow new ones. Such a process takes motivation, effort, time, support, and sustained practice. . . . Organizations increasingly are providing training and development that is explicitly labeled as 'emotional intelligence' or 'emotional competence' training. However, the EI models apply to any development effort in which personal and social learning is a goal. This would include most management and team development efforts as well as training in supervisory skills, diversity, leadership, conflict management, stress management, sales, customer relations, etc. . . . The current interest in promoting emotional intelligence at work has to be a serious, sustained effort, rather than just another management fad.[6]*

Project Management Is a Discipline

As a techie, you already have a great IQ and analytical skills. All you need to do is to appreciate and accept the importance of project management as a discipline and realize what it can do to make project a success. Becoming a project manager can be a natural step in your career. You need to develop

---

[6] Cherniss, Goleman, Emmerling, Cowan, Adler, "Bringing Emotional Intelligence to the Workplace: A Technical Report Issued by the Consortium for Research on Emotional Intelligence in Organizations," http://www.eiconsortium.org/reports/technical_report.html

communication and other soft skills, as discussed. You will also need to master standard project management frameworks described in the Project Management Institute's PMBOK and PRINCE2 resources. Both PMBOK and PRINCE2 give a comprehensive framework on how project management should be practiced in the real world. They detail processes in scope, schedules, cost, quality, human resources, risk, and other important knowledge areas of project management.

Literature on project management is available in abundance on the internet for all levels of expertise. There are discussion forums and specific interest groups available on social media sites like LinkedIn. They bring to your doorstep the experiences of managers from all over the world. You can ask for specific advice or simply read through the discussion chains. And you know that learning from the experiences of others can sometimes be more rewarding than learning on your own. I am member of a couple of such forums on LinkedIn, and I find that it adds great value to my ability to manage.

Joining clubs like Toastmasters International can give a boost to your public speaking and communication skills. And, it would also be wise to ask a more senior colleague to be your mentor. So let's tighten our belts a bit and get ready for a rewarding career in project management. Good luck!

Summary

There's a need to view project management from a different angle. Understand and appreciate functionalities like financial and legal issues, risk management, and the role of the PMO. It's also important to appreciate the transition and change management that is a part of almost every project, and to recognize that it also needs to be managed formally like a project. In many large projects, there is a separate person designated as a transition and change manager. Finally, soft skills are important. Your emotional quotient can be improved by proper training efforts. I strongly believe in the school of thought that says great managers can be developed. You don't need to be a born leader.

Case Study: Project Team Learns to Understand the Client's Business

During my early days as a software engineer, I interviewed with a couple of multi-national corporations. In one interview, after a technical round, the hiring manager said, "Well! Shailendra, you know a lot about technologies but what do you understand of my business?" It was a manufacturing company and luckily I started my professional career as a production engineer with an aerospace company. I could answer the question to his satisfaction and I was hired.

If you know the client's business in addition to its technologies, you are way above the lot. Luckily I had one incident that emphasizes the business aspect of a project that gave the project team a great advantage. I am presenting it here.

The Lesson

How important is it for a project manager to have a business perspective? Our client was a young team of four second-year MBA students from a leading business school in North America. They won an idea contest sponsored by the business school and, as a result, the school partly financed their idea and also gave office space to support their start-up company.

The students contacted my company in India in a bid to reduce the costs of developing their product, which was software for the health care industry. After a long chain of group meetings and teleconferences, we received an initial draft of the requirement documents from them. We went through it many times and discussed it with the clients, to discover that nobody from their side had a clue about what was required. Even the client team leader was not sure exactly what they wanted in the software. Only vague and high-level features were getting discussed again and again in all the meetings.

With each passing day, the cost pressure was piling up at our end. We had formed a team of four and also had a full-time project manager. Office space, salaries, and other overhead were adding to project costs, but we had not one single billable hour. At one stage, we thought of abandoning the project. We decided against it because it would have been a sheer loss to the company in terms of revenue already spent. Plus, we would lose an opportunity to work with a start-up with a bright idea and ready funding.

After lots of brainstorming, we decided to invest further and take some well-thought-out, calculated risks. We decided to invite the originator of the idea to our Chennai office. He agreed to come and pay all the costs associated with his trip. This showed the client's eagerness and determination to succeed, and it justified our decision to take more risks with the project.

That gentleman came to our office on a designated Monday morning. He was a young and enthusiastic person in his late twenties. Before going to business school, he had a short stint as a business analyst in a leading software company in North America. Having more ambition than to simply complete his MBA, he was betting big on the business idea that won the prestigious idea contest at his business school.

Our journey had just begun. In a couple of hours it became clear that the task ahead was going to be much more challenging than any one of us had thought. The client wanted much more than what was initially provided in the draft requirements document, and much more than what was discussed in teleconferences. As we went forward with discussions, it also became very clear that none of us in the Chennai office had any clue about the segment of health care domain that our guest was talking about. We were not able to relate to what he was saying, and at the same time he was not able to give us requirements in a form that could be used as a base for software development.

After a series of meetings in person, we decided to relay our difficulties to the client. Fortunately, he agreed to give some business background to our team. For the next week we simply received business tutorials from our client at his expense. He had to extend his stay. Once our team was charged fully, we held our first technical meeting in a pub. For the next two weeks, it was our show. We also included a technical writer in our meetings. In these two weeks we took the client far beyond his own ideas of what the software should look like, and it was not a surprise that most of the workable suggestions came from the project manager and his team. The client never considered many of the new functionalities that we added to make his software more useful and user-friendly.

Our team prepared a requirements document as a result of those charged-up meetings and, not surprisingly, it was signed immediately by the client. We also engaged a graphics design team and prepared a fully functional and navigable-click prototype in HTML. It was a pictorial presentation to the client team on exactly what they were going to get. The project's revised scope was now many times more than what was originally proposed by the client.

Needless to say, the financials worked out. It was win-win-win for the client, my project team, and my company. And it was a result of teamwork—a team that showed the courage to get involved in knowing the client's business! Top management support earned by the project team was simply superb. It was teamwork, a great relationship with the client, our willingness to take risk (and the client as well), and enthusiasm that made this project a case to remember. The project team showed extraordinary willpower to fight all odds and make the project a great success.

We're now in the sixth year of the relationship with that client, and the additional revenue has multiplied many times in dollar terms. The software, by the way, has been successfully implemented as a product in more than 24 countries.

CHAPTER 3

Delivery and Program Management

The next logical step in your IT career may be to assume the job of a program manager. Many terms are used for this role, including delivery manager, senior manager, and delivery director. The job content also varies from company to company. But this is common: at this level you manage a single, large project that is of strategic importance to the company; or you handle multiple projects in parallel. Either way, it's a big step above managing a single, lower-level project.

The terms "program management" and "delivery management" are used in different ways by different companies. This chapter presents more widely accepted and authentic definitions of these functions.

This chapter takes you through the differences between program management and delivery management and later discusses the concepts PMO (Project and Program Management Office), metrics, and the reporting applicable to these roles. The challenges in the life of a program manager and the critical factors required for success are also discussed. The chapter ends with a case study on the program management of a *Fortune* 500 company.

What Is a Program?

According to the Project Management Institute (PMI), *"A Program is a group of related projects managed in a coordinated way to obtain benefits and control that are NOT available from managing them individually. Programs may include elements of related work outside of the scope of the discrete projects in the program. Some projects within a program can deliver useful incremental benefits to the organization before the program itself has been completed."*[1]

Program management therefore acts as a crucial link between different active projects in the organization and performs coordination and resource optimization across the portfolio of projects. Prime functions within program management include the prioritization of resources, cost management, and risk management. Projects are finite in nature with fixed end dates, while a program can be an ongoing entity. Many companies run only a single program that contains all ongoing projects. This single program is often called a *project portfolio*.[2]

The Difference Between Delivery, Program, and Project Management

Delivery management is much broader than project and program management. It includes people, processes, and technologies, all combined into a comprehensive plan to achieve the required client deliverables. Delivery management may contain many projects and programs, along with their organization, administration, and supervision. So we say program management covers many related projects, and delivery management can cover many programs and projects.

The person in charge of delivery management is typically called an account manager or a delivery manager. A delivery manager supervises at a very high level, while a project manager gets into the minute details of project deliverables. A delivery manager has a much wider area of responsibility,

---

[1] PMI, *The Standard for Program Management,* Second Edition (PA: Project Management Institute, 2010).

[2] Wikipedia, "Program Management," http://en.wikipedia.org/wiki/Program_management.

and she has more experience than a project manager. She may be more involved with executive management, third-party vendors, and clients. Managing the client's executive management may also be part of the job.

It's the delivery manager's responsibility to see that projects and programs are executed smoothly, with proper risk management in place. Delivery management also fits into the broad framework of "initiate, plan, execute, monitor and control, and close," which is derived from the PDCA (Plan-Do-Check-Act) cycle popularized by quality-control professionals. The delivery manager is involved in each of these areas.

The Program Manager

A program manager may belong to the program office, which typically manages a portfolio of projects and programs. Some strategic projects may not fall under any program and, so, get managed individually. The job responsibilities of program managers may vary from organization to organization, but they typically manage programs and don't directly manage people.

Program management involves centralized program management software, maintaining complex dashboards, and reporting. The day-to-day work of a program manager includes effective speaking and active listening skills, managing vast amounts of information from end users and clients, comprehending complex topics and presenting them to nontechnical stakeholders, preparing crisp summaries, and preparing complex technical reports. The required soft skills include negotiation, conflict management, and dealing or coordinating with difficult people.

The Program and Project Management Office

In large organizations, a PMO might be referred to as a program and project management office. In that case, a set of related projects can be combined to form a program and a PMO would manage multiple programs. There may also be strategic projects that don't belong to any program that are directly managed by the PMO. The basic aim of the PMO is to optimize resources and get better visibility across programs.

The PMO can function at the department or the organizational level. Examples of the project functions of a PMO include resource allocation, risk management, controlling, and monitoring. Enterprise functions might include training, project achievements, best practices and lessons learned, managing dashboards and reporting, monitoring and optimizing processes, and participating in strategic initiatives.

Figure 3-1 diagrams areas covered by a PMO. Everybody is familiar with the word *supervision*: it's about making sure the work allocated to subordinates is completed per stated objectives, which include quality, schedules, accomplishing a task, or completing something within budget. *Troubleshooting* is another familiar term. "Trouble" in this regard is anything that halts the completion of stated objectives within cost, quality, and schedule parameters. Trouble may come on the technical front, from management, or from the client. It's the PMO's job to get these problems solved if they are beyond the control of a project manager.

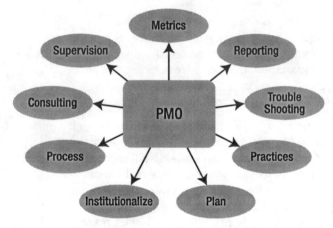

Figure 3-1. Project and Program Management Office activities

As for *plan*, the PMO, in a broad sense, is the owner of the overall project schedules. Project managers may need the help of the PMO to prepare project plans if the project is large or there are too many stakeholders involved who can have an effect on the successful completion of the project. The PMO also owns the project management *processes* and best *practices* within any organization. They maintain the process documents and update them with accounts of best practices and lessons learned, as contributed by project managers.

Note: I will discuss Metrics and Reporting of Figure 3-1 in the next section of this chapter.

Ultimately, the PMO has a responsibility to institutionalize processes across the organization. A PMO may also be involved in consulting on project, program, and delivery management challenges because they possess the best of the organizational knowledge in these areas. They may offer suggestions to the executive management on strategic projects. They may even consult with project managers if they see the need or a project manager specifically requests it. The PMO may also suggest closure of a project if it sees the benefits are low when compared to the costs.

Metrics, Dashboards, and Reporting

There are many variations in reporting requirements and methods, depending upon the size and nature of the program. It can also depend upon what upper management wants to see in program reports.

Let's take a look at something increasingly common in business: dashboards. A dashboard is a means of tracking key indicators like adherence to schedule or budget. Depending on the audience, it starts with a high-level executive summary. Preferably the dashboard is a visual. In demonstrating trends, arrows are typically used to show improvement or decline.

Figure 3-2 shows an actual company dashboard. Resources, timelines, and infrastructure are given a green (good) status. Scope is flagged yellow, which signifies an alert. To view details, you would click on the Scope hyperlink to take you to the project that is challenged in managing scope.

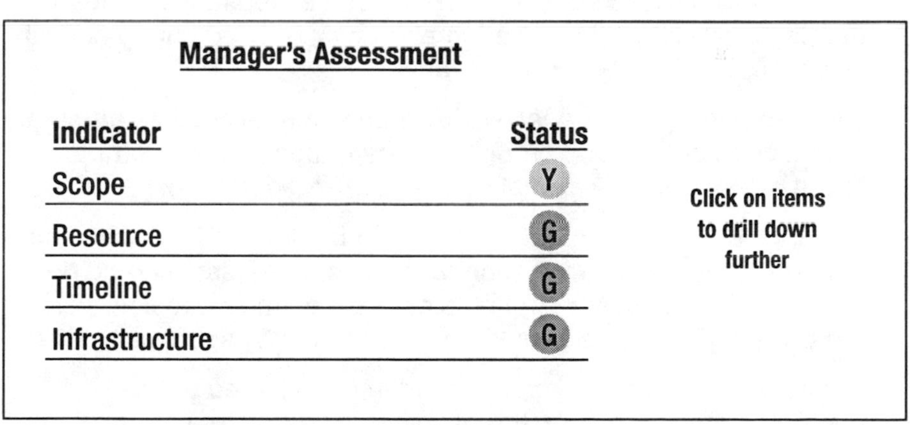

Manager's Assessment		
Indicator	**Status**	
Scope	Ⓨ	**Click on items**
Resource	Ⓖ	**to drill down**
Timeline	Ⓖ	**further**
Infrastructure	Ⓖ	

Figure 3-2. A simplified, high-level program dashboard

If we use the analogy of automobiles, a dashboard is the control panel in front of the driver that houses instrumentation and controls for the operation of the vehicle. Similarly, in a business dashboard, all the project or program measurements are presented in the form of charts, tables, and so forth. The PMO needs to measure a mix of criteria to judge project and program health and to keep better controls. These measurements are called *metrics*, which can be defined at the project or program level. Any project or program generally has a minimum of the following metrics.

- Time (on or behind the baseline schedule)

- Cost (on, under, or over the baseline budget)

- Resources (expenditures, personnel, materials, etc.)

- Scope (scope creep or in line with expectations)

- Quality (measurements against the set quality standards)

- Actions (internal or client-reported actions that may be pending)

To show current status, a typical traffic light approach can be used. Greens indicate that we are well within where we need to be; yellows range between 10 to 15 percent, and red is anything above a 15 percent deviation. These numbers can change based on requirements. The following list shows possible variables and indicators used on a dashboard.

- *Project-wide expected value*. This is shown with the help of multiple fields. Baseline budget, YTD total expenses, YTD total earnings, project payback period and any expected changes (with reasons), and the Net Present Value (NPV).

- *Detailed earned value analysis*. Earned value tells what portion of the planned budget and time should have been spent, compared to the amount of work completed so far. (Need based).

- *Variance in allocated budgets*. This can be depicted by color and percentage variance from approved value. Forecasts should be shown as money spent YTD plus estimated amount to complete the project. This figure should be compared with approved values.

- *Project baseline schedule*. Indicated in color based on the percentage variance from the baseline schedule (of project plan).

- *Scope*. Shown in red, yellow, or green. Red is used if scope cannot be completed.

- *Risk.* Shown as the probability of occurrence, with the impact in dollar terms. Red is used if the probability and impact to budget and schedule are high.

- *Realization of accounts receivables against outstanding and unbilled revenue* (optional).

- *Profitability analysis and revenue projections* (optional).

- *Components of costs in project and programs* (optional).

- *Attrition rates in projects* (optional).

- Any *outstanding issues* that need the attention of executive management.

The information for program dashboards can be summed up or aggregated starting from projects to the program levels and on through to the organizational level. In the presentation hierarchy, the information is aggregated in the following order:

1. Projects

2. Programs

3. Portfolios

4. PMO (Project and Program Management Office)

5. Organization

Along with challenges that need higher management attention, program managers need to gather routine information for reporting. Program managers feed essential information to delivery managers. They need to create ways and means to summarize and present information in a meaningful and intuitive manner. A generic dashboard template may not fit because metrics and reporting requirements can radically differ from one organization to the other. It may make more sense to create a template than try to customize a generic one. Templates are often spreadsheet based or slide presentations made in Microsoft PowerPoint. A metrics representation for the full program on a single slide presents better view and objectivity. Please refer again to Figure 3-2, which represents a single-slide view for a big program's state of affairs. It looks too simplified, but such dashboards are in common use across the industry. Clicking the links for different attributes drill down to lower-level details.

Let's consider the following list as a basic dashboard template used by a company. To maintain consistency in reporting, the template applies a set of standard reports across projects.

1. Actual hours for each project under different heads (monthly)

2. Charts showing planned vs. actual hours (monthly)

3. Project-wide expense details (monthly at line-item level)

4. Monthly costs in real time, by project and including overheads

5. Project cost summary that shows current month and YTD against budget

Depending on the type of project, other metrics might be included. They can be based on risks, issues and action items, defects data, and so on. But remember: too many metrics might be almost as bad as too few.

From a PMO perspective, looking at general resource capacity, current workload analyses, and resource availability might help ensure productivity and permit you to create realistic schedules. A PMO keeps track of all project resources (skill availability, common business components, etc.), and ensures optimum utilization by leveraging commonalities among the projects.

The PMO should be able to communicate clearly to stakeholders when new projects can be initiated. This allows senior managers to prioritize at an organizational level. Actual expenditures on existing systems and projects can be higher than expected, so realistic estimates are very important in helping executives decide if new initiatives can be taken up.

Key Success Factors for a Program Manager

Success factors for a program manager revolve around three key result areas. The first is proactive management of risks (like doing a quantitative risk analysis at the start of the project) and critical oversight to keep the project on track and on budget. The second focus area is accountability—the efficient and effective utilization of program resources. The third result area is a standard program management approach that employs the best practices mentioned in this section. Program management is a challenging task, but the use of proper tools and techniques can increase the chances of success.

The following list suggests some important steps in managing a successful program.

1. Secure a strong executive sponsorship.

2. Identify program stakeholders (both internal and external) and actively manage their perceptions.

3. Master program management tools and techniques.

4. Practice effective change management.

5. Employ scientific risk management by doing a comprehensive qualitative and quantitative risk analysis before the start of a project.

6. Produce a streamlined plan for the program.

7. Maintain an action log.

8. Use a standardized approach to help save time.

9. Create customized templates depending on the project/program.

10. Use the best people. A team of competent people is very important because it's people who will execute the processes and work towards quality deliverables. Team building is a very important skill for a successful program manager.

Project managers, delivery managers, and program managers have closely related roles. As a tech lead, you may start your career in delivery with smaller projects that have smaller risk content. This is a good time to develop the skills required to manage larger projects, or multiple projects of substantial value.

A Typical Day in the Life of a Program Manager

A program manager's day-to-day functions can differ drastically from organization to organization. Some organizations may incorporate delivery function responsibilities with program management. No matter the scope of the job, meetings with program managers and senior managers are an integral part of a program manager's daily life.

Many program managers use a centralized project management software tool to allocate and oversee resources, and to create schedules. This can save a lot of time and effort. Some program managers make high-level schedules for strategic and important projects, and then leave the details to the project leads.

A typical day may start with a regular review meeting with all the project managers involved in the program. Regular meetings with individual project teams may also be required, especially when the project is strategic in nature. These meetings can discuss the future course of action, solve a problem, or simply bring everyone to the same page.

After a meeting, the program manager might get to work preparing one of the many complex reports and dashboards to show progress at the program level. These reports can be weekly, monthly, quarterly and yearly—almost all are required by management to help them monitor the progress of program. Of highest concern to management will be resource utilization (which can sometimes be based on timesheets), revenue and profits (both running and projected) at project level, revenue and profits at the program level, schedule variance, cost variance, customer issues, and so on. The reports can be automated, but a lot of time is often spent on spreadsheets.

There are also meetings with functional managers to resolve issues and allocate resources. In many cases, program managers don't have formal authority over these functions, but still must get the work done on a priority basis. These priorities are important since the support functions may have many tasks in parallel and a program manager's task is just another in the queue.

As a part of the PMO, a program manager can also be involved in resource allocation and team building. A manager has, for example, to build a training session into the day to help a project team work together more effectively. In some companies the project bench (human talent) is also maintained under a PMO, or it has a say in the allocation of projects and assignments to the team members. Sometimes the PMO has a request for a skill, and the PMO might know someone with that skill who is not fully utilized in some other project.

Program managers may also meet with clients. Here, strong interpersonal and communication skills are key. The program manager listens to client feedback or may help the client flesh out new requirements.

At the end of the day, the program manager may meet with executives for a wrap up. This meeting can discuss the general progress of the program, new resource requirements, escalations, and the status of projects in the pipeline. Here the program manager may want to draw attention to some customer matters that are beyond his control. If it's a project-based organization, the program manager may have a say in helping make policy.

A couple of days at the start of a month may be reserved for preparing monthly or quarterly reports for the executive management. Some days of the month, a typical program manager may also be busy answering requests for proposal (RFPs) and requests for information (RFIs) from prospective clients.

A program manager's day is varied and busy, but can be exhilarating. Program management is very rewarding for the right kind of person.

Pick Good People and Review

If you are managing multiple projects, the role of the tech lead in each project becomes very important. Generally it's the program manager who picks the tech lead and key team members. Technical team members are selected with the help of the tech lead. Sometimes the client also has a say in the selection of tech leads and key team members. It's important to have competent people in the team, as they are the ones who deliver the goods at the end of the day.

Another key to succeeding in delivery is to review at every stage. As a manager, you need to reduce risks by personally reviewing the scope, document requirements, and design of the software. You must also make sure code reviews are done rigorously. Stringent code reviews can be the single most important factor to drive a project towards success. Code reviews reveal the reality of claims made by developers. And while a program manager usually can't get down to the level of doing code reviews, she needs to ensure it's a top priority for project managers and others who do them.

Summary

Program management is more or less like running a small independent business. Program managers are primarily responsible for the delivery of projects as promised per budget, schedule, and quality standards. They have the sole responsibility of keeping the program within the profit targets set by the company. Their job involves team building, planning and execution, monitoring and control, budgeting, reporting, and maintaining a healthy work environment. It's a very responsible position generally held by mid-level executives. The next level of promotion typical for a program manager is to general manager or assistant vice president.

Case Study: Program Management in a *Fortune* 500 Company

As we have seen in this chapter, delivery and program are made up of multiple projects that take time to build. A program may have only a couple of projects at the start, but with time many more related projects get added to the program. A typical program, for example, may have application development, maintenance, and support (ADMS) services for all manufacturing IT systems in the organization. This type of program may cost several million dollars to run annually.

This case study demonstrates how an actual program is built and set up. It shows the program constituents, its governance structure, and management of deliveries in a large ADMS program. It should help you visualize delivery and program management in a project-based organization.

This case belongs to a large US-based IT services company (called "company") and its *Fortune* 500 European client (called "client"). The relationship started with a couple of Y2K assignments that gave way to work in Java- and Oracle-based web applications. The work comprised both the maintenance of existing applications and new development. For a few years the team size remained below 50 members.

Then engineering assignments in CAE (computer-aided engineering) were added. These projects involved design and analysis using popular modeling and analysis tools like AutoCAD, Unigraphics, and Catia. The quality of the work, the dedication of the team, and low offshore costs helped take the relationship between the company and the client to the next level. The IT company's strong portfolio of satisfied customers prompted the client to also offshore some ERP assignments. The account grew steadily and the company eventually employed more than150 developers and CAD (computer-aided design) engineers.

In a newsworthy major event, the company won a $300 million deal spanning eight years from the same *Fortune* 500 client. Suddenly, almost 70 percent of the client's own IT organization found its way to the IT company's premises, both onsite and offshore. The new deal involved ERP, Lotus Notes, J2EE, and .NET, just to name a few. The account strength grew to more than 1,500 employees. Now too big to be handled as a single entity, the account was organized into two programs, Application Development, Maintenance, and Support (ADMS) and Engineering Services, with each program having its own program manager.

The annual revenue from both programs ran into the tens of millions of dollars. The profit and loss (P&L) was aggregated at program levels and finally at the account level. Each of the program managers was responsible for the P&L accounts of their respective programs. There was an account delivery manager responsible for the overall delivery and P&L at account level that included both the programs. Both program managers reported to the account delivery manager. Naturally it was an important account (often called the strategic account) for the company, and the account delivery manager directly reported to the department head, who was a vice president.

The ADMS program had many logical technology groups that included ERP, web applications, and legacy applications, just to name a few. Major functional areas were service delivery management (production support) and the development of new applications and functionalities. Application maintenance and bug-fixing were grouped under service delivery. Sixty to seventy percent of team strength and budget was devoted to existing application support and maintenance. The remaining budget was allocated to new enhancements and developing new applications. The ADMS program had many project managers working for ERP, legacy applications, and web technologies. Each of these streams had technology-specific team leads, which typically had 10 to 15 developers with them.

There was a governance board for the account, comprising the account manager and other senior executives from the company and the client. The board was responsible for policy matters, overseeing strategic business relationships, and handling major escalations (problems needing resolution at higher levels). The program managers had the delivery responsibility for their respective programs and the account delivery manager was responsible for the whole. The delivery manager had sole responsibility for everything at the account level, including operations, new business development, client relations, reporting to the top management, and commercials, which are the contractual and financial aspects of an engagement.

So how did the programs get managed efficiently? First, timesheets were entered by the staff in a homegrown tool that also generated timesheet reports. Project managers had to approve the actual hours logged by team members against planned hours, which were typically generated by project schedules. In time and materials projects, actual hours were used to bill the customer directly. In a fixed-bid projects, actual hours were used to determine the project profitability. The program manager had to ensure the group achieved the profitability levels set by the senior managers. This data was also typically used to determine the quarterly incentives for the program manager and project managers.

A web-based SAP project/program management tool was used for project schedules, resources, costs, expenses and overheads, which were entered by respective project managers. An open source tool was used company wide for bug management. The timesheet tool and the SAP-based program management tools were two main supports provided by the company. Still, program managers spent several hours weekly on spreadsheets to provide reports and dashboards required by corporate and the client. Much of the number crunching and charts were later automated using Excel.

Yet seamless interfaces between a number of tools were needed to make managers more productive. The organization implemented an integrated enterprise tool for the program management office, making the job of the PMO a lot easier. Now, all the program data was available in one centralized place. Reporting became a lot easier: by just one click of a mouse, it was possible to learn a project status and the resource needs of any project. If a project had a surplus of resources, it immediately became evident to the PMO and redistribution was made without losing precious time.

This case study gives a glimpse of the challenges in managing large programs. These challenges include resource ramp up, relationship building, outsourcing, management in multi-technology environments, reporting, the governance structure of large programs, and other delivery operations.

Does it excite you enough to take up the challenge of becoming of a program manager?

Service Delivery Management

This chapter is about production support, otherwise known as service delivery management. In the past few years, it has emerged as a major revenue earner for the traditional IT services companies across the world. Service-level agreements (SLAs), process automation tools, and many other things that you need to know about service delivery management are also discussed. The chapter ends with a case study on service delivery in a *Fortune* 500 company, discussing the company's service delivery organization (SDO), its real-time SLAs, and much more.

In most of my client engagements, around 80 percent of IT budgets were spent on supporting and maintaining existing applications. It's very likely that an IT manager will spend a few years of her career in support and maintenance jobs. Useful tips in IT support work are provided throughout this chapter.

What Is Service Delivery?

The service delivery process is the production support that deals with sustaining information systems once they go live for end users. This process deals with service or incident requests, from inception to closure. There are many time-tested third-party software programs available that handle incoming requests, route them to the correct work-flow group for decision making, and maintain and track a complete record of the process in real time. They have automatic escalation and expedite mechanisms for timely resolution of trouble tickets.

Service delivery process automation software reduces cost and minimizes error by automating change, configuration, provisioning, release, and many other related tasks. In today's complex IT scenario, it's impossible to imagine the service delivery function without the use of such software.

To maintain the support levels, service-level agreements and periodic customer satisfaction surveys are an integral part of the service delivery function. I will talk more about them in the following sections.

Let's recall the definition of a project: a task that has a definite start and a definite end. Service delivery or production support is a continuous or ongoing process with *no* definite start and end. So technically speaking it can't be classified as a project. It's better classified as an operation. The main functions of service delivery are

- Service-level agreement (SLA) management
- Capacity management
- Continuity management
- Availability management

In many companies today, up to 80 percent of the IT budget is spent on service delivery or production support activities. That makes financial management a very important aspect in the service delivery process.

Differences Between a Service Delivery Manager and a Project Manager

A project manager takes a project through standard phases of initiation, planning, and execution. Then she hands over the application to a service delivery manager, who is responsible for sustaining the application. A service delivery manager maintains service levels as set by end users.

Project managers have set deliverables. They move on to the next project when they are done. Service delivery managers oversee the continued delivery of the service. Service delivery thus is an ongoing effort that includes service-level agreements and metrics reporting, as defined in Chapter 3.

Transition and Change Management in the Service Delivery Process

Change management, in the context of service delivery, is the process of planning, executing, and controlling changes that have a direct impact on effectively managing applications in production environments. Transition and change management are crucial and unavoidable for service delivery managers. Indeed, the life of a service delivery manager revolves around change. Change management may be required when an application is handed over to production or in legacy transformation, technology upgrades, business growth, application maintenance, and problem fixing. Whenever a major service request has been handled, for example, the manager needs to ensure it has been implemented smoothly and all the change management steps and training requirements were handled.

Change can involve applications, underlying networks, databases, and other infrastructure and system elements. Organizational structures, governance models, processes, and business models are also a part of the change management processes. The process adopted for change management and the way transition is managed largely governs the time taken and degree of success realized.

There are many change management methodologies found in literature. I like leadership expert Dr. John Kotter's eight steps for change management.[1]

1. Create a strong urge for change.

2. Create a platform where all the stakeholders can collaborate.

3. Develop a comprehensible vision statement that strongly supports the change.

4. Communicate the vision to all the stakeholders and make sure you meet them regularly in this regard.

---

[1] John Kotter, *A Force for Change: How Leadership Differs From Management*. (New York, NY: Free Press, 1990).

5. Form a strong team that has sufficient powers to deal with all the challenges that come in the way of successful implementation of change.

6. Make sure you show some early wins to demonstrate to the stakeholders and keep up the morale of entire team.

7. Follow an integrated approach. Consolidate from the past, present, and keep moving.

8. Make sure there is strong leadership to constantly review and derive the change. It may be wise to have a fallback plan ready in case the change is not successful.

Change management skills are often required of IT managers. In project management strategies, change management points to a process in which changes to a project or a program are introduced and approved by design. Change management involves creative marketing strategies that enable communication between the employees or population affected by change. Change management becomes easier if managers develop a social understanding of group dynamics and leadership styles. Team integration, managing group expectations, effective communication, and training are important to facilitate any change.

What Is an SLA?

A service-level agreement (SLA) is a contract between the IT service delivery organization and the end users that specify the level of service to be provided. SLAs are invariably defined in measurable terms so that service levels can be justified, or perhaps compared with industry standards or organizational levels of service.

Some common metrics specified in SLAs include

• The availability of services (the percentage of the time that services will be available)

• The availability of support (the portion of the day, week, month, and year that support will be available)

• The schedule for maintenance and down time

• The number of users that can be served simultaneously

• Performance benchmarks to which actual performance will be compared

- The mode of incident logging (online requests, messaging, e-mails, voice, etc.)

- Help desk response time for incidents

- Resolution time

- Ticket reopen rates

- Penalties for nonperformance, if any

- Statistics to be provided in periodic reports and dashboards

Types of SLAs

SLAs are living documents, and so nothing is cast in stone. Condition-driving SLAs may change from time to time, so they are reviewed and updated regularly to maintain their relevance.

There are many different types of SLAs. Some are very basic and general purpose, defining application performance and availability. Others can be much more focused and precise and can vary from user to user in the same organization. Most large data centers, for example, have multiple computing environments. For users with mission-critical and time-dependent workloads, general purpose SLAs have little or no meaning. Users in production and development environments usually require different service levels. Often, you'll find relaxed standards for the users in the development community because their resources are not exposed to the end users and the application is still under development. Response time requirements can differ drastically at different hours of the day; though usually, more stringent response times are observed during business hours. SLA definitions can differ based upon whether you are providing services to internal or external customers, or whether a vendor is providing services to you.

SLAs can also govern infrastructure availability and performance. These are not really aligned to the customers or the business directly. They are mainly technology-centric, proactive SLAs that have more to do with planned maintenance to ensure the smooth-running availability of technology. This is in contrast to customer-centric SLAs that are based upon incident/problem response time or restore time.

To achieve infrastructure-based availability and performance service standards, maintenance actions are planned proactively to avoid the slightest probability of incident occurrence. Incident-based SLAs for end users are reactive in nature, so measurements should be based upon the quality of service as experienced by the customer or end user.

SLAs are negotiated by the top management in an IT organization. This process is typically done once every three to five years. Most of the time, the IT support team is working on SLAs set by existing contracts.

Service Delivery Organization (SDO)

Without a fully developed service perspective, IT organizations tend to focus on the management of technology domains, which in effect act as large silos that are isolated from each other. It is important to manage these silos well in respect to domain-based goals related to availability, capacity, security, and financial accountability. These goals represent only the first stage of effective IT management.

The two biggest silos found within an IT organization are the application groups and the infrastructure management groups. Each of these groups sees a further breakdown of management structures based on application types or technology platforms. On the positive side, each group manages its budget and objectives with reasonable effectiveness. But little or no thought is given to IT planning in a larger perspective, or to service delivery, which should be a main objective. SLAs are often based on the application in isolation from its supporting infrastructure components.

Transforming a traditional IT organization into an efficient service delivery organization is often an uphill task. And organizations that don't make this transition are in danger of losing competitiveness and credibility. Challenges are faced on technical, organizational, and cultural fronts. Effective service delivery ultimately depends upon the ability of an organization to redefine and simplify business processes to a level at which IT can use technology to automate and manage them. This transformation of business processes invariably requires cooperation between different departments and their ability to balance multiple and often competing objectives. Applying the principles of Lean IT and enterprise architecture discussed in Chapter 1 greatly helps in cutting across the silos and achieving high IT service for the entire organization.

Some important tasks for the IT service delivery organization are

- Establishing a service delivery governance structure

- Participation in business process design / redesigns

- Performance metric design, reporting, and dashboards
- Service-delivery strategy and planning
- Service-level definition, optimization, and management
- Portfolio management

SDOs have the important tasks of establishing governance processes for efficient service delivery, to identify trade-offs that will cut costs without any adverse effect on service levels, and to eliminate non-value-added work. Figure 4-1 depicts the important functions of a service delivery organization. Table 4-1 is linked to this figure and details some important functions of service operations, transition, design, and strategies.

Note: The term "ITIL" in Figure 4-1 stands for Information Technology Infrastructure Library www.itil-officialsite.com. The ITIL provides a framework on IT service management.

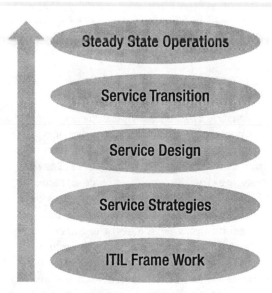

Figure 4-1. Service delivery in action

Table 4-1. Functions of the Service Delivery Organization

Service Strategy	Service Design
• Service Portfolio and Economics	• Service Portfolio Design
• Service Demand Management	• Service SLA management
• Service Outsourcing Strategies	• Service Vendor Management
	• Service Capacity, Availability, and Continuity
	• Service Design for Information Security

Service Transition	Service Operation
• Service Transition and Change Management	• Service Incident Management
• Service Configurations	• Service Request Management
• Service Knowledge Management	• Service Access Management
• Service Release, Deployment, Commissioning, and Transfer	

Service Delivery and SLA Management

Effective SLA management ensures that the desired service delivery levels are maintained. SLA parameters that are under control allow a service delivery manager to sleep peacefully at night. The minimum requirement in SLA management is ensuring effective SLA monitoring and control. Service delivery managers need to objectively measure the performance parameters and report the results in periodic SLA Compliance reports. These can be a part of a program's weekly or monthly status report. There should be indicators to demonstrate whether results meet or exceed the SLA performance objective(s) and comment on any apparent performance deficiencies. The methodologies on how SLAs are being monitored and measured need to be clearly documented and benchmarked with minimum requirements. This is important because SLA measurements can be very tricky and the validation of compliance reports might be the day's challenge for a service delivery manager.

SLA monitoring and control usually requires a lot of end-user interaction, number crunching, and reporting to stakeholders. Numerous functional groups from IT and business can be involved. This reminds service delivery managers that they do not have complete control in all places, so overall IT governance in service delivery organizations is very important. A combination of policy, process, and controls are needed for a desired level of service and customer satisfaction. Consistent and reliable sources of data on IT service offerings and the means to effectively utilize it are also needed. IT governance is successful only if it is aligned with overall corporate governance requirements. The bottom line for effective service delivery: the SLA objectives should always be in line with overall business objectives.

For effective SLA management, we need to thoroughly understand not only the information systems but also the business and service delivery processes like application management, performance management, service desk management, network management, and database management. Equally important for a service delivery manager is understanding information system security management, which is concerned with the security aspects of the entire IT infrastructure (including hardware, networks, software, and physical assets). Process standardization, security considerations, and automation are critical factors in effective service delivery management. Given the complexity and sheer magnitude of today's IT organizations, it is absolutely necessary to create a repeatable way to get the job done right.

Customer Satisfaction Surveys

Customer satisfaction surveys are an important part of any service delivery organization. Each survey is an informal performance appraisal for service delivery managers and their teams. Customer satisfaction surveys help minimize recurring problems and enable the IT organization to act proactively. This can reduce the number of service incidents, which in turn might significantly reduce the maintenance and support-cost burdens of the IT organization. These cost savings can be diverted to new IT initiatives and continuous improvement programs. Customer satisfaction surveys also help achieve improvements in service response time, professionalism, courtesy, communication with end users, and process effectiveness. These surveys provide good feedback on the IT help desk, application support, hardware, the network, and other services provided by the service delivery program.

Survey ratings provide a clear indication of service levels in terms of performance and end user satisfaction. These ratings indicate the effectiveness of the overall service delivery organization. User comments and suggestions are actionable items for the continuous improvement of the service delivery organization's program. Surveys may also provide compliments from end users—something the business always expects; but these keep the entire service delivery team in high spirits.

Challenges in the Life of a Service Delivery Manager

There are ever-increasing demands by business managers for quick and easy access to IT services, quick response to requests and fast turnaround for problem resolution, and to maximize the use of IT investments.

A dimension of these challenges is stringent SLAs across a complex and wide range of IT systems that have an amazing variety of domain functionality and technology platforms. Added to this is the limited availability of skill to perform these complex jobs—the IT staff usually prefers to work on conventional software-development jobs than ticket-based service delivery tasks that may also involve working in shifts. Support activity is typically round-the-clock. In multinational companies, the teams can be exceptionally large, diverse in terms of skills, cross cultural, and spread across the globe in different time zones. Maintaining support in different time zones worldwide is sometimes referred to as "follow the sun" support.

SLA monitoring and control is a tedious task at times. It involves enormous data collection from a variety of sources. And we know from experience that collecting quality data is not an easy task: data presentation, reports, and dashboards all require lots of data and data processing. This processing can occur using various service delivery tools and spreadsheets, and might also need final consolidation at the presentation tier. The quality of the content and the timeliness of the delivery and distribution of these reports are rigid: any miss can result in penalties or answering to authority. Possible penalties, which are generally mentioned in contracts for violating SLAs, can be stiff. Penalties for mistakes against external clients may be in dollar terms, and penalties for mistakes against internal clients may impact the IT manager's contract or service terms.

Love challenges? Get into service delivery…

Summary

We can easily summarize service delivery in the following terms and phrases:

- 24/7

- Always under the lens of top management

- A game of numbers and cold facts

- Incidents or tickets

- Metrics and SLAs

- Cast-in-stone processes

- Data collection and number crunching

- Reports

- Customer satisfaction surveys

- Large teams

- A determined team behind a tough man or woman—the service delivery manager

Case Study: Service Delivery for a *Fortune* 500 Client

Let's build upon the company and client case that we started in Chapter 3. As discussed, service delivery was a part of one program, and that up to 80 percent of the program budget was consumed by this department. Naturally service delivery took the maximum portion of total efforts spent by the program manager. Service delivery had a whopping team size of more than 300 IT support personnel, including subject matter experts and business analysts. The program had close to 15 project managers and many more team leads. They all belonged to specific technology streams in ERP, web applications, legacy applications, and so on.

There were close to 150 individual applications to be supported that included multiple ERP, mainframe, and other infrastructure applications. Intensity of support is always an issue, and in this case the teams were divided into three categories: mission critical, important, and ordinary.

Three categories of SLAs were defined as type 1, type 2, and type 3 support. Sometimes users called them gold, silver, and bronze.

Gold class was the most stringent. It had 24/7 support for all 365 days of the year. Once an incident was reported, the support agent had to respond to or acknowledge it within 15 minutes. All urgent issues had a resolution time of one hour, and other categories within gold class had a resolution time of two to four hours, depending upon the urgency and severity of the incident. The support team for gold class, mission-critical applications carried client-provided mobile devices that received incident information (along with a high-level summary). As per the SLA, within 15 minutes, the agent had to send an SMS (a short message on a mobile phone), e-mail, or a voice message acknowledging the incident. During odd hours, a portion of the team had to be on-call and connect to the client's system using notebook computers.

In most cases, it was possible for a team member to resolve the issue remotely from home, but in cases where a team effort was required to resolve an issue, there was no choice but to report to the office, even if it was two hours past midnight.

The gold class support team was divided into three groups that rotated shifts. Gold class SLAs suffered heavy monetary penalties if even a single incident was not resolved per the set performance standards. Any reopening of a ticket also attracted heavy penalties. Any end user could reopen the ticket if she was not completely satisfied by the fix provided by the support team.

In contrast, as many as 15 days were allowed for the resolution of tickets under some categories with bronze support. This support team had only one shift during general office hours. Bronze-level support teams mastered applications within a few months and thereafter the average ticket resolution time was continuously reduced.

The client was aware of this phenomenon and the company had to offer a 10 percent discount in support costs every year. The support cost of the second year had to be 90 percent of that of the first year's cost, and for the third year it had to be 90 percent of the second year's cost. This continued until the contract costs were reviewed after five years. The challenge to the program manager was not only to offer the annual 10 percent discount to the client, but also to absorb the cost of inflation and the salary raises of support staff.

All the learning and expertise therefore had to be documented very meticulously. Maintaining continuity in services while training new staff was another challenge. There was absolutely no room for a newcomer's lengthy learning curve.

Program managers had to collect data from all over and report the metrics and SLA compliance. There was incident management software that tracked applications support and calculated the impact on SLAs. Still, there was a lot of work in spreadsheets, which was later automated using Visual Basic applications that had interfaces with the incident-management application. All incident and SLA data was accessible to the client on a real-time basis.

One of the program manager's jobs was to constantly push the team to meet the SLA performance standards in order to demonstrate SLA compliance to the client with objective evidence.

For every major incident, a root cause report was a mandatory requirement. The team had to explain their actions so that incidents wouldn't repeat themselves. This was accomplished with an "action taken" report. Quarterly customer satisfaction surveys for all functional streams were mandatory, and they were conducted by the client with their end users. Passing marks for the program manager were an average rating of 4.5 on a 5-point scale.

Is this kind of work challenging enough for you? Does it at least sound interesting? Then you might make a good service delivery manager.

Portfolio Management

This chapter explains the concepts of project portfolio analysis. It ends with a real-time case from a *Fortune* 500 company. I have noted frequently in this book that big corporations may have hundreds of legacy applications. Many of these organizations are still using obsolete technologies and outdated business processes that don't represent fast-changing business realities. Often, nobody in the IT department knows the exact inventory or functionalities of these applications.

As an IT manager, you need to keep track of what's going on when, for example, an enterprise resource planning (ERP) system is updated to accommodate legacy applications or when decisions are made to transform the organization's business processes—because today this is the trend. A portfolio analysis of existing applications and projects is the single most important step that companies are taking to clean up the hodgepodge of applications and processes that have accumulated over the years. At some point soon, you may be called upon to help transform the business in an important and fundamental way. This requires a close look at existing systems, processes, and applications with an eye toward optimizing the mix to save money and increase the power of the IT infrastructure.

What Is Portfolio Management?

Today, most established companies have made major investments in their IT departments to support business operations. Over the years, systems evolve to support changing business environments. These systems tend to become complex, intertwined, and interdependent. In most cases, inefficiencies creep in over time. Keeping control of the growing application landscape and its complex web of interfaces is not easy. The return on investment becomes questionable as a result of increases in support costs. Acquisitions and mergers with other businesses bring in yet another set of IT systems to integrate, which may further add to the problem.

Many companies need an effective process to determine their IT budgets and to uncover opportunities for streamlining operations and improving efficiencies. Today's competitive business environment demands optimal investment choices as opposed to those that are merely "good enough." The IT budget should be linked to a company's overall business strategy, but this is usually not the case. Simulation and optimization modeling techniques can enhance the company's ability to quantify risks and maximize business value. Project portfolio management (PPM) is one such method to optimize IT investments across applications and projects.

PPM techniques help determine the investment strategy for the entire IT portfolio across the organization (or a division). Managers determine what types of projects or applications should be included in the portfolio, evaluate and prioritize planned projects, and construct a balanced portfolio that will achieve the objectives of the organization through prudent IT investments. Managers then monitor portfolio performance and adjust the contents of the portfolio in order to realize the desired results. IT asset portfolio management helps control IT expenditures, balance contending priorities, and provide a method of investing along the lines of the department and enterprise priorities.

Taking a broad view of the entire enterprise application portfolio is the first step in this direction. Improved resource management, facilitated through portfolio management processes, enhances IT credibility and efficiency.

In fact, before starting any business transformation project, it's important to carry out an effective portfolio analysis on existing applications and projects. As you'll see, the techniques used in the world of finance (managing capital assets, for example) will help drive and communicate productivity improvements for IT assets across the organization.

Why Use Portfolio Management?

Most large companies are reeling from the weight of supporting and maintaining redundant applications and PMO departments. AMR Research (now part of Gartner) states that "85 percent of IT budgets are spent on maintaining current operations," and "75 percent of IT organizations have little oversight over their project portfolios and employ nonrepeatable, chaotic planning processes."[1]

Often these statistics are a result of factors such as the following:

- A buying splurge during the dot-com days.

- Multiple mergers and acquisitions that have created a complex application network and interfaces.

- Inadequate planning or lack of direction. Different business units following different paths (silos) to meet their IT requirements.

- A "*lost team approach*" meaning different departments work in isolation from each other when it comes to development of IT systems.

These factors indicate why most companies have accumulated redundant applications that might duplicate the functions of other applications within the organization. This leads to repeat processes and redundant data sets that create integrity issues. Process upgrades are not consistent, as many applications have the same processes. Mergers and acquisitions of companies also pose a big challenge to the integration of IT systems, as there might be similar processes in merging entities. Both, for example, probably have payroll and human resources (HR) processes, and database applications. Similar processes of merging entities might be maintained until a solution is found to remove the redundancies. The same applies to databases as well.

In such disorganized conditions, project portfolio analysis techniques are becoming an increasingly important tool, given that they provide a holistic view of all the IT projects and applications across the organization. Project portfolio analysis, combined with project management best practices, allows an organization to apply more control over projects and IT spending while at the same time delivering more value to the business. The analysis ensures

---

[1] Todd Datz, "Portfolio Management Done Right," http://www.cio.com/article/31864/Portfolio_Management_Done_Right, 2003.

that IT resources that are limited and costly are not being allocated in an ad hoc or reactive manner.

A well-built portfolio management program does the following:

- Maximizes the value of the company's IT return on investment (ROI) while minimizing the risks

- Limits the number of redundant projects and applications and helps managers make a decision to discontinue projects

- Develops better communication and alignment between IT and business leaders

- Allows planners to marshal resources more effectively

- Encourages IT and business leaders to think in terms of teamwork

A portfolio analysis program indicates redundancies in processes and identifies those that can be removed over time. The analysis will reduce the costs of IT support and maintenance. A portfolio analysis will also point out unproductive and unnecessary projects by challenging the existence of every project and measuring its usefulness in terms of parameters such as net present value, a project's alignment to the organization's business strategies, and so on. As a result of portfolio analysis, the team will get a handle on IT assets because information about them and their functionalities will be documented at one place. This will be a big positive step toward effective asset management within the organization. Also, such documentation provides a way to address the redundancies and deficiencies.

In addition, PPM ensures that a CIO, working in concert with an on-demand infrastructure (such as cloud computing), plays a critical part in ushering in the next era of e-business. Some CIOs have claimed that PPM has reduced their overall IT application expenditures by 20 percent. Support and maintenance costs have gone down by almost the same amount. Eric Austvold, a research director at AMR Research, says companies doing PPM routinely report substantial annual savings in their IT budgets.[2]

Tools and Methodologies

There are many ways to manage a project portfolio. Different vendors, consulting companies, and academicians offer various models, tools, and

---

[2] Todd Datz, "Portfolio Management Done Right," http://www.cio.com/article/31864/Portfolio_Management_Done_Right, 2003.

methodologies. Organizations often develop their own ways of conducting portfolio management, sometimes on a simple spreadsheet. Off-the-shelf software tools are available from a variety of vendors including IBM, but many obstacles still exist to doing PPM well. There are, however, many best practices and key logical steps that will get the job done admirably.

Following are the key steps that can be used to create and manage a project portfolio:

1. *Initiate*: Perform a project inventory.

2. *Evaluate*: Flag the projects that match the company's strategic objectives.

3. *Prioritize*: Score and categorize the projects based on first identifying a few key strategies (like reducing support costs, reducing number of technologies, and so on) that will govern the whole PPM process. You should have at least one objective criterion per strategy component. You will need to devise a simple scoring methodology and assign appropriate scores to each strategy criteria.

4. *Match resources*: Match prioritized initiatives with resources to implement them.

Any methodology used to manage an IT portfolio must align IT with the organization's business objectives, promote the use of IT to improve operational efficiencies, and help in managing new IT initiatives effectively. Overall risk management and effective communication are keys here. Taking a portfolio approach will not only help IT departments to prioritize, categorize, and evaluate IT initiatives, but it will also help in enhancing the value of existing investments and aligning IT with business.

The sole goal in implementing portfolio analysis should be to simplify and modernize the company's IT portfolio in order to achieve better efficiencies and reduce costs. The analysis will also speed up and extend the effectiveness of IT with increased awareness of the availability of application portfolios. After the first round of PPM analysis is implemented, the need is to maintain and increase IT effectiveness, taking advantage of the new capabilities and enhanced agility made possible through PPM initiatives.

A big corporation in Europe went through this exercise and found it very rewarding. It is using PPM as a routine business process now to keep a handle on its large number of legacy systems. The company has a centralized board to consider any new software development requests from the whole of the organization. This board finds the best way to provide the requested business functionality—by enhancing an existing legacy system, buying a third-party compatible application, or by extending the existing ERP system. If any of these doesn't work, the board considers new development projects and ensures that the new application gels well with existing applications in terms of the company's overall business objectives, technology, data, and business processes.

The company has an IT system to take the requests for enhancement to existing applications and new developments from all over the world. The centralized board considers each request on its merits before giving approval. Only about 20 percent of the requests have been given approval. For the rest, the board finds ways to accomplish the tasks through existing applications and processes, thus saving the organization from an unnecessary littering of uncontrolled IT applications that are more trouble than help. How is this made possible? By maintaining an up-to-date inventory of applications and performing an ongoing process of portfolio analysis.

Key Challenges

Portfolio management is desirable, but it requires a strong commitment from both business leaders and IT. Following are some of the challenges of implementing the PPM process:[3]

- *Getting consensus isn't easy.* Portfolio analysis may disturb power equations within an organization. Some business leaders may fear losing power if applications in the portfolio are retired or merged with other enterprise applications as a result of the findings from portfolio analysis.

- *Getting quality information isn't easy.* The project and application database has to be updated regularly. Constant status updates for each project are required to ensure fast reaction to any market changes.

- *A single software application doesn't exist that can perform all the functions in an organization.* There are excellent enterprise applications that perform many jobs, from resource management, to manufacturing support, to account maintenance. But many

[3] Todd Datz, "Portfolio Management Done Right,"
http://www.cio.com/article/31864/Portfolio_Management_Done_Right, 2003.

other jobs will require you to deploy different process-specific applications.

* *Portfolio analysis can create an additional workload on executives.* The processes and meetings involved in any serious portfolio management exercise may be a major time challenge, because most people in companies are already overstretched and may not have the required bandwidth.

* *It's tough making decisions on whether to keep or throw away projects.* Again, people with entrenched interests will defend their turf.

PPM is not a simple management tool, as others might be. It can alter the power equations in the organization. Managers might worry about losing power if their applications are retired or merged with others. So PPM must have a high level of support from the top management. In fact, it should be led by somebody from executive management.

Critical Success Factors in the PPM Process

The factors leading to success in implementing and maintaining effective project portfolio management are many. Defining the key objectives of the PPM exercise comes first in the list. Then you need to identify projects and applications that fit into the objective criteria determined by the overall strategy of the exercise. Doing these things provides a framework for analyzing projects within the context of the overall business objectives. In the first round, focus on just a small portion of the organization's systems. The selected applications may belong to the stream of manufacturing, for example, leaving finance and HR legacy systems for rounds two or three of the PPM exercise. The next step is to take all stakeholders into confidence and create a sense of urgency among them about the whole process.

Next you need to gather, score, and categorize an accurate inventory of all IT assets under the study. Portfolio review and decision-making tools must be used under well-thought-out implementation models and metrics to keep a tap on quality and progress of the whole exercise. After you complete the initial rounds of the PPM exercise with success, you need to institutionalize PPM as a core business process and actively manage it.

Case Study: IT Portfolio Analysis in a Big Corporation

It all started with ABZ Inc. inviting bids for the business transformation of a majority of their legacy applications and processes. A comprehensive portfolio analysis was a part of that exercise. ABZ is the world's leading supplier of capital equipment used in the fabrication of integrated circuits. (The numbers presented in this section are indicative but changed to maintain the company's confidentiality.)

ABZ Inc.'s Worldwide IT Portfolio

ABZ had more than 1,200 different systems being used within the company. These included mission-critical business applications, management information systems (MIS) and decision support systems, and administrative and support function applications. These applications could be further categorized as internal facing (used in-house and by vendors) and external facing (used by customers). On an average, 60 percent of the applications were internal facing. A large number of these applications were redundant, and the exact inventory and documentation of the applications' functionalities was not available. Getting that done was one of the aims of this portfolio management exercise.

The PPM analysis was a mandate from the CIO level. The driver was the business transformation exercise taken up by the organization. Gaining control over existing business applications was necessary for the success of the company in the long run and the goal of the PPM exercise. IT engineers at the lowest level were involved in collecting inventory and assessing the functionality of applications from all over the organization. Department IT managers were responsible for the analysis of the portfolio of applications falling under their purview.

It was a big job. Application inventories had built up over a couple of decades, with many applications developed in relative isolation. Obviously, many of them duplicated the functionality of others. So it was probable that some redundant applications and projects or those with a smaller ROI would be retired. For any application or project to survive this PPM exercise, it was a prime requirement that it should be in line with organization's overall business strategy.

We started with a well-structured Microsoft Excel sheet with lots of columns and rows relevant to the PPM exercise. The rows represented application, and the columns represented the attributes on which the applications were rated. We evaluated a couple of out-of-the-box tools for this PPM but finally decided in favor of our own customized Excel sheet. And it worked well.

All applications (represented in rows) were weighed on a scale of 1 to 5 for each attribute (represented in columns). The attributes were cost reduction by offshoring, cost reduction by technical and functional cross training, retiring redundant applications, merging with ERP, application integration and so on. Each application in the organization was given a score for each attribute. A high score for an attribute represented a high degree of alignment of that application with the goal of that attribute. Using a weighted average method, the overall score for each application was computed. A high score for an application represented the positive alignment of that application towards cost reduction and the overall objectives of the PPM exercise.

All the concepts and discussions presented earlier in this chapter were put to use. We even had a three-day training workshop for the PPM team. It was organized by our consultants for ABZ.

Four-Step PPM Methodology at ABZ

We used the following four-step methodology for ABZ:

1. Devise a model for the PPM process.

2. Develop a prioritization and evaluation framework.

3. Determine the critical success factors.

4. Establish a review framework to check the status periodically.

The key here was to have an analysis criterion under a PPM prioritization and evaluation framework, and to have a mechanism of regular reviews of the implementation process.

Inventory of Applications at the Corporate Level

We conducted an inventory of existing applications and systems. We also documented their functionalities and determined where these applications fit into the overall organizational structure. As it turned out, these included multiple ERPs and other core systems that helped run the business at the corporate level:

- Supply chain management (SCM), ERPs, and manufacturing resource planning (MRP II) applications

- Logistics and purchasing systems

- Sales and marketing applications

- Shop-floor scheduling systems

- Inventory and spare-parts management systems

- Finance and payroll applications

- Human Resource Management Systems (HRMS)

- Business intelligence (BI) and data warehousing applications

- Reporting systems at various levels

All applications for supply chain, logistics, marketing, shop-floor scheduling, inventory, BI, and reporting were on different platforms, distributed among three ERPs and many homegrown applications. These applications required a complex web of direct interfaces and batch processes so that they could talk to each other and maintain consistency of information among these disparate systems.

Inventory of Need-Specific Applications

Next, analysts drilled down another level and uncovered many more applications. These applications were relatively localized and represented sales, quality, bid management, and other business process–specific systems, as follows:

- Resource (labor) availability and assignments applications.

- Post-sales applications such as those related to installation and warranties.

- Product-quality management applications.

- Supplier-quality applications.

- Contract maintenance and bid management applications.

- Applications designed to maintain legal requirements of international trade (imposed by the US government for sensitive technologies and products).

- Systems for controlling functional changes in IT infrastructure.

- At the group level, dozens of localized applications involving work flows. Some were stand-alone applications, and others interfaced with other systems.

All told, these systems literally ran into the hundreds, and managing them was a real challenge. Each application or system was categorized as follows and is shown graphically in Figure 5-1:

1. *Strategic*: Focusing on strategic elements of an enterprise, like making major investment decisions.

2. *Tactical*: Focusing on ways to make improvements by changing or replacing the existing processes or procedures. An example of this might be updating an old business process like order entry.

3. *Operational*: Focusing on existing processes with an aim to find ways to improve efficiency or reduce costs. Routine applications like payroll processes will fall under this category.

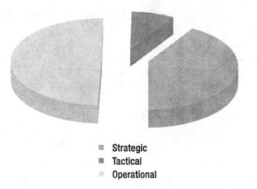

■ Strategic
■ Tactical
▒ Operational

Figure 5-1. Overall application breakdown at ABZ

Figure 5-1 shows the overall classification of applications at the organizational level. The majority of applications fell under the category Operational. Many measures were taken in this category to improve operations efficiency—for instance, by putting in a load balancer, buying more-advanced hardware, and tuning and improving application performance. The operational category is followed by tactical and strategic applications.

Besides strategic, tactical, and operational, each IT asset was rated and categorized on another scale based on the analysis. As Figure 5-2 shows, the applications were divided into three broad categories—New, Enhancement, or Maintenance:

1. *New*: New products or those to be built

2. *Enhancement*: Applications that require new functionality

3. *Maintenance*: Applications with errors that need to be fixed, features that need updating, or features that have become obsolete and need to be replaced or scuttled

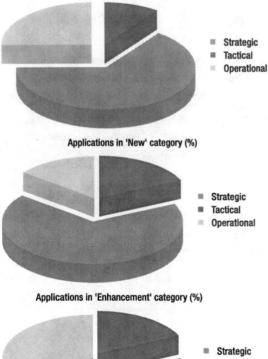

Applications in 'New' category (%)

■ Strategic
■ Tactical
░ Operational

Applications in 'Enhancement' category (%)

■ Strategic
■ Tactical
░ Operational

Applications in 'Maintenance' category (%)

■ Strategic
■ Tactical
░ Operational

Figure 5-2. Category of applications at ABZ

In all three categories, the applications were further subdivided into Strategic, Tactical, and Operational. Although the data is changed slightly to maintain the company's confidentiality, the charts well represent the methodology used.

We also listed the number of technologies that were in use at ABZ. This was important because the number had a direct impact on support and maintenance costs. From Table 5-1, it's clear how many technologies can find their place in the IT department of a large organization. This list represents practically every existing technology—and it's just a partial list. This should give you an idea of the magnitude of the challenge. Each heterogeneous platform requires a large IT staff to maintain and augment applications. That results in phenomenally large support and maintenance budgets. The applications and their interfaces become too complex to be managed.

The PPM exercise and subsequent business transformation (BT) had a clear and extremely valuable goal: to simplify the system and reduce the number of technologies for ease of support and maintenance.

Table 5-1. Technologies in a Large IT Setup

SAP technologies	Microsoft Office
Technologies specific to other ERPs	Mail servers
Oracle Forms, Procedural Language / Structured Query Language (PL/SQL)	GUI design tools such as Adobe Dreamweaver, Photoshop, and Flash
Oracle9*i* and MySQL data bases	Integrated development environments (IDEs) including Eclipse, WSIDE (Web Sphere Integrated Development Environment)
A host of operating systems including Linux, Unix, Windows XP	
Application and web servers	Test management tools such as HP QuickTest Professional (QTP) and Quality Center (QC)
IBM WebSphere, Apache HTTP Server, JBoss Application Server	
Netscape Application Builder	Service delivery management tools
Java 2 Platform, Enterprise Edition (J2EE); Hibernate	Messaging systems
Microsoft .NET Framework	Document management systems such as EMC Corporation's Documentum
Microsoft SharePoint	Search engine–related technologies
Microsoft Visual SourceSafe (VSS) and other version control systems	Data Warehouse, reports and BI tools such as IBM Cognos, SAP Crystal Reports
Microsoft Office Project Server and other Systems Development Life Cycle (SDLC) computer-aided software engineering (CASE) tools	Pipeline management tools (for movement between development, QA, and product)
Open Text's Livelink	Defect- and issue-tracking systems such as WEBsina's Bugzero
IBM Lotus Notes	Build and release management tools

Problems Uncovered at ABZ

The PPM initiative revealed the following problems at ABZ:

- An inventory of large and disparate IT systems that were very much silo based.

- A huge base of hardware, software, and proprietary applications. More than 1,200 applications were running on various platforms and technologies, including multiple ERP systems. In addition, there were countless homegrown Lotus Notes applications developed by the various business groups.

- Specific challenges regarding the inability to focus on core business and new initiatives.

- Numerous sourcing issues as a result of multiple external vendors, resulting in high management and support costs.

- High costs in maintaining legacy applications.

All of the preceding points reflect ABZ's inability to focus on its core business, very high application maintenance costs due to a large number of uncontrolled running applications, and a large number of IT vendors that had no coordination among themselves. As much as 80 percent of the IT budget was spent in support of existing applications. Existing ERPs were also highly customized, and looming upgrades presented a big challenge to the IT department. After the PPM, ABZ was seriously thinking of adopting a single ERP (instead of the current three) and dramatically reducing the number of technologies used in the organization. They were considering mySAP as a single ERP.

Numerous legacy systems and ERP interfaces formed a complex web of applications and interfaces at ABZ. All these applications were subjected to the objective criterion set for PPM analysis. The main criterion was the overall alignment of any application with the business strategy, eliminating redundancy, and providing a higher return on investment. As a result of the portfolio analysis (and a BT exercise after that), some redundant applications were decommissioned and some of the application portfolio was be transformed into mySAP. The CIO had to ensure that the mission-critical applications continued to run smoothly at minimal costs to the company.

Realized Benefits

The portfolio analysis paid off big time for ABZ. Following were the measurable results:

- The company reduced total IT spending by 20 percent, in terms of support costs.

- Process simplifications and productivity improvements were done on more than 400 applications.

- Better project management and training lowered costs on more than 200 applications.

- IT managers created 31 process groups to provide a common pool of resources that would work across those groups. In other words, the initiative helped removed silos and silo-based thinking.

- About 30 percent of work previously done onsite was sent offshore to low-cost regions, with no detriment to quality or production.

- IT managers found 120 applications redundant and retired them.

The notable highlights were reducing IT support costs by 20 percent and retiring a significant number of applications. The 20 percent savings represented a substantial amount of money each year. This saving was made possible by cross-training employees, sending work offshore, combining functionalities, and retiring many redundant applications. And cost savings would continue, of course, thanks to simplified operations and systems.

Other Benefits

The most prominent nonmonetary benefit was the knowledge gained in performing a PPM. It yielded concrete strategies for maximizing the ROI on IT investments by relating the project and application portfolio to business strategies. The overall alignment of applications and projects ensured that the organization's business strategy had the maximum potential to succeed. This was achieved through better cooperation and removal of silos. The whole process of planning, budgeting, and resource allocation was greatly streamlined.

Most important, the IT organization got a firm handle on all applications and processes in the organization. All applications surviving the PPM exercise became aligned with the overall business strategy of the organization, which greatly enhanced the credibility and efficiency of the IT organization.

Summary

This section covered the topic of project portfolio management through a real-time case study. The first part discusses the principles involved, and the second part contains a real-time case study. The principles covered included initiating PPM, taking inventory, and understanding critical success factors. PPM can be an eye-opening exercise for any big organization that is taking it on for the first time. It may uncover a large number of redundant applications and increase company awareness of those remaining. Many companies undergo a PPM exercise before a business transformation exercise like the one described. Process improvements and PPM go hand in hand.

Project management processes invariably evolve as business needs change. CIOs must drive the continuous improvement of projects, programs, and portfolio management processes. They must also ensure that project managers follow best practices and show effective project management, before moving them to the next stage of helping with PPM.

Regular PPM exercises are a must in order to effectively control an organization's project and application portfolio. PPM also gives us an effective way to objectively evaluate new development and enhancement requests coming from all over an organization. Creating investment categories and evaluation criteria is a prerequisite for achieving a balanced portfolio. Logical investment categories can help allocate resources intelligently. Objective evaluation criteria based on business drivers, familiar financial measures, and risk can be used to rank initiatives within each category. The consolidated scores indicate their relative importance in each category.

PPM requires a coordinated effort on many fronts: process, framework, governance, application clustering, right mix of resources, accountabilities, training, and tools, to name a few. Senior management can use PPM as a scorecard and an ongoing methodology to review the company's current status and understand areas that need improvement.

Acknowledgments: I sincerely thank Laxmi Naraya Sahu and Radhika Unni for helping me in the initial versions of this text. Special thanks to Venkat Paturi for his encouragement and guidance throughout this study.

Presales, Bid Management, and Sales and Marketing

This chapter takes you through preliminary concepts relating to sales and how deals get made, and then introduces third-party consultants and their role in large deals. It also discusses the role of onsite relationship managers. The major real-time case study at the end will help you understand how presales efforts affect your world.

This is important stuff. Sales, after all, pay your salary. What's more, many techies end up in sales or marketing, or participating in bid efforts, at some point in their careers.

Bids, sales, and marketing are an integral part of any IT company, whether it's a product company or a services company. Large deals can run up to or even beyond $500 million. Solutions architects and third-party bid management consultants are an essential part of such deals. A role in presales and marketing departments can get you executive slots faster than anywhere else in your company. The bottom line is this: a thorough understanding of these roles and an understanding of what it takes to get great results can propel your career. So gear up! In this chapter, you'll learn some useful tips that you can apply immediately.

Presales and Bid Management

Presales involves generating leads and following up with potential clients, preparing solutions, creating final proposals, providing product demonstrations, establishing proof-of-concepts (POCs), and many other marketing-related activities—a cycle that is not completed until the customer is acquired. Bid management is a vital presales support service that provides copywriting, administrative, and technical resources to the salespeople to ensure the quality of proposal documentation and presentations.

Usually working in conjunction with field sales reps who get wind of an opportunity, a bid manager's role is to present a proposal to a client that meets that client's business and cost objectives, while minimizing business risks and maximizing profit margins. The bid manager is the owner of the proposal-making process. That person studies the request for proposal (RFP) documents from the client, which can be very comprehensive and legal in nature. The bid manager plans the proposal-making effort like any other project and is solely responsible for maintaining quality, watching costs, and overseeing the schedule for the whole bidding process.

To coordinate the preparation of a winning proposal, the bid manager needs to work closely with sales, technical, delivery, and commercial teams (finance, legal, and so on). The sales, delivery, and technical teams can belong to different verticals (departments or functions in an organization) and might be scattered across the globe, so effective coordination and interpersonal skills are key here. A bid manager may not have any direct control over any of the teams involved. For participating executives from different verticals, proposal making may be a large addition to their already tight day-to-day schedules, so getting quality time from them can be one of the biggest challenges in the process.

The concept of a *winning proposal* is important here, because if you don't win, the whole exercise will become just a big chunk of overhead to the organization. And how much of these costs can your organization absorb without having them significantly affect the bottom line?

Following are the main functions that can be categorized under presales and bid management:

- Qualifying and prioritizing proposals and RFPs.
- Coordinating with the sales, solutions (technology and high-level architecture), delivery, and finance departments.
- Ensuring the availability of complete, quality information from each source within set timelines.
- Documenting proposals.
- Making the final presentation to the client, with a sales team. The presentation may require technical consulting and product demonstrations.

Who Makes a Good Presales/Bid Manager?

A good fit for a bid manager is a person who knows the company and its offerings inside out. Good communication, coordination, presentation, and interpersonal skills are usually required. It will help if this person has worked in similar projects or products (as required by an RFP) and can appreciate their commercial as well as technological aspects. The bid manager will be required to do a lot of number crunching regarding schedule, cost, and scope, and quick "'what if" computations to deal with variations in these factors. A thorough understanding of the industry segment involved will be a big plus. Stress and round-the-clock work under the pressure of deadlines can be an integral part of this job.

The Organization for Presales and Bid Management

The department handling presales and bid management will vary from company to company. In IT services companies, a few people may be working in the presales function at each department level. Typically, the effort is headed by the manager for presales. For large deals, a presales group may be working at the corporate level to help presales managers in different departments. A corporate-level presales group might include very senior and seasoned professionals as far as the whole process of bid management is concerned. Whenever the organization receives an RFP, the presales group may need to draw people from different departments depending on the expertise required in making the proposal. Technical writers, financial managers, and legal managers are invariably required for large deals. A different bid manager could be designated for each RFP, depending on the size of the deal. For smaller deals, a single bid manager might take over multiple bids.

A bid manager is like a project manager with the responsibility for the complete bidding process. The bid manager typically belongs to the presales organization, but there can be variations. If the stakes in a proposal from a particular vertical are higher, senior managers may want to appoint the bid manager in consultation with presales. After the bidding process is complete, experts from other verticals may go back to their regular assignments.

Role of Third-Party Consultants in the Execution of Bids

Companies typically specialize in a particular line of business. Floating or issuing an RFP may be an altogether different ball game as compared to conducting their usual business. This is true especially when the stakes on the buyer side are high and RFPs are floated globally. Fortunately, consultants are there to help. In the process of bid management, consultants can be employed by buyers as well as sellers.

The buyer's side may find it an uphill task to manage the bidding process. Consultants can therefore help in writing documents for the RFP and managing the bidding process until the right vendor is selected. Consultants hired by the buyer may sometimes take the role of transition and change managers after the deal is signed.

The RFP document is important because it tells exactly what goods and services are required along with location, price, constraints, and other terms and conditions. It's a legal document and forms the base for writing the proposal on the supplier's side. Third-party consultants can help buyers evaluate the proposal. Consultants can also take the role of a bid manager on the supplier's side, coordinating verticals as required and managing the bidding process.

When third-party consultants are engaged by the buying organization, they are the sole contact points for vendors for the entire bid life cycle. These consultants ensure the quality of the RFP and supporting documents, the right placement of the RFP (selecting qualified vendors), the assessment of vendor capabilities and fit, the quality of the documentation and adherence to agreed-upon standards, and the assessment and rating of the vendor proposals. They may also monitor the transition and change management for the buyer and typically oversee steady-state operations for an agreed-on period.

Buyers generally employ third-party consultants to help in large deals. Many buying organizations don't have the expertise to deal with the bidding process. Third-party consultants in these cases bring their expertise and valuable experience to large deals. By employing consultants, a buying organization can concentrate on its day-to-day business. Buyers need to oversee only the overall bidding situation; individual transactions are carried out by the consultants.

Role of Onsite Customer Relationship Managers

Let's switch gears here. After a bid is successful and the deal has been made, the work begins. Often, the winning bidder will place a customer relationship manager (RM) at the buyer's site to provide a point of contact for the buyer and to get the project moving.

RMs are typically seasoned IT professionals who have technical or marketing backgrounds. One of the most important skills an RM needs is the ability to multitask and utilize various skill sets depending on the assignment at hand. Each day can bring its own set of unique responsibilities and challenges. For example, the RM might be anchoring a series of client meetings to discuss a large proposal for outsourcing infrastructure and ERP maintenance. The RM might be attending a networking event to assemble important stakeholders, from both business and IT, for a big project. Managing several tasks at the same time can be challenging.

The variety of responsibilities an RM has in order to keep the business and relationship running can be interesting. For example, back in the RM's office, there can be reviews of ongoing projects with a couple of meetings per week. There can be one-on-one meetings with the client and other stakeholders. There might be meetings with offshore teams late in the evening. The job can get complicated—many projects are spread across locations, with people working offshore and onsite. These projects are referred to as working under the onsite-offshore model. Offshore locations might be in Europe, Japan, or low-cost regions such as India and China.

Effective presentation and negotiation skills are important for an RM. The RM will probably give periodic presentations to the client's CIO on the overall engagement or might give a presentation regarding a resolution to a major breakdown in IT services. At times, the RM is there only to listen and work out with project owners the details on project scope or upcoming contract conditions.

RMs as Onsite Detectives

One major task for the RM is to learn about new bid opportunities and other initiatives. A good RM keeps an ear to the ground to learn about new RFPs and to relay the information back to the home office. Also, the RM is one of the few people present on the client side (from the vendor team) and so is the one who will witness the first reaction from the client regarding both good and bad results from the offshore teams. The RM needs to be a true diplomat, and then work with the home office to work out problems if things go poorly.

Onsite RMs are often the first to know that something right is going on at the target customer's place and that more business is in the offing. They may bring in a lead for a future order, often before the official RFP is floated. They also help ensure that their company is a party to the bidding process, because in many strategic deals, the RFP may not be floated publicly. Instead, the buyers place it with select companies they believe have the capabilities to deliver on the requirements.

Onsite coordinators can thus bring in vital information about buyer groups, managers, and their motivation behind floating a tender. Sometimes, an approximate budget is also known. All this information can be critical in bringing in a winning proposal, in fine-tuning the financials, and in taking care of other details at the last minute if required.

After a contract is awarded, onsite managers play a lead role in the transition and ensure required levels of cooperation from the client's end. It's the familiarity of onsite coordinators with client managers and their business (and also on "what will fly") that makes them a crucial link in the whole process. Onsite RMs are maintained for large contracts and important customers. They do exist in smaller as well as large organizations.

RMs vs. BRMs

You are now familiar with the role of customer relationship managers in solutions selling (i.e., selling a software solution). The role of a business relationship manager (BRM), on the other hand, is relatively new in IT organizations.

The BRM is strictly an internal job that links IT and business managers. The BRM needs to have significant knowledge pertaining to both technology and the business function. The BRM generally talks for the business, relating strategies and goals, within an IT organization, without any additional responsibilities to sell products or work on upcoming business deals. The BRM role was created by CIOs as a solution to how business can see IT as a barrier. Many times business executives don't understand how swiftly the IT department can or cannot respond to their fast-changing needs or simply don't appreciate the capabilities of IT. The BRM is supposed to fill this communication gap.

As already stated, the BRM needs to know both business and technology. This position also requires an ability to understand the business adequately to communicate the substance of projects to technology teams. On the other hand, the BRM also needs to comprehend the technology sufficiently to communicate its complexity in simple terms for the business.

Sales and Marketing at IT Companies

Many of us do not appreciate the fact that sales are an important part of marketing. Marketing is everything you do to promote your business. If you have an apt marketing strategy, most of the sales job is done. If customers value your products and services, they will make an effort to buy them. And you may need little or no sales effort at all. The primary job of marketing is to create customer interest in your company's products and services. Marketing strategies deal with business development, selling techniques, communication, and customer relationships. Marketing creates value for your customers as well as the company.

Still, salespeople capitalize on marketing's work by connecting clients to your solution. They are the human face of the organization to potential customers and hence are irreplaceable.

When we talk of IT marketing, we are generally concerned with selling our solutions, services, and products. (For the purpose of this discussion, a solution is a mutually agreed-upon answer to a recognized problem that should provide some measurable improvement.)

There are two processes in any business scenario: purchase and sale. The solution sales process depends more on the buyer, who must feel the need for the value your organization provides, something beyond the standard product or services being sold. If it's the sale of a standard product or service, it won't be called a solution sale. It will be a simple routine sale such as selling a standard Microsoft Windows 7 package. If a buyer is asking for SAP ERP software that is customized to that company's specialized needs, this will qualify as a solution sale. The buyer must also perceive the prospective seller as having the credibility to deliver that expertise. At the same time, the buyer must trust the supplier to discuss the problem and share information that may be crucial for the buyer's survival. Again, this is where the salesperson becomes essential: establishing trust. It's only after establishing the trust that a supplier may be allowed to do due diligence (a study of buyer's systems) and offer a solution and associated commercial terms to the buyer. So now you understand the difference between a buyer in two situations—selling solutions and selling standard products and services.

Critical Success Factors in Solutions Selling

Much has been written in management literature on how to successfully sell solutions. Let's discuss only a few of the key points for the sake of completeness:

Believe in the value and benefits of your solutions: In addition to a technical and business understanding of your products, you need integrity and a strong belief in your offerings. The buyer needs to see that you care about your solution and its ability to help.

Know how to find qualified buyers: Meaningful selling happens when you can find people who have a certain need that you can fill.

Establish trust: Selling always requires building relationships and determining the buyer's true needs before you make a sales pitch. If you can't establish trust, selling a solution will be extremely difficult.

Match the buyer's needs and wants to the product's benefits: It is critical to understand the buyer's true needs and to be able to match them to the solution's benefits.

Ask for the sale and deliver. Simply presenting the benefits of a solution isn't enough. You must be able to ask the prospect to take action in the form of placing an order. After the order is placed, you must be able to deliver on what you proposed. These abilities are directly linked to your credibility to make the next sale to the same customer or in the greater marketplace.

How a Technical Background Helps

There might be a future in sales and marketing for you. It is difficult to find people who are well-versed in selling technical solutions. Companies are investing a lot of money in training qualified people with relevant technical backgrounds so they can find the right solution for their customers.

An effective solutions sales executive should be capable of processing a potential client's business needs, comprehending the technologies available, and helping design a solution that delivers desired value to the customer and maximizes profits for the company. Most successful solutions sales people have good engineering or business backgrounds. They have the right soft skills and a thorough understanding of the market. The key soft skills that count here are business communication, public speaking, conflict management, and negotiation.

Summary

It's important to understand the terminology used in the bidding cycle. To summarize that cycle, let's discuss some important terms. *RFI* stands for *request for information*. This request is made by purchasers of services to vendors. The RFI is designed to obtain information on products and services offered by a vendor. There is no commercial or financial obligation involved from either side. RFIs are usually sent to many vendors. After RFIs are completed and returned to the buyer, that buyer chooses, or *short-lists*, vendors that will later be sent the RFP. The RFP is usually sent to a small percentage of the vendors who sent in information. Note that a *request for quotation* (RFQ) is a synonym for an RFP.

Multimillion-dollar deals are generally referred to as *large deals*, and in many companies a separate group of employees works on large deals. This group consists of seasoned professionals from technology, legal, finance, and business departments. Bid manager positions may exist with the buyer, the seller, or with third-party consultants. In large deals, a temporary team is sometimes drawn from different departments to help bid managers and the large-deal group.

Contracts may be written by the buyer's legal people with the help of IT and business managers. Vendors may suggest some amendments before finally signing the contract. Before signing a contract, commercial details and pricing are negotiated between the buyer and the seller. Technical writers, graphics designers, and legal people are an integral part of the team that prepares a response to the RFP.

When any large deal and underlying projects are executed, transition and change management is important. Transition management, in particular, may be required before the projects are taken over by the firm that won the bid. Contracts often call for operations well into the so-called *steady state*, when solutions are in place and processes are, ideally, working smoothly. At this point, the staff is comfortable working with the project as per contract terms and service-level agreements (SLAs). After the steady state is reached, the contracts or purchase department on the buyer side keeps track of whether contract terms are followed by both the sides.

Case Study: A Complete Bidding Cycle for a Multimillion-Dollar IT Outsourcing Deal

Earlier in this chapter, I mentioned that large commercial deals are an integral part of the IT world. That's true for both product as well as services companies. As an IT manager, you must understand the bidding cycle and the role of third-party consultants. Down the line, you may be an important stakeholder in such deals. The contract, for example, might affect the applications that you are handling. Or in a more direct case, you might be handling the bidding process as a bid manager or a solutions architect.

Now to the case: Y Inc. is a US-based IT outsourcing company dealing in information technology products and services. It has marketing and development offices in more than 50 countries all over the world, with sales revenue reaching billions of dollars from services alone. The services IT portfolio covers almost every segment, ranging from high-end ERP consulting, to the Internet, to mainframes, to legacy applications. It has development centers in all Indian metropolitan areas, with its staff exceeding

40,000 people in India alone. ERP services and web applications are the two areas that earn the most revenue throughout the globe.

Receiving the RFP

Y Inc. received an RFP from a European conglomerate (AtoV Inc.) for managing its IT operations worldwide. AtoV wanted to outsource its entire IT operations in order to achieve better operational efficiencies, substantially reduce IT operations costs, and have the ability to focus more on its core manufacturing and retail business. AtoV has diverse interests throughout the world that include heavy engineering, consumer goods, household electronic equipment, electric distribution grids, automobiles, and retail businesses. It also has a fully owned IT company (IT Ltd.) that is supposed to manage IT operations for all of AtoV's other companies. However, IT Ltd. is seriously short of skilled manpower to support AtoV's other companies in a cost-effective manner. Also, there is a lot of interference in the operations of IT Ltd. itself by AtoV. Moreover, IT Ltd. is not free to price its services as per market standards. Many times, IT Ltd. is forced to provide resources free of cost or at nominal rates to other companies in the conglomerate. Appointments at the top level in IT Ltd. are also dictated by AtoV. There are many more such reasons IT Ltd. is fast becoming too expensive in providing IT services to the group.

AtoV corporate executives were forced to look outside for better options (vendors) that are market driven and can be held responsible in case of nonperformance. This was the first occasion in the past several decades where AtoV had floated an RFP outside its group empire for outsourcing IT operations. AtoV executives were extra cautious and took every possible effort to make the RFP a success.

Placing the RFP

The RFP was not advertised publicly. Only a few major players across the globe were invited to submit proposals. AtoV thought these were the IT services companies who could provide services up to their standards in terms of quantity, quality, and reliability. Nine IT service providers (including Y Inc.) were invited to participate in this prestigious worldwide bidding exercise. Each one of the participants had annual sales revenues well exceeding $1 billion. All were global players. They all had expertise built up over the years in the areas desired by AtoV.

These nine service providers were selected based on a comprehensive research project undertaken as a part of preparing formal RFP documents. The selection of the final vendor would depend on how well these service providers understood the requirements of AtoV and presented a customized solution. Pricing and other financial terms of the proposal were to play an important role. However, the contract could be awarded to a vendor whose quality and solution most closely suited the needs of AtoV. In that case, the pricing could be second or even third best (among all the bids submitted). Pricing was not the sole criteria. The total pricing of goods and services requested by AtoV was likely to run into several hundred million dollars, spread over the contract period of many years. Depending on the annual performance reviews, the contract was likely to be extended up to five years.

As expected, this bidding exercise attracted the attention of the business press worldwide. In India, the RFP was in headlines in national business newspapers, because much of the contract was likely to be executed from India, which is a low-cost region. Almost all the companies vying for this contract had a major back-office presence in India.

Using a Third-Party Consultant

Executives of AtoV had no prior experience in dealing with a bidding process of this magnitude and geographical spread. So they engaged a third-party consultant (TP Cons), which specialized in bid management for large deals, to manage the selection of the most suitable vendor for them. TP Cons was given complete responsibility from concept to closure. The selection of a suitable vendor was the closing point of the bidding process. TP Cons was also supposed to monitor the transition and work out a plan for change management. Both AtoV and TP Cons were headquartered in California.

TP Cons started talks with various department heads and top executives of companies within the AtoV group that were likely to be parties in sending the IT work offshore in this off-shoring exercise. TP Cons required almost a month's due diligence to figure out the IT needs of various participant companies. AtoV finally decided to contract out IT operations in phases. For the first phase, infrastructure management services (IMS) and ERP were chosen. These services badly needed an overhaul and were consuming most of the IT budget in almost all cases. After everyone agreed in concept on inviting proposals in order to contract ERP and IMS, the first step was to write an RFP.

Creating the RFP Document

As you know, an RFP is a comprehensive document focusing mainly on the scope of goods and services requirements and conditions that govern the bidding process and the contract thereafter. As stated, this was to be a multimillion-dollar contract spanning five years.

The RFP document itself was running close to a hundred pages, including many appendices. The main document had many sections. The first section included company background and the intentions behind floating the RFP. Various acronyms used in the main RFP document and its appendices were defined. The RFP listed contact points—AtoV personnel—for those vendors with questions. It also had proposal submission timelines and terms and conditions governing the process of proposal making. It had the general requirements that a vendor and its proposal needed to fulfill as a prequalification note. It had an executive summary of the overall scope of the job being outsourced. And as main content, it had two sections on the scope of goods and services sought from prospective vendors. One section contained a detailed description of ERP services and the other one contained detailed infrastructure service outsourcing requirements. It had a nondisclosure agreement (NDA) to be signed by prospective vendors because AtoV was sharing a lot of confidential information regarding its applications and infrastructure.

All this information was vital to the prospects to help them produce an accurate proposal. The RFP also had a template (an outline format) for the proposal and broad guidelines on what the proposal should contain in terms of solutions, financials, legal, and other terms. Apart from the details in the main body of the RFP, there were a number of supporting documents, including some detailed spreadsheets. These documents included NDAs, formats for financial documents, legal terms and conditions governing the proposal, an overview of the application landscape and the interface details with multiple ERPs in the scope of proposal, details of servers and diagrams of network architecture, and many other details to work out the solution and financials of the proposal as accurately as possible.

Proposal and Transition Terms

After AtoV issued the RFP, the suppliers were given a chance to raise their questions regarding the proposal and bid processes. Each proposal was to be submitted by e-mail before a stated due date and time of day that was to be followed very strictly. After creating a proposal, each one of the nine prospects was to be given the chance to make an oral presentation to a selection committee comprising senior executives from AtoV and TP Cons. The period between floating the RFP and the final award of contract was approximately two months, a period typical of deals of this magnitude. After the contract award date, there was a transition period of three months to transfer application and infrastructure services to the bid winner.

TP Cons was to chalk out and execute a plan for transition and change management. During the transition, all expenses were to be shared 50-50 by the bid winner and AtoV. Expenses included salaries for both firms, all overheads, software/hardware, and whatever it took for a smooth transition of services to the bid winner. The transition was to work under an onsite/offshore model, with India as the offshore base. Main onsite locations were spread throughout North America, the United Kingdom, Germany, Japan, Singapore, and Australia. After all transition was done, TP Cons was to monitor the steady-state operations for an additional quarter.

Forming the Response Team

After Y Inc. officially received the RFP, it formed an RFP response team. The first member was the bid manager from the presales team, as happens in many cases. He was the project manager for this mega proposal-making exercise. Team members were added from the infrastructure and ERP groups as per the needs of the RFP. Almost all the elements of IT infrastructure such as mobile devices, phones, copiers, PCs, servers, data centers, software, networks, and the processes including those of the help desk were involved, but IMS was the biggest component of the RFP. Three to four senior experts were needed to cover all the areas of IMS required in the proposal. As usual, the required people were already busy doing other billable projects. Producing a proposal was important to the organization, but it couldn't be billed to other clients. So taking a project manager out from a billable role for a couple of months was a difficult call for any functional head.

For the ERP stream, Y Inc. required both technical and domain experts on SAP, Oracle Apps, and PeopleSoft HRMS systems. Though the size in terms of dollar value of the ERP stream was smaller compared to the IMS project, Y Inc. needed many more members there because of the diverse nature of functionalities involved, and Y Inc. had three core ERPs to support. In other streams, the story was the same—all designated members for proposal making were busy in other billable roles. At first, the members in both streams were put in dual roles of working in their regular jobs and contributing to the proposal as well. All the team members including bid manager started with studying and analyzing the RFP documents from the client. Legal and finance teams also studied the proposals.

Answering Questions from Vendors

Y Inc. sent about 35 questions from all the streams to the client for clarification. Sending too many questions would be considered bad form—as if you had not done your homework in analyzing the information supplied in the RFP. At the same time, sending too few questions could also be seen to mean that you had not studied the RFP in the depth required for making the proposal. So it was a fine balancing act.

All nine prospects sent in their list of questions to AtoV for more information and clarification, which they thought were required to make a decent proposal. AtoV executives took about one week to get back with answers. The questions from all nine prospects, and AtoV's answers, were combined and circulated to each participant. This is a typical practice to make sure that each prospect benefits from the questions raised by others and that all of them have the maximum possible information before they start working on their proposals. AtoV, along with TP Cons, also hosted a pre-bid face-to-face meeting in which all the prospects could discuss the answers and ask any remaining questions. This was the last chance for all the participants to raise their questions or ask for more information. After the closing of this meeting and until the submission of final proposals, any officials from the potential vendors were not supposed to talk to anyone from AtoV except the designated contacts. Any such attempt could disqualify the prospect from making a proposal.

Working on the Proposal

With all this information, it was imperative for Y Inc. to work on the proposal on a war footing. Y Inc. had 40 calendar days, and the team was not in place yet. Except for the bid manager, nobody else was confident regarding the content, clauses, and scope of the proposal. Y Inc. decided not to engage a third-party consultant for writing a proposal. Being an IT services major, Y Inc. routinely wrote such proposals. Moreover, it had a specialized team under presales for such large deals. Even with the large-deals team, the experts were to come from the respective teams of ERP and IMS competency verticals. Including the bid manager and two members from the large-deal group, a total of 14 members were identified who would help produce the proposal. All had prior experience in making such proposals. Two technical writers were also included in the team. One of the team members from the large-deals group was of the level of general manager.

The day came when all the designated proposal team members were detached from their regular work and packed in a conference hall of the corporate office. They had no land lines in the conference hall and no cell phones—only hot discussions! These discussions were sometimes useful and sometimes not so useful. But all the team members were available in a room to exchange ideas, and the technical writers, who were ready to take notes and make the proposal presentable.

First, the bid manager presented a schedule on how to produce the proposal on time as well as who would do what by which date. The manager set a 30-day program—no days off, not even weekends. The team would start by 7:30 or 8 a.m. and work until half past midnight sometimes. Coffee breaks took place with snacks made available inside the room, and all meals were made to order. The motto—only one: Get it done, whatever it takes. Employees could take their days off later. (Of course, the team would be given extra incentives to make up for the hard work if the RFP was won.)

Some model proposals were studied, and the proposal started taking shape. But when the first draft version was ready, everybody was disappointed. A senior member from large deals wanted everything to be redone. The onsite manager insisted on the inclusion of everything in the proposal as per Information Technology Infrastructure Library (ITIL) standards, because that was important from the client's perspective. One ITIL expert and one graphics designer were added to the team. The first draft was then ready. Technical writers had to compile 485 pages for it. But finally, the proposal started taking shape.

Suddenly, a new policy decision came from the client side. A written proposal was okay, but more emphasis was to be put on oral presentations. So Y Inc.'s work was redone on Microsoft PowerPoint slides—thanks to the timely inclusion of a graphics designer on the team. Financials took about a week, but they occupied only two slides in the final proposal. The final bid was close to $300 million. Real strategic for the company! They wanted to win it at any cost. Eight to ten "what-if" scenarios were worked out, using different combinations of schedules, efforts, resources, onsite-offshore ratios, scopes, and rates. Approval for all of them was given by the corporate and the finance departments in advance. These scenarios were created in order to accommodate any last-minute changes prior to or during the live proposal presentations. Excel worksheets were kept ready to work out additional custom scenarios if required. In the last minutes, input from the sales team become important, and the financials changed accordingly.

Defending the Response

On the final day, in a San Francisco hotel, three different committees consisting of the AtoV and TP Cons officials congregated. Final presentations were made by all the prospects. Written proposals were submitted a couple of days advance via e-mail, and seven print copies were placed in sealed envelopes. All were dropped in a designated physical mail box.

After the presentations, there was a follow up round of questions from the client side. AtoV and TP Cons raised a lot of questions to clarify the promises and solutions made in the presentation. A time of three days was given to answer these questions. The bid manager from Y Inc. again formed a team to answer this final round of questions. The team sent around 30 pages of clarifications to the client.

AtoV wanted a month to study different aspects of all the proposals. Word came back in just two weeks. The winner? Y Inc.!

Performing the Transition

Now it was on to the transition and a huge number of applications and infrastructure issues. TP Cons was the boss, so TP Cons officials explained the process to the transition team. They provided around 30 elaborate templates and forms to be filled for each stream at each step. All this was to be loaded in an orderly fashion on a web portal designated for the transition. The progress of transition in real time was now available to everyone, including top management of Y Inc. and AtoV.

There was one more challenge, probably tougher than making the winning proposal: main transition sites were offices and plants in Texas and New York. A couple of them were added from Germany, the United Kingdom, and other places too. Y Inc. roped in four transition managers—one each in California, Texas, and the Indian cities of Chennai and Noida. The transition team structure was 50 percent onsite and 50 percent offshore. A large onsite presence was required to cover the learning curve and attend face-to-face learning sessions with AtoV subject matter experts. Later the onsite-offshore percentage was to be reduced to 20-80 and finally 10-90 in the long term.

TP Cons deployed not more than three members, who did everything from RFP until the transition was over. The transition took a total of six months, end to end! TP Cons walked away with a handsome consulting fee.

Summary for the Case Study

This case brings you a high-level idea of how a typical bidding cycle operates. With expertise in participating in the bidding process, drawing up contracts, offering technical solutions as a solutions architect, and understanding financial and legal aspects, you can expect many exciting opportunities for you within IT departments of large and small corporations, third-party bid consultants, outsourcing companies, and legal firms. You may take the role of bid owner with a buyer. You can even look for opportunities as a bid manager for a bid management consultant or a vendor who has the responsibility of preparing a winning response to an RFP. You can look into the legal side and draft contracts in coordination with IT and business managers. In preparing a response to RFPs, solutions architects play an important role in terms of offering technical solutions to client-specific problems. They also prepare effort estimates that are used in working out the final pricing for the contract. Solutions architects need to keep multiple solutions ready in response to a given problem at the client's place so that contract negotiators from the vendor side have some good options. All these positions of bid owners, bid managers, third-party bid consultants, and solutions architects are very well paid in the industry because they are crucial to business for buyers as well as sellers.

Acknowledgements: The author wants to give special thanks to Venkat Paturi, the senior vice president, Mahindra Satyam, for his guidance in preparing this case study.

Infrastructure Elements

You need to appreciate the functioning of infrastructure management services (IMS) in order to claim top IT slots. For readers with only a software background, this chapter will be a quick go through of the challenges faced by IT infrastructure people. The content is general and will be equally useful to both technical and business people. This is an overview; if you want a more in-depth understanding of this topic, you should read books focused specifically on this subject. The list of references at the end of the book in Appendix C will be a good start.

This chapter starts by defining IT infrastructure elements and then further discusses capacity planning and performance management. It also covers SLAs, tools, and challenges specific to IMS. The chapter ends with a case study that discusses an interesting real-time IMS deal.

Many of the IT outsourcing deals in large corporations across the United States, Europe, and Asia are related to infrastructure. Infrastructure elements are also part of IT outsourcing deals that contain software such as SAP and other legacy applications. Managing IT operations also in most organizations includes infrastructure elements such as data centers and networks. Therefore, as an IT manager, you must appreciate the infrastructure side. Most CIOs, for example, have a very good handle on IT infrastructure—both hardware and software. Knowing only software will get you only a limited leg up the ladder of any IT organization. That's especially true for companies in which IT is a support department, such as in manufacturing companies. So pay attention here—your career growth depends on it.

What Constitutes Infrastructure Elements?

Elements such as phones, copiers and printers, servers, PCs, software, data centers, networks, and the processes associated with them make up most of the world's IT infrastructure. For most organizations, the IT infrastructure is growing at a very fast pace. It is becoming more difficult to manage with each passing day. Large companies have centralized data centers that are supported by massive networks and distributed storage elements on storage area networks (SANs). This infrastructure technology and related processes are evolving very fast.

Ongoing efforts within an organization are always designed to make the existing IT infrastructure leaner, more flexible, more resilient, and smarter. We want the infrastructure to respond swiftly when business really requires it to. Efficient management of IT infrastructure can help contain costs while reducing complexity and enabling businesses to reach productivity goals. Efficient management can also help maintain security and resiliency-as your organization develops new business initiatives.

Infrastructure management services in such environments calls for management of geographically distributed network resources, monitoring and management programs to ensure enhanced service levels, reduced response times, near-zero down times, and proactive support across all layers of technology and business architecture. Ensuring performance and high availability at peak load is one of the prime goals. In a similar fashion, lean periods in business have to be handled cost-effectively when the IT department might have a surplus in resources. Some of the important functions under IMS are briefly described in the following sections.

Server Management

Server management is a function that might involve monitoring and administering key system resources. These include server configuration, performance, availability, and utilization. Server administrators need to work in real time, sometimes around the clock, to ensure effective functioning of company servers and proactively act to prevent problems from occurring. Managing servers might include the following:

- Round-the-clock monitoring and administration of servers and data center resources to ensure that set performance and availability goals are met.

- Server administration and incident management might also be possible to do remotely by using sophisticated tools. Doing this from low-wage regions can significantly reduce costs.

- Operating system upgrades and system administration. This might involve administering security and patches as supplied by vendor(s) from time to time.

- Management of network bandwidth, load balancing, and web site traffic.

- Optimization of server storage and CPU performance.

Network and Storage Management

Effective capacity planning is required for network devices such as firewalls, load balancers, routers, switches, and hubs to maintain optimum performance levels. You also need to manage and administer network usage effectively along with regular monitoring of network thresholds. Proactively detecting network degradation before it becomes a service bottleneck is important. Monitoring bandwidth utilization trends, looking into spare capacity, providing network security and bug patch notification, administering firewalls, performing event analysis, creating and monitoring watch lists, and conducting overall network fault management find a place in day-to-day activities. Anticipating growth over a three- to five-year period is also important when dealing with bandwidth and network issues. This will require making accurate predictions of growth in the business and having the IT resources required to support that growth.

Asset Management

Management here requires collecting data-related assets, tracking assets as they move about, and maintaining inventory records. Infrastructure assets can include servers, desktops, notebook computers, handheld devices, other software, and hardware. Asset management might also involve facilities planning, budgeting, and compliance activities. Asset management is often automated with the help of third-party software. Corporations can also have multilocation, complex SANs. Performance and availability requirements in this case can be very stringent to ensure that critical business data is always available. Like servers and networks, SANs also require 24/7 real-time monitoring. Maintenance activities are similar to those in server management. In addition, SAN management processes must ensure the perfection of data backup and replication.

Application and Security Patch Management

This category involves application delivery, program installation and removal, application updates, application configuration, and repair. Software usage in servers and desktops is monitored by using software tools that present real-time reports on the location of software, number of licenses installed, and usage data such as time and frequency of use. Common now as well are centralized security patch administration and the detection of vulnerabilities. It is important to make sure, through testing, that security and other patches don't have a negative impact on production systems.

Performance Optimization and Application Tuning

This function often has four major tasks: network optimization, capacity planning, storage optimization, and application tuning. Optimization is done by collecting and correlating the various aspects of the organization's present and future needs, something that arises out of short- and long-term business plans. Major cost savings are often achieved by outsourcing in this case.

IT Security and Business Continuity Planning

This function involves the design and implementation of an IT security-management architecture that fits the organization's risk-management needs. It requires the real-time, active monitoring of company networks, analyzing the security of a company's information systems and infrastructure, and gathering and scrutinizing intelligence related to information systems at a global level. Another set of activities performed in this area includes log file analysis, vulnerability scanning, penetration testing, device tuning, and compliance risk monitoring.

Business continuity planning is mission critical for any business. What happens, for example, if a fire consumes a building that houses your servers? What if hackers infiltrate a key process? Continuity planning involves making sure processes related to critical business procedures can still run in a disaster. It also involves emergency procedures and data/process recovery.

Database Administration

The stability and reliability of an organization's data is one of the top concerns for any company. All company data is maintained by database administrators, and their jobs demand very high skill levels. The related technology is evolving fast and is too complex for any individual to perform all database management and administration tasks. The risks and costs involved are simply too much.

There are several major tasks involved when we talk of database (DB) administration: DB installations and upgrades, managing tablespaces, round-the-clock monitoring, routine troubleshooting, and archive and log maintenance can be listed under day-to-day administration activities. Capacity planning, compliance for security requirements, performance tuning, DB replication, backup, and recovery procedures are some other activities undertaken by the database team of the infrastructure management services group.

Help Desk Services

Help desk services are the most visible part of the IMS group. Generally, the help desk has 24/7 operations for technical and functional problems raised by end users. Help desks act as a one-stop shop for all the IT-related problems in your organization.

Users can ask questions and report problems related to software and other IT infrastructure elements that include personal machines as well as company networks. The end-user interaction can be through multiple media, including voice, e-mail, instant messages, and logging incidents in centralized help desk software.

There can be multiple levels in support, typically named L1, L2, and L3. L1 usually relates to simpler and direct user problems such as setting up a user, solving PC and printer setting problems, and other things that can be solved in real time over the phone or with the help-desk agent remotely taking control of a machine for the purposes of resolving an issue. The more issues you are able to resolve as L1, the greater the user satisfaction levels will be.

Definitions of L1, L2, and L3 supports can vary for different setups. Sometimes there can also be an L4 layer. Broadly speaking, L2 refers to a technical problem that is not simple enough to be resolved in real time. L3 support comes into the picture when a serious software bug is reported by end users. There are usually stringent SLAs defined for L1, L2, and L3 layers that govern the response time and other performance terms.

Help desks are sometimes categorized as functional or technical. Functional help desk services deal with domain- and process-related difficulties raised by end users. A business user, for example, will call a functional help desk if she has difficulties with an SAP production order process. The application is working correctly, but she may have problems with the meaning of a couple of fields or she doesn't know the proper sequence of user interface screens involved in the process. On the other hand, she will call a technical help desk if she is a seasoned user of SAP but in a particular instance is getting technical errors such as, "The page can't be displayed" or "Unknown error—contact your administrator." In most companies, there is a common call center (called the *L1 help desk*) for both technical and functional challenges faced by end users. If the L1 help desk can't solve a problem, the company brings in functional or technical people from higher levels.

Challenges in IT Infrastructure Management: A 10,000-Foot View

On multiple occasions, I have discussed the importance of lean IT—IT that is flexible enough to accommodate business demands that arise as a result of operating in highly interconnected global markets. IT must also respond flexibly because an organization's performance these days is influenced by events outside its control. Organizational success today depends on the speed with which a company responds to changing market conditions. As the backbone of any IT organization, IMS obviously has a crucial role to play in the whole game.

Effective management of IT infrastructure is made possible by employing the best people, processes, and technology. It is therefore important to understand how these elements work together in harmony for excellence in service delivery. You must understand how existing and emerging technologies can be applied to deliver support services in cost-effective and energy-efficient ways. Service delivery depends on a foundation of multiple facilities, networks, storage, servers, and applications. All these are different technology domains. The IT department needs to figure out innovative ways to ensure optimum resource usage and top levels of security. IMS also needs to meet or exceed stringent SLAs set by the business. These typically pertain to performance, availability, capacity, energy, and costs.

Capacity Planning

We have seen that IT is always driven by business needs. IT simply enables the business to reach its goals, so investments in IT—and for that matter, in the growth of IT—should always be business driven. We also know that the economy tends to fluctuate, and the demand for goods and services along with it. It's the job of executive management to read the market and economy and provide projections for growth of the business in the near and long term. Any planning activity in the organization, including that of planning IT infrastructure, will depend heavily on these growth projections. We can't simply extrapolate the last five years of data to plan for growth in infrastructure elements such as networks and storage.

IT directors need to sit down with business executives to get the business projections and translate them into the required capacities of the various infrastructure elements discussed in earlier sections. And these meetings between top IT and business executives are required at regular intervals; business plans are often fine-tuned based on market feedback and many other conditions. So, as you can see, capacity planning is not a simple activity nor is it a one-time task. It's important to keep in mind emerging trends such as cloud computing and service-oriented architectures and come up with a clear road map on how the required growth in IT infrastructure will be supported. Not everything can be done in-house. After you have an idea of the requirements for the future state of infrastructure, it's time to see how well current needs are fulfilled by existing IT infrastructure and strategies. This will be used to do a comprehensive *gap analysis*—the distance between where things stand and where they need to be. The results will be useful in making intelligent purchasing decisions.

But wait. Some homework is still required before you approach the market with a bag of money. Can you consolidate servers? Eliminating a server can save you a lot of money. Technical decisions such as these must be carefully worked out. A carefully worked out consolidation exercise is likely to bring savings in cost and operational simplicity because of the fewer number of components. Server virtualization with VMware may also be considered to reduce costs. But keep in mind that server consolidation may not be good in all cases. Depending on the specific functions, server consolidation can in fact be dangerous. More often, you'll need to be prepared to buy new hardware and integrate it with the existing infrastructure.

Performance Management

Performance degradation in IT infrastructure can adversely affect business processes and users. There are system variables related to CPU usage, memory utilization, storage, ports, and network segments that can be monitored to discover whether performance is below predetermined levels. In addition to these regular infrastructure elements, there are other key indicators including system latency, connection time, errors per second, and discarded frames per second. These variables are individually monitored to detect possible degradation in the associated element of infrastructure.

Best practices in incident management, capacity management, availability management, and service-level management together contribute to the effective performance management of IT infrastructure. By implementing these best practices, you will know in advance of problems when infrastructure elements such as server capacity, router memory, and circuit bandwidth need upgrading. Many companies have IT performance-management services that have a proactive and cost-efficient approach to managing infrastructure elements. These services can monitor the performance of networks, servers, desktops, laptops, printers, and other elements on a 24/7 basis. The focus is to keep IT systems operational, available, and secure so that attention and energy can be devoted to revenue-earning activities.

A performance management system needs to monitor and record the patterns of changes in workload, utilization, and other factors indicating the quality of the user experience. The system administrator should be notified of any break in thresholds. That administrator should be well equipped to take proactive and corrective steps. These steps can include reallocating workloads among hardware or increasing capacities to maintain utilization within acceptable limits. The indicator most worried over is degradation of resource performance (for example, CPU usage or memory utilization in servers). Both will degrade with increases in application load and cause the system to slow down.

Many powerful performance-monitoring and management tools are available that provide an integral view of IT infrastructure and overall system health. These tools perform routine checks such as monitoring CPU usage and memory utilization, and monitoring disks and interfaces in case physical and virtual elements of the infrastructure show problems. The tools can also identify bottlenecks via comprehensive traffic monitoring and analysis. They also verify (through features such as synthetic traffic monitoring) application integrity for communication protocols such as HTTP, SMTP, and FTP. These infrastructure performance-management tools also provide key metrics for business applications including Oracle Apps, Microsoft SQL, and Microsoft Exchange, as well as operating systems such as Unix and Linux.

Summary

Infrastructure management services forms an important part of IT operations. All ranks in the organization are stakeholders and customers of this department. For example, in a typical emergency situation, the CEO of the organization may spend hours in the data center to oversee resolution of a crucial breakdown in services that is affecting millions of dollars in business per minute. Any critical infrastructure breakdown immediately gets escalated to the levels of CIO and CEO, because it may affect the ability of the company to do business. Every IT professional needs to handle IT infrastructure services at some time or other in his career, especially if he has his eyes on the top slot of CIO, CTO, or IT director. So good luck!

Case Study: Infrastructure Operations

The client in this case is a global manufacturing company called M Inc. This company supplies various engineering goods across the globe. M Inc. has a multiyear outsourcing contract with Y Inc. to manage its entire IT infrastructure, including the help desk. Y Inc. is a US-based outsourcing company headquartered in California with offices across the globe, including India.

The infrastructure elements transitioned were operating systems including different flavors of Unix and Windows, around 700 servers, and an EMC storage area network. The contract involved support to around 120,000 employees across the globe in eight time zones in North America, Asia,, and Europe. The transaction also involved noninfrastructure items that included ERPs such as SAP and Oracle applications, Oracle databases, and a host of homegrown applications.

The contract involved an L1 and L2 help desk that was operational 24/7 for cases involving the ERP and databases. Y Inc. had to guarantee a 5 percent reduction in costs each year over seven years. All help desk support involved SLAs and penalty clauses in case of nonperformance. An important part of the contract was that many surplus employees of M Inc. had to be added to Y Inc.'s payroll. This arrangement was a great help to Y, which got trained employees in the areas required by the contact. Taking over trained employees considerably shortened the learning curve and difficulties in transition for Y Inc. These newly hired employees brought along with them valuable information in terms of insider knowledge and an understanding of M Inc.'s culture.

As a part of the contract, the ownership of relevant assets from M Inc. were transferred to Y Inc. It was a huge transition that involved transfer of people, processes, assets, and office locations. Some mission-critical services were taken over by Y Inc. but were still delivered from M's locations. Others, such as the data center, were moved to low-cost regions where Y Inc. had offices. In all cases, extensive testing was done by vendor staff before the assets and processes were formally transitioned. SLAs remained more or less the same, regardless of whether they were located at M Inc. or at Y Inc. All performance, compliance, and security obligations were taken up by Y Inc. The contract involved managing other smaller vendors and subvendors that fell under the purview of functions overtaken by Y Inc.

For implementation, Y Inc. followed a three-phase approach. A separate data center environment was created at Y Inc.'s Chennai location, and all the systems marked for takeover were reconfigured and tested in this new environment. This included the ERPs and all other software and hardware. The transition period was two months, during which the client systems were taken over in phases. The last phase was steady-state operations. All the care was taken to secure and replicate the data as a part of business continuity planning at new locations and with new management at client locations. This required prior approvals from client business units and periodic meetings for status reporting and inspections.

Starting in the third month, SLAs were applicable with all their penalty clauses. Now Y Inc. was directly responsible to the end users of the client. The service levels were gauged through periodic customer satisfaction surveys. For all the functions they took over, Y Inc. was responsible for all regulatory compliance, certifications such as International Organization for Standardization (ISO) 20000 series, and benchmarking against industry standards. The client wanted a Six Sigma quality process applied uniformly to all the facilities.

Note: Six Sigma quality processes were pioneered by Motorola in the late 1980s. They identify and remove the causes of defects or errors in order to achieve exceptional quality levels of 3.4 defects per million.

The Benefits

This deal enabled M Inc. to concentrate on its core business. Because of the resulting savings and energies, the IT organization was able to give technology support to new business initiatives. The vendor also brought in a high level of technical expertise and a valuable knowledge bank in terms of experiences working with other customers. In tangible terms, the overall contract reduced support expenditures at M Inc. by 35 percent. In a typical year, the savings were close to $20 million. That was about 15 percent of M's annual total operating expenditures. Just as a benchmark, many IT-savvy companies spend close to 10 percent of their annual sales revenue on IT.

Being hands on in IT infrastructure planning and operations is a big plus for any IT professional. Remember, almost 80 percent of the total IT budget goes into the support and maintenance of existing applications. Much of this falls under infrastructure. A great and fast-track career waits for those who understand infrastructure—both hardware and software elements—and the core business of the company.

CHAPTER 8

The Cloud

Fundamentals, Strategy, and Economics

This rather short chapter discusses everything that you might need to get started with clouds. It discusses cloud environment fundamentals and *cloudonomics*—the economics of cloud computing.

Clouds are the "in" thing. They provide IT infrastructure on demand. Pay per use without the complications of investing in hardware and software. They are highly scalable too. Clouds are currently a very hot topic of discussion among CIOs. Many of them are implementing clouds in order to achieve lean IT operations so that the organization can concentrate on its main line of business and not IT. As an IT manager today, you must have a working knowledge of clouds and the associated economics in order to stay current on the technology landscape and to implement the decisions that executive management makes to achieve lean operations.

Understanding Cloud Fundamentals

Cloud computing is a relatively current trend with a great potential to increase agility and lower costs in enterprise computing. It's Internet-based, on-demand computing that very much resembles an electricity grid that is scalable on demand. You pay only for what you use.

Cloud computing provides shared resources (such as software), information, and physical infrastructure (such as like servers) that can be on employed on a pay-per-use basis. End users don't own the resources they use. Instead, they save on immediate capital expenditures by renting usage from third-party service providers. Many cloud providers employ the *utility* computing model—much like traditional utility services for electricity and water. You subscribe to these cloud services and pay for only what you consume.

You need not install the applications and enterprise hardware. You simply access them over the Internet by subscribing to the cloud service provider. Cloud computing provides an efficient computing model by centralizing processing, memory, storage, and shared physical infrastructure. Figure 8-1 provides a simple view of cloud computing: users access infrastructure from a big, common pool located offsite.

Figure 8-1. Cloud computing: a layman's impression

Cloud computing can be broken down into three major segments: applications, platforms, and infrastructure. And infrastructure service is the backbone of whole cloud concept.

- *Application clouds*: Cloud providers host applications on their centralized servers that can be accessed by subscribers through the Internet. A subscription fee is charged under different models of payment. Major players include Concur Technologies, Salesforce.com, Cordys, Google, NetSuite, and Taleo. They provide a variety of services including remote patch management and upgrades, accessing standard packaged software on a network, enabling custom application access over the Web, and providing delivery under a model in which many different clients access the same instance of an application (for example, many stock brokers using services from a single application hosted by a cloud provider).

- *Platform clouds*: This service delivers a computing platform that facilitates the deployment of applications without buying the underlying software and physical infrastructure layers. Major players include Amazon Elastic Compute Cloud (EC2), Google App Engine, NetSuite SuiteFlex, Microsoft Windows Live, and Cordys Process Factory.

These service providers enable deployment of custom and standard applications without the hurdles of investing and managing in the required hardware. They can provide hardware servers and operating systems, and so forth, under a pay-per-use model. Under the platform cloud model, instead of you buying the computing platform, the cloud provider buys it and provides you with access that you pay for based on your use of the service.

- *Infrastructure clouds*: Providers of infrastructure cloud services, also called *platform virtualization services*, provide clients with the equivalent of data centers and other hardware elements. A client, using these services in fully outsourced mode, need not invest in an IT department at all if desired, except for the supervision and coordinating staff. Providers include IBM (managed hosting), Google (managed hosting and development environment), Amazon.com (cloud storage), and Rackspace Hosting (managed hosting and cloud computing).

This whole cloud delivery model can significantly reduce IT costs, while optimizing workload and the overall service-delivery model. Cloud computing models have built-in scaling capabilities that allow them to grow as your business grows. Clouds are associated with new, Internet-driven economies that make sense for many businesses.

Developing the Right Cloud Strategies

Cloud computing can dramatically reduce the cost and hassles of managing the technology and associated infrastructure. But like any other offering, you should do some research before you decide to apply cloud services to a specific business problem. The cloud may not be the right answer to every business problem within your organization.

You also need to consider the company's strategy regarding capital expenditures (CAPEX) and operational expenses (OPEX). For example, you need to pay for any bills provided by a cloud service provider as an operational expense. That can be a problem if the company accountants would rather buy a piece of equipment and depreciate it over time.

You also need to consider the type of cloud to be used as well as the right service levels. And what about legal and other compliance issues as your data goes to external clouds? Finally, you must place a lot of faith in the providers who will store your information. Many IT people don't like the idea that they can't back up data locally.

You can use clouds to get the infrastructure required to test your new product line. You can use clouds for e-mail services for the entire organization. And you can use clouds to test experimental business simulations that later become mainstream business models of your company. To arrive at any effective cloud strategy, therefore, you need to first have a look at your company's business strategies and the role that your technology infrastructure plays in that strategy. You need to assess how loosely or tightly coupled the systems are in your organization and determine whether it's safe and feasible to take some noncritical systems to an internal, external, or hybrid cloud environment. A similar analysis needs to be done with the current state of data centers to determine feasibility, cost, and safety considerations.

The ultimate aim of this exercise should be, as always, to simplify operations and to cut operational and capital expenditures significantly. Security, privacy, and compliance for data and processes may be the deciding factors in many cases. In developing cloud strategies, you need to first assess the current state and then decide on rules and policies that will govern the whole transition. To succeed with your cloud strategies, your people, processes, and technologies need to be organized effectively. Cloud-enabled business strategies can knock down functional and information silos while focusing on outcomes that drive business performance.

You must get answers to the following:

- Do you know all the whats and whys of existing and new services and how they can be moved to the cloud?

- Have you assessed all financial, security, legal, internal compliance, privacy, and feasibility issues?

- Do you have a clear road map for moving from the current state to the cloud?

- Have you documented all the desired benefits to provide a benchmark for the experience?

- Do you have transition and change management plans for moving to a cloud environment?

- Do you have a business continuity plan in case the cloud service provider collapses or is out of business?

- Can you later switch the service provider or move to internal clouds or come back to the original state?

- Does the cloud provider have connectivity and service-level contracts and does the provider have the capability to support them? Penalty clauses can be an option.

- How does the cloud service provider ensure the privacy of your data and the services offered?

- Is your data safe? Can you back it up and restore it?

- What is the market standing and reliability of the cloud service provider?

- What will be your cost for, say, the next five years?

You'll have other questions unique to your business that will affect your operations or reputation.

Managing and Securing Cloud Environments

In March 2009, Google discovered a security challenge with its Google Docs service. The documents marked as confidential were getting shared because of some application bugs. Google Docs contains millions of documents, many of them very sensitive. This incident may be enough to open the eyes of IT managers, who perceive cloud computing services as free of day-to-day management hassles.

Any organization that opts for the cloud should treat the cloud service provider just like any other third-party vendor. The contract clauses have to be reviewed very thoroughly to ensure that they can hold the cloud service provider responsible for security and other lapses caused by their mistakes. All security risks need to be considered and proper insurance coverage taken. Like any other third-party vendor, the cloud provider needs to be actively managed. While the data might be residing on a cloud vendor's systems, the responsibility for that data is not fully transferred. Organizations are responsible to their clients regardless of whether they are using cloud services or they are hosting all their services internally in a conventional manner. Choosing and managing a vendor is, therefore, equally as important as, or even more important than, it is in conventional bidding scenarios.

Organizations must remember, too, that employees of cloud service providers will have access to your sensitive data. You must be able to trust them before subscribing to their services. In cloud scenarios, all the considerations apply that are deemed important while selecting vendors in conventional strategic deals. These include understanding the firm's financial position, undertaking periodic audits, and reviewing security certifications. After selecting the vendor, continuous monitoring is equally important in steady-state operations. Organizations using cloud models should make sure that their insurance covers cases of security breaks occurring at the cloud provider's location. In a nutshell, proper risk management and continuous monitoring are two key management principles to be employed for safely working under cloud environments.

Working with clouds often creates an additional layer of complexity in managing applications. Applications usually need modifications to accommodate the additional layer introduced by clouds, and that makes the version under the cloud environment different from that of original. Third-party tools such as integration scripts, virtual private networks (VPNs), and encryption software can be used to help integration with clouds. Each version of this software comes with its own life cycle. Each may need further upgrades and maintenance, like many other third-party software programs. This applies to every image deployed into the clouds.

Comparing the Cloud to Service-Oriented Architectures

In a cloud computing model, enterprises use a variety of services hosted on third-party servers through the Internet. In SOA, enterprises use integrated applications in the client-server model that may be more lightweight than traditional legacy systems. SOA is used over both the Internet and intranets.

The cloud forms a very logical hosting platform for services. SOA is a methodology to build applications. SOA is also a way to integrate applications. Clouds, in contrast, present both infrastructure services and a delivery model for applications. SOA, as the name suggests, is an architectural style of building loosely coupled with application or software infrastructure. Using SOA, applications can be integrated and presented at the enterprise level. SOAs can be much like a cloud environment.

Exploring Cloud Economics (Cloudonomics)

Cloud computing users avoid CAPEX on hardware, software, and services when they pay a provider only for what they use. Companies have low management overhead and immediate access to a wide range of applications. The contracts with cloud service providers can be terminated at short notice, so the risks involved in getting locked into unnecessary IT investments are minimized. IT is becoming more standardized and more like a commodity—it's now nearer to its true role as a business enabler. In situations where the capital expenditures would be small, or where companies prefer CAPEX over recurring expenses, the cloud model may not make economical sense. Cloud computing makes sense for short-term initiatives or short-term surges in business demands that will require some extra CPU and storage capacities. Cloud computing can be financially viable when your organization is performing software evaluations and testing that might require specialized software and infrastructure on a temporary basis.

Moving a data center or a portion of it to clouds requires extensive analysis in terms of calculating the current running costs and the costs involved with capital investments. Any data center would have sizable investments in servers, networks, storage, and data center physical infrastructure. Added to this are investments in infrastructure and help desk software licenses. Operational costs would come in the form of salaries and business processes such as software maintenance, backup, disaster recovery, help desk personnel, and other operational support. All these costs should be taken into account when considering any cloud solution. Costs are also required to maintain service levels and compliance. When switching to clouds, you'll have visible costs including the entry fee, ongoing billable hours, and other expenses charged by the provider. But you should also consider the hidden costs pertaining to the evaluation of cloud vendors, planning, transition and change management, backup and fallback plans, and many more things. This makes the whole feasibility study for switching to clouds a complex task requiring patience. Sometimes the benefits of switching over are very much apparent even without a detailed analysis, but it's still better to play it safe and do a comprehensive cost-benefit study.

Clouds Help a Pharma Company

A pharmaceutical company with offices mainly in the Asia–Pacific region recently went to the cloud. The company was looking for significant improvements in IT efficiencies and also wanted to "go green"—primarily use less energy—in its five data centers. Company officials achieved this through virtualization offered under various cloud models explained earlier in this chapter. The cloud operations not only reduced their overall costs but also provided a cost-effective IT platform for business innovations that required major simulations in their work of discovering new molecules.

Summary

This chapter covered the fundamentals and trends under various cloud operating models. It also covered the economics of using cloud models. The cloud is a promising but relatively new trend in infrastructure services. Not much literature is available in terms of its experiences in the industry. So managers need to be extra cautious. They should know exactly what they need before approaching a cloud vendor. Data security and data privacy might be prime challenges while working with cloud vendors. Your data or your client's data is exposed to the cloud vendor's staff. Depending on how the cloud is set up, your data could be exposed to other customers of the cloud, or breached by hackers. So you, as a manager, must assure yourself of the practices followed by the cloud vendor for data, service continuity, and other legal issues. A cloud vendor must be treated just like any other third-party vendor, whose services need monitoring for quality and content.

PART 2

IT Business Issues

The Fascinating World of Finance

Many decisions that you make, no matter what level you are in the organization, have a financial impact. For you to grow on the job, and within your organization, you must understand financial data at a basic level. This will enable you to make better decisions in both your professional and personal lives.

This chapter therefore aims to provide a basic awareness of accounting and finance for anyone in information technology, marketing, operations, and human resources. The contents of this chapter will help you gain a better understanding of the financial objectives of your organization and how they intertwine with such things as IT strategy, product development, project management, and so forth. This chapter will thus help you put your new understanding to use in your respective functional area. It will also help you work out the financial implications of your day-to-day decisions, help you make decisions that have a positive impact on the financial health of business and, finally, prompt you to make better use of the resources allocated to your projects and administrative division.

This chapter will discuss financial statements and decision making broadly, but for a detailed treatment you might refer to more specific texts on finance and accounting. The concepts discussed here are not limited only to IT companies. They are general knowledge to understand any business—be it of yours or that of a client's. You need to appreciate both for all-around professional success.

Economics and Finance

It's important to understand the difference between economics and finance to know how your organization relates to world markets and other important factors in the big picture.

Economics is a branch of social science that is mainly concerned with the manufacturing, consumption, and distribution of goods and services across the world. It's a science that deals with high-level concepts like price and supply and demand. It explains to us how economies work internally for different countries and how they interact with each other to shape world trade as we see it today. Economics is mainly the study of the goods and services moving among world markets.

Economics is usually divided into two categories. *Microeconomics* deals with the dynamics of individual markets. Microeconomics also focuses on supply-and-demand relations. *Macroeconomics* deals with topics similar to microeconomics, but on a much larger scale. Instead of focusing on individual markets, it focuses on things like gross domestic product (GDP), trade flows between countries, inflation, unemployment, per capita income, the national debt, and so forth.

Finance, on the other hand, mainly concentrates on the maximization of wealth, while economics is all about optimizing valued goals. Finance is more like a subset of economics that deals with money management. Finance, for example, is all about the saving, investing, spending, and lending of money at the granular level. Financial institutions like banks and stock markets play an important role in these activities. Concepts like time, risk, and money are crucial in the world of finance. In fact, risk management is a discipline unto itself, and financial institutes spend millions of dollar perfecting it. Further divisions in finance include personal finance, which deals with the finances of an individual or a family, and corporate finance, which deals with funding activities essential to the working of the companies like yours. Public finance is a term used to describe the financial activities of public entities like a country, state, or city.

Supply, Demand, and Market Pricing

Supply and demand is one of the most basic concepts of a market economy—and one that has an impact on your organization on a daily basis. Demand tells us how much of a product people want to buy, while supply tells how much is available in the market. In a competitive market, the price of any specific good varies until an economic equilibrium is reached. At an economic equilibrium, the demand (by consumers at current price) equals the supply (by producers at current price). If there's excess quantity of an item, the price tends to fall. If the item is scarce, the price tends to rise. The market supply is dependent upon a number of things, including manufacturing costs, technology used in production (which may allow mass production), the number of suppliers in the market, prices of related goods, and general expectations about future market prices.

If the manufacturing costs are high, there may be fewer producers in the market. Mass production lines make the cost per unit cheaper and allow for a larger quantity of goods to be available in the market. The number of producers in the market decides the level of competition and thus the quantity and price of a good or service. The greater the number of producers, the more competitive the prices will be.

Finally, if companies expect prices to rise for anything they sell, they may release fewer goods into the market to reap the benefits of price increases later. This may create an artificial shortage, resulting in higher prices. On the other hand, the expectation of higher prices may encourage others to jump into the market, eventually lowering prices. The price of a specific variety of goods can also be affected by the prices of related goods. Let's take the example of a component used in a product that is manufactured to order. The manufacturing cost of that component may be high in absolute terms, but since it's used in a high-value, customized product, it may be economically manufactured in fewer quantities.

Individual supply and demand patterns for specific goods are usually differentiated from those of markets. On the other hand, market supply patterns are the summation of supplies from individual suppliers. So individual items may or may not reflect broader market trends.

Market price is a topic of interest mainly in microeconomics. Manufacturing costs, availability of goods, affordability to consumers, strategic goals, competitor's prices, the number of producers in the market, market maturity, and brand value are some of the factors that determine the prices of goods or services in the market. The rules of supply and demand are always at work in a competitive, free-market economy. A business might revise the price if the demand for its product is too high or low. Similarly, a price correction may be applied if the current prices of the product are on the higher or the lower end. Prices charged by the competition also have a great effect.

There are some conditions under which the natural law of demand and supply may not work, at least right away. According to John Maynard Keynes, a noted economist, prices might become "sticky" and not react to variations in either demand or supply. This is likely to occur when prices in the market are declining. An economic dictum tells the story: Prices are flexible upward, but not downward. There are certain situations where either a buyer or a seller has the power to dictate the prices in the marketplace. In such situations, the natural law of demand and supply has a smaller role to play.

Business Cycle or Economic Cycle

Every nation goes through periods of economic contraction (recessions or depressions) and periods of expansion (so-called booms). Such cycles may last from a year to more than a decade. In the United States, recessions seem to occur every ten years or so. Do business cycles have an impact on you? Ask yourself that question when you are standing in the unemployment line during a recession! Conversely, boom times tend to spark an increase in salaries because employers try to ensure that valued employees stay with the company.

In this context, it's necessary to understand the nature of recession and recovery. A recession starts when some factor or measurement of aggregate economy (a macroeconomic activity) starts declining and has cascading effects on other key measures of economy. For example, if sales decline, it will naturally cause a decline in production. In a cascading effect, a decrease in production will cause a decline in employment rates and in income levels. This will cause further decline in sales and the cycle will continue. A continuous two quarters of negative growth in GDP is generally taken as a measure of an economic recession.

At some point, this vicious cycle will break and a positive, self-reinforcing cycle begins. In this upward and positive cycle, there is an increase in output, employment, and sales, all of which support each other. At this point the recovery of the economy starts.

Examples of Basic Economics in Decision Making

Modern business conditions are becoming so competitive and complex that intuition and experience alone might not be adequate to make the right business decisions. Economics offers a range of analytical tools and models that can assist you in making decisions. Today, a number of such tools and theories are available but I'll keep the discussion here to just two of the most valuable concepts: opportunity cost and discounting (net present value). These are used by almost every practicing manager.

- *Opportunity cost:* The main point is to assess what you are giving up by pursuing a given action. If any decision doesn't involve sacrifices, then its opportunity cost is zero. Let's say you have $10,000 in cash. You can put this money in the bank at 3 percent interest or invest it in a business that might earn more or less than that bank interest. The opportunity cost of investing $10,000 for a year is $300, which is the interest your money would have earned in the bank. Knowing the opportunity cost, you can decide whether to invest in a business, hold the money, or simply put it in a bank. In this case, you'd probably invest in the business only if the likely annual income is much more than $300, because the risk is much higher.

- *Discounting principle:* This principle is based on a basic rule in economics—a dollar tomorrow is worth less than a dollar today! The reasoning is not hard to understand. The future always involves risk. If you pocket one dollar today and wisely invest it in a business or in a bank, it will earn interest. You'll get more tomorrow than you have today. But you may not invest it wisely or the bank may fail. And if you simply hide it under your bed, inflation will eat away at its value. There is an old saying that supports the discounting principle—it's not wise to sacrifice today's pigeon for tomorrow's peacock. Then again, nothing ventured, nothing gained.

Business and the World Economy

The phrase global economy generally refers to the economies of all of the world's countries. The world economy is typically judged in monetary terms—usually in US dollars. The twelve major economies, not necessarily in order, are the United States, China, Japan, Germany, France, the United Kingdom, Italy, Russia, Spain, Brazil, Canada, and India. Recently, China surpassed Japan as the second-largest economy in the world. Some studies say that by 2012, India will post the highest growth rates compared to all major economies. Currently China holds this position, followed by India (9 percent) and Russia (8 percent). Growth rates in many of the developed countries are well below 5 percent. The predictions are that, in GDP terms, India will be the third-largest economy within two decades. Naturally, companies in fast-growth economies are well positioned to ride a powerful wave.

The years 2008 through 2010 were an extremely difficult period for the global economy. World trade contracted by 12.2 percent in 2009—probably the sharpest decline in the past 70 years. Economic forecasts, at any given point in time, depend a lot upon oil prices, the strength or weakness of major currencies, and the stability of financial markets. World trade ultimately affects national economies, which are very important factors in deciding the financial health of corporations. Our jobs and compensation are also very much dependent on the health of the national economy and, in the era of globalization, the world economy.

In the wake of the global financial crisis and the collapse of companies like Lehman Brothers, financial gurus are advocating more openness in financial sectors. That could mean more foreign investments in and imports to developing countries like India.

The IT sector in India, for example, is traditionally dependent on exporting and offshoring by countries like the United States, the United Kingdom, and Japan. World Trade Organization (WTO) rules are specially framed to fight against protectionist measures taken by some countries that are seen as barriers to free world trade. Free and fair international trade is strongly viewed by many as the engine for world economic growth. Easy availability and affordability of trade finance (one component of which is the credit to exporters in emerging markets like India and China) is also seen as a booster of economic growth. The bottom line now is the fact that collective emerging markets, which are economically bigger than the United States right now, are steering the global economy.

Politics and the Economy

Political issues all have an impact on business. These issues include taxes, pace of regulatory and economic reforms, importing of skills from foreign countries, rules governing patents and intellectual property rights, and funding for social and educational programs. Business decisions to hire more employees, make capital expenditures, set inventory levels, buy imports, get affordable credit—all depend upon government policies and the state of the economy. Inflation, consumer buying power, interest rates, labor availability, labor cost and quality, cost of capital, regulatory framework and bureaucracy, competition from large businesses and multinationals, social safety cover and unemployment benefits—all are critical for almost any business. And they all are directly controlled by government policies. Corruption and bureaucratic red tape in the public sector can also have a huge effect on the way business is conducted.

A country's culture and history have a big impact as well. Businesses operate differently depending upon whether they are located in a capitalistic system like in the United States, or in a country with a different ideology like China. A lot has been written about the Japanese style of doing business and its correlation to their culture. India started economic reforms in the early 1990s. Economic reforms pioneered by Dr. Manmohan Singh—as a result of political decisions that came from the highest levels of Indian government—have increased the size of India's economy dramatically. Politics and the economy always sail in the same boat.

The Financial Institutions

Our financial systems are very complex and comprehensive. They consist of federal banks (as regulators), public and private banks, markets, financial instruments, and services. A financial system plays a vital role in the growth of any economy. Financial institutions act as intermediates between those who save a part of their income and those who require capital to invest in productive assets like businesses. Financial systems may exist two ways: as organized or formal institutions and as an unorganized sector in urban and rural areas. This is commonly referred to as "financial dualism." An example of unorganized sector is money lending by private parties that are not registered with the government. This type of money lending sometimes fulfills the microeconomic needs of certain sections of society and needs few formalities. The organized sector is bound by a very tight government regulatory framework that takes care of investors and the public's common interest.

Formal or organized financial institutions come under the purview of the central governments, federal regulatory banks, statutory bodies that regulate stock exchanges, and many other regulatory bodies. A well-functioning financial system needs a strong legal and regulatory framework, sound banking system, well-functioning securities markets, a central bank (federal regulatory bank), stable money, well-managed financial institutions, and robust information systems that integrate the whole system.

A federal bank regulates the country's monetary policy, which affects currency exchange rates with all major currencies of the world, interest rates for lending and savings, and rules governing foreign exchange. The aim of monetary policy is to keep inflation in control and maintain a healthy availability of cash (liquidity) in the system. For example, if the cash availability in the system is high, it may trigger inflation. The federal bank's regulatory framework will act in a way to suck the extra liquidity out of the system by increasing interest rates and making it more expensive to borrow.

Inadequate monetary resources on the other hand can disrupt the payments system. The federal bank tries to strike a proper economic balance through its policies. Liquidity, exchange rates, lending rates, and stability of currency have a direct impact on the financial well being of our corporations. For example, when the Japanese yen becomes stronger with respect to the US dollar, Japan-based goods and services companies become less profitable in terms of yen. For every dollar earned in profit from the international market, they now get a lower return in local currency. To ensure smooth international transactions, it is necessary to maintain the external stability of the local currency. Incidentally, confidence in the local currency outside any country also depends very much upon domestic price stability. Furthermore, federal banks in some countries also maintain and manage foreign exchange reserves to sustain this confidence.

Well-developed financial institutions like capital markets, banks, investment institutions, insurance companies, and mutual funds prime the economic engine and help it run faster and more powerfully. Businesses are dependent upon capital markets, investment banks, mutual funds, and venture capitalists to fund their short- and long-term capital requirements. These requirements can be day-to-day running expenses, called *operational expenses* (OPEX), or they can be for longer-term expenses, *capital expenditures* (CAPEX), which pay for equipment, software, and other infrastructure needs.

In the organized sector, some countries may have separate markets dealing in short- and long-term securities. Financial markets, in some countries, are also be classified as primary or secondary markets. A primary market comes into picture for new issues (for example, when a start-up from the Silicon Valley comes out with a public issue and its shares will be offered for the first time to the general public). Once securities are issued they can be traded further in secondary markets (any subsequent buying and selling of shares for that start-up will now take place in secondary markets). The same financial institution like the New York Stock Exchange (NYSE) can act both as primary and secondary market.

The Role and Functioning of Financial Markets

From a microeconomic viewpoint, the primary goal of financial markets is to assign available savings to the most productive uses in business. If a particular economy or market does not allocate national savings to the most productive assets or uses, it will grow at much slower rates. A well-functioning financial market system fuels economic growth. When we talk markets, by the way, we are talking of stock and bond markets, markets for goods and services, and so on. Markets are all interrelated. A problem in one market can have its roots in a different market.

In the primary market, new securities are issued. Stocks and bonds are the most commonly traded securities. Whenever a corporation or a civic body needs funds, it issues securities. These securities can be common stocks or bonds or one of many other forms. Investment banks assist in issuing securities in the primary market by guaranteeing (underwriting) securities. They ensure a minimum price for a primary issue. The primary market does less business compared to the secondary market, since it does business only in issuing new securities. A vast majority of capital transactions find their way into the secondary markets. These include stock exchanges like the New York Stock Exchange (NYSE), the Bombay Stock Exchange, the Tokyo Stock Exchange, options and commodities markets, futures and bond markets, among others.

The international capital market is composed of a number of closely knit markets. The key benefit of the internationalization of markets is that investors can diversify their investment risks. Investors, including individuals, major corporations, and even countries, work hard to diversify the risks in financial portfolios. If a particular industrial sector is not doing well in a developed economy like the United States, it may be doing much better in a developing economy like China. A diversified portfolio of international securities could therefore yield better results investing beyond the United States, for example.

American Depository Receipts (ADRs) or Global Depository Receipts (GDRs), as they are called, are used in US markets. They are the certificates issued by depository banks, which represent shares or stocks of foreign corporations held by those banks. In India, Infosys started the trend with ADRs and now many Indian companies have a listing in foreign stock exchanges like the NYSE. These Indian companies are successfully raising cheaper capital from foreign markets to leverage their operations. In today's open economy, global capital markets have become vital to the development of industry. Lots of foreign direct investment (FDI) is coming to India through these capital markets. If these investments are used wisely in productive assets, borrowing economies like India can benefit in a hugely positive way.

Common Financial Instruments

Quite a few financial instruments are currently available to investors. These include equity and preference shares, government securities, commercial paper, certificates of deposits, industrial securities, and call money markets.

- *Industrial securities:* Big corporate bodies issue these to accomplish their long-term working capital requirements. Debentures—bond-like securities not backed by collateral—and equity shares fall under this category.

- *Equity shares or common stock:* Ownership shares in companies are often high-risk/high-return instruments. Equity shares have no fixed period of maturity and also no fixed return rates. When investors buy stock or the common equity of a company, they get ownership of a portion of that company's assets and earnings. If a company does well, the price for its stock rises. Those who bought stock at a lower price then make profits, if they wish, by selling their equity holdings in the secondary markets. Stock prices in the secondary market depend upon the general health of the economy, on how well that industry sector is doing, and of course the health of the corporation. There are many other factors that affect stock prices.

- *Preference (or preferred) shares*: These instruments have fixed dividend rates and special rights to dividends, when compared to private equity shares. Preference shares are usually redeemable with a fixed period of maturity, though sometimes the maturity dates are far in the future. Therefore, they are also called hybrids.

- *Debt securities*: These instruments represent loans from investors to a corporation or government body. Investors of debt instruments are seen as creditors, or debt holders. The most common debt instrument is the bond. Bonds are issued both by civic bodies and corporations. Bonds earn interest payments at a fixed rate until they mature and can be redeemed.

- *Derivatives*: Derivatives are also financial instruments, like common stocks, but they derive their value from an underlying entity (stock or commodities, for example). Derivatives can be traded in markets independent of their underlying asset base. The value of derivatives changes as the underlying asset changes. Futures and options are exchange-traded derivatives.

  An option is a derivative. It's a contract between two parties that is concerned with the buying and selling of assets in a specific time frame. An option is an obligation to the seller and a right to the buyer. A buyer can purchase an option from a seller for purchasing X amount of securities at a specific price within a specified time frame. The buyer pays an option premium for entering into this agreement with the seller. Then it becomes obligatory for the seller to honor the transaction (per the time frame set in the contract) and give the X amount of specified securities at the specified price. The option buyer, however, is not required to buy the specified securities. An option holds good for a specified period stated in the agreement. Again, an option is derived from an underlying asset like a common stock, a bond, a currency or a futures contract. In principle, an option can be created for any valuable asset. The option premium is the money that a buyer pays to a seller for entering into an option agreement. The price specified at the time of activating an option is called a strike price or an exercise price. An option not exercised by a buyer before the expiration date automatically becomes null and void.

  A "call" option gives a buyer a right to buy. A "put" option provides a right to sell.

  A future is also a financial contract between two parties. In a futures contract, a buyer has an obligation to purchase an asset. And the seller has an obligation to sell. An asset in this case can be a physical commodity like oil or corn or a financial instrument (like US Treasury securities) that has a predetermined future date and price (as per contract). A future is different from an option in that, unlike an option, it's mandatory for the buyer to purchase the underlying asset. (They can also sell the contract before taking delivery.) Futures are used in speculating or to hedge against price fluctuations in the underlying asset.

For example, a farm producer could use a futures contract to lock in a certain price on a commodity and reduce his risk. This way, he is using it as a hedging instrument. Another example, by taking short positions (you expect a price to go down) or long positions (you expect the price to rise) using futures, you can speculate on the price fluctuations of farm produce or many other physical commodities.

- *Commercial paper (CP):* These instruments are issued mainly by corporate business entities to fund their working capital or business expansion needs. Commercial paper has short maturity periods. Commercial paper is not as secure as bonds and is subject to market risks. Therefore, corporate bodies with a good credit history only use this financial instrument.

- *Certificate of Deposit (CD):* A CD is similar to commercial paper, but it is issued mainly by commercial banks.

- *Government securities:* State and central governments and authorities like state electricity boards, municipal corporations, and others issue these securities. Commercial banks and other institutional investors are the biggest investors in government securities. The government uses this money to finance infrastructure development projects or it is used in various other government expenditures.

- *Call money market:* The call money market is mainly an interbank market. Banks that need cash for short terms borrow capital from the call money market. The interest rates on these loans are dependent on market rates, which in turn depend upon the current state of the banking system as a whole.

Objectives of an Enterprise: Shareholder Wealth Maximization

The objective of any for-profit enterprise in a capitalist system is to maximize the shareholder's wealth. That translates into effectively managing organizational resources, including human capital, to achieve maximum profitability. Put another way, any enterprise needs to maximize the return on investment made by shareholders.

To achieve this objective, an enterprise needs to maintain healthy growth patterns, develop infrastructure, develop required expertise, and maintain adequate levels of liquidity (access to cash or things that can easily be turned into cash). To keep growth steady, enterprises also need to develop and maintain an organizational environment conducive to new business initiatives, innovation, and productivity, and also ensure an ethical, fair deal for employees. Adequate design capabilities, facilities for manufacturing, business development, and diversification form another set of activities for achieving the goal of profitability for shareholders. Business needs to be conducted in the most ethical manner, while complying with all legal and social commitments, and contribute towards a healthy, ethical, and creative society. If you take away nothing else from this chapter, remember this: shareholders do not look at a business as if it were a charity. They expect a good return on the money they invest.

Basics of Accounting for an Enterprise

In this section, I discuss some basic accounting terminology and then analyze a simple balance sheet. Most businesses use what's called a double-entry accounting system. That means that any transaction results in a simultaneous entry to both the debit and credit side of the ledger. For example, if someone buys an item from you for cash, you would debit cash and credit sales with the same amount. It's mandatory for corporations to maintain accounts using the double-entry system. The so-called "single-entry" accounting system used in the old days by money lenders and landlords made ensuring transparency and detecting fraud extremely difficult.

Let's take a quick look at some standard accounting terms you should know. A *journal* is a book in which an account of transactions is kept prior to transferring entries to the ledger. A journal is like a rough book where running transactions are recorded as they take place. The *ledger* is the book (or more commonly these days, a part of a computer program) in which transactions are transferred from the journal. The ledger maintains final and more precise entries of transactions compared with the journal.

The chart of accounts (COA) is the structured list of a company's general ledger accounts. The chart of accounts can be prepared to best reflect and suit a company's needs. The accounts at the top level are generally grouped by type. In charts of accounts, the typical group headings are sales revenue, costs of goods sold, and the long list of expense accounts. Expenditure heads include administrative, selling, distribution, establishment, or financial expenses.

Bank reconciliation is a process in which figures from the company's accounting records are compared and matched against those on a bank statement. The accounting department needs to ensure that both statements match. The primary purpose of the bank reconciliation process is to make sure all the transactions with the bank are reflected on the bank statement and that final cash balances in bank accounts exactly match expectations.

Accounting standards are a set of detailed rules or codes that are imposed by government or other authorities to maintain and audit public accounts. The purpose is to maintain uniformity in preparation of accounts and financial statements like balance sheets. They also help us in detecting fraud and financial malpractice. Financial audits based on widely accepted accounting standards like GAAP (Generally Accepted Accounting Principles) create a sense of confidence among the users of financial statements and investors.

Any company wanting to list in a stock exchange can pass the required reliability and credibility criteria only when the books of accounts are maintained per official accounting standards. The Institute of Chartered Accountants (CA) in India, for example, has issued a number of standards that members follow while auditing the accounts of corporations.

The *balance sheet* and *profit and loss statements (P&L)* are two general financial reports that are required from every public company (although nearly every business makes use of these statements). Of the two, the balance sheet is the most important financial statement. It gives a snapshot of the business' assets, liabilities, and equity on a specific date. The balance sheet also serves as a bridge between consecutive accounting years. The P&L lists transactions over a fixed duration of time: monthly, quarterly, or annually. A P&L indicates how net revenue is transformed into net income, while a balance sheet summarizes an organization's financial status at a specific point in time.

Profit and Loss Statements

The sample profit and loss statement in Table 9-1 shows some common accounts for expenditures and income. An actual P&L (or income statement, as it is also called) can be very detailed and run multiple pages. The entries in Table 9-1 are self-explanatory. The things to be noted are the style and the total amounts in the columns at the end of the statement.

Table 9-1. Sample Profit and Loss Statement

Sample P&L Statement for Example XYZ Trading Co. Ltd.
For the accounting period 4/1/2010 to 3/31/2011

Total Sales Revenue	$180,000
Minus returns and scrap	10,000
Net Sales Revenue	170,000
Material costs	
Inventory, April 1	50,000
Purchases	10,000
Transport & handling	10,000
Minus Inventory March 31	10,000
Total Cost of Goods Sold	60,000
Gross Profit	**$110,000**
Expenses	
Staff Salaries & wages	$60,000
Utility bills	5,000
Rent and maintenance	7,000
Office consumables	3,000
Insurance	2,000
Promotion	3,000
Communication	6,000
Travel and Entertainment	4,000
Taxes	10,000
Total Expenses	**$100,000**
Net income	**$ 10,000**

Balance Sheets

A very simple balance sheet is presented in Table 9-2. Please note that shareholders' funds, share capital, and retained profits (undistributed), while equity related, are shown on the liability side because proprietors are holding money on behalf of their respective owners. On the asset side, the entries typically belong to that of a small business.

Note: The sample balance sheet shown in Table 9-2 should be taken as a starting point. For more complex financial statements, refer to books dedicated to accounting. Or, if you work for a publicly held company, get a copy of the annual report. It will have balance sheets and incomes statements covering the past year.

Creditors are companies or individuals to whom money is payable (owed). Debtors are people or companies that owe money for goods sold or services rendered, or due to contractual obligations. The money owed by debtors is known as *account receivables*.

Table 9-2. Sample Balance Sheet

Sample Balance Sheet for Example XYZ Trading Co. Ltd.
For the accounting period ending 3/31/2011

Liabilities and Equity		Assets	
Accounts payable (Creditors)	$500	Land & buildings	$10,000
Bank overdraft	500	Plant & machinery	5,000
Short-term (current) liabilities	1,000	Accounts receivable (Debtors)	6,500
Shareholders funds	9,000	Stock	500
Share capital	10,000	Cash	500
Retained profit (undistributed)	2,000	Closing balance	500
	$23,000		**$23,000**

Ratio Analysis for Reading the Health of an Enterprise

A balance sheet can tell much about the financial health and the state of current affairs of a company. Intelligent financial analysts can read between the lines and draw some usable intelligence about the company. Details like working capital, capital employed, net worth of the business, and return on equity or assets, can be determined with a complete balance sheet.

A balance sheet can also be used as an instrument for valuation. There are some limitations though. The real worth of an asset can be determined only when it's up for sale. Most reputed asset appraisers can also differ in their valuation of the same asset. Valuation itself is largely subjective. The value of an asset is often influenced by factors external to the organization. Details on how to do these calculations are beyond the scope of this book, but any book on the basics of accounting can assist you in this regard.

There are limitations inherent to financial statements. For proprietary concerns or partnership firms, there is no statutory provision for an audit by a qualified accountant. In public firms (limited companies), however, there is more authenticity. The statements are signed by the company's secretary and the board of directors, and it is formally audited and signed by external auditors. Auditors can also add notes before signing the balance sheet to cover any special requirements that may need further investigation. Corporations, in their own interest, aim for complete transparency in their financial statements and compliance with all applicable regulations.

When it comes to investing, financial statement information becomes very important. The massive amount of data in a company's financial statements can be very confusing. Through financial ratio analysis, these numbers are worked in a more organized fashion. There are dozens if not hundreds of useful ratios, but they can be grouped as

1. Liquidity Measurement Ratios

2. Profitability Indicator Ratios

3. Debt Ratios

4. Operating Performance Ratios

5. Cash Flow Indicator Ratios

6. Investment Valuation Ratios

Let's keep it simple and discuss only return on investment (ROI). This ratio is very basic and used widely. For a more comprehensive treatment, Investopedia.com provides a detailed description of these ratios along with numerical examples that are linked to actual published financial statements.[1] It's worth the time to visit this web site in order to see how the pros make use of ratios to dissect a business and its opportunities.

Return on Investment (ROI) allows an investor to evaluate the performance of an investment and compare it to others in his or her portfolio.

The return on investment formula is simple:

ROI = (Gain From Investment − Cost of Investment) ÷ Cost of Investment

So if you make an original investment of $170,000, which turns into $193,000—a gain of $23,000—the ROI is 13.5 percent.

ROI is generally expressed as a percentage. While calculating ROI, the gains or returns can be adjusted for taxes or inflation (or both) depending upon where you are using it. The higher the percentage obtained, the better. A negative percentage means the investment lost money.

You can bet that ROI calculations are made at the topmost levels in your organization. Executives give the green light to projects that provide a better potential return than others competing for corporate resources. In the process of capital budgeting, projects with maximum ROI are selected to maximize the wealth of company shareholders. In the process, executives may also compare parameters like payback period, average rate of return, net present value, internal rate of return, and profitability index.

ROI values can be easily employed to make or assess personal financial decisions. You are looking at different things when you invest in low-risk bank savings accounts or certificates of deposits than with high-risk investments like stocks or mutual funds. In low-risk investments you look at the effects of compounding or reinvesting the savings amounts over time. In high-risk investments you tend to consider the effects of capital gains and price volatility on returns. Please refer to Wikipedia for a great treatment of ROI.[2] In sum, ROI is used extensively by managers making investments and budget allocations. As a manager, you'll need to know when and how to make ROI calculations in decision making.

---

[1] Investopedia, Richard Loth, "Financial Ratio Tutorial," http://www.investopedia.com/university/ratios/.

[2] Wikipedia, "Rate of Return," http://en.wikipedia.org/wiki/Return_on_Investment.

Let's discuss an example involving numbers. Suppose you have $172,000 to invest. If you invest this money in the fairly stable US markets, suppose the gain (ROI) over time is 6 percent. But if you invest the same money as a foreign investor in the markets of booming economies like India and China, the gain is 20 percent. Assuming the risks in both places is similar, where you would like to invest? In booming economies, provided your investment is safe and the procedures to make the investment are hassle free. That's why, given the current political stability in China and India, these countries are attracting a lot of foreign investments from the United States and other Western economies.

Cost Leadership and Competitive Advantage

In a fiercely competitive business environment like we have today, a robust cost leadership strategy might be required of an organization for its survival. As Michael E. Porter of Harvard Business School points out in his book *Competitive Advantage* (Free Press, 1998), the foundation of above-average performance within the industry is a sustainable competitive advantage that can be achieved through cost leadership, differentiation, and focus. *Cost leadership* means low cost for a quality product. *Differentiation* means the company's products are unique in the market. *Focus* means market segmentation—finding a profitable niche. Market segmentation is a narrower scope than cost leadership and product differentiation. Companies with lower market share can be successful because they focus upon a smaller but profitable market niche.

Any one or a combination of these three strategies can give a competitive advantage over rivals. In the text that follows, I will talk about cost leadership and costs.

Like it or not, given a chance, people buy on price. Yesterday's high-priced innovation is today's cheap commodity. In price-sensitive markets, it is imperative for companies to have a thorough understanding of their costs and the things that drive costs to pursue the cost leadership strategy. Companies need to fully understand their customers' opinions on quality: What are they looking for in a product or service? This knowledge helps determine the features offered in a product, and avoid those that add cost but not increased customer satisfaction. Knowing this helps companies achieve competition-beating low prices.

Cost leadership is a goal of every organization. An effective cost leadership strategy can enable them to defend their market share, expand in the existing markets, create new markets, defend supplies, build entry barriers, weaken the threat of substitutes, protect against rivals, and reduce the cost of capital.[3]

Components of Cost

The final cost of any finished product is made up of components like material cost, labor cost, different overheads, and taxes. Let's look at these cost components in detail, using an example in the IT industry.

Software projects are perceived to be never on time and never on budget. Software is built in fast-changing business environments with flexible development models. The designs practically never get frozen to better accommodate last-minute changes. Consider software development projects like batch processing, online, and real-time applications. The cost components of each one of these may differ.

Following is a representative list of project cost components that need to be considered in costing out a software development project. This list is not intended to be exhaustive, but it is a fair representation of cost components in real-life projects. These include direct costs like testing or design costs that relate directly to the project; fixed costs, like equipment; and variable costs, like labor or materials.

Project cost components directly related to the SDLC (systems development life cycle):

- Requirements/scope analysis
- Application prototyping
- Design
- Construction
- User interface planning design and construction
- Performance
- System security

---

[3] Cost Leadership Strategy Blog, "Cost Leadership Strategy," http://www.costleadershipstrategy.com, February 26, 2011.

- Code documentation
- Testing
- System testing
- Application/functional testing
- Performance testing
- Test automation

Project cost components peripheral to SDLC:

- Additional documentation (end-user manuals, etc.)
- Knowledge transfer
- Install kit
- Data migration

Project cost components related to delivery support:

- Support during system testing, performance testing, and user acceptance testing
- Network and server configuration support
- Installation/implementation support

Project cost components related to training:

- Technical training (on specialized software and hardware)
- End-user training
- Communication training

Project cost components related to fixed costs:

- Facilities
- Machines
- IT infrastructure
- Lease
- Rental

- Interest in invested capital
- Research

Project cost components related to overhead (from a project manager's viewpoint):

- Unplanned iterations (for example, in iterative and agile development methodologies)
- Performance (for example, in real-time applications)
- Security (a stringent requirement in defense and mission-critical applications in enterprises)
- External interface (for example, in ERP and web applications)
- Cost overheads due to unplanned travel, expenses in additional software and hardware tools used in testing and performance monitoring
- Location overheads for multi-location projects (expenses generally not taken into account at the time of formal estimates)
- Project management and other administrative expenses
- Unplanned quality assurance and inspection exercises (on-site and offshore)
- Coordination and follow-up with clients, support functions, and management (more in cases of multi-location projects under the onsite/offshore model)
- Unplanned meetings and conference calls
- Project contingencies
- Scope changes that a manager needs to accommodate
- Risk management that includes mitigation and insurance expenses
- Wait time due to constraints and dependencies
- Other unplanned activities that differ from project to project (better to accept their existence and plan them as contingency)

As you can see, costs in IT projects depend upon the type of application, development methodology, scope, risk-management approaches, environmental factors, estimation techniques, and more.

This is a pretty exhaustive list of project cost components. You would have to make some alterations in the list based upon the peculiarities of your project. The basic components will remain the same, though, for most projects.

Accurately forecasting project costs is very important in ensuring profitability. The labor component may represent the single largest cost factor in your project.

Skill categorization is needed so that you can assign the right person to the job. For example, for release-and-build management, you may not need someone with ten years' experience. You can assign a programmer who's been on the job for two years. Some project tasks can be allocated to the newly hired or even to interns.

Proper scope management and the early recognition of hidden requirements, like performance, can also save a lot of money. Other cost-saving tasks include reviewing work at every stage and evaluating and managing risks. These can also help you achieve project objectives regarding cost, quality, and schedule.

Allocation of Overhead

Accurately understanding costs and cost drivers is very important. Major categories of costs, as we have seen in the previous section, include direct materials and labor, and overhead. Direct costs are relatively easy to calculate. On the other hand overhead is not so easily calculated. Overhead involves every business activity or material that is used to conduct business that is not directly attributable to your project. There are two methods that are generally used to allocate the overhead.

The direct method uses a predetermined overhead rate (OHRATE) to multiply a cost driver for any of the firm's products. For example, the OHRATE for a software company may be $18 per labor hour. The firm uses this rate in all its processes to determine overhead. Companies, naturally, have long-term and short-term projects. But in using this method, long-term projects carry too much overhead and they become overpriced while the short-term projects are likely to stay underpriced. This is seen as a major drawback of this method.

The second method, Activity Based Costing (ABC), uses many cost drivers in determining overheads. Organizations closely monitor projects to take note of what activities they are using. Overhead calculations for projects are based on every activity connected to the project. There are advantages of using ABC. For one, thing, it can result in very accurately determining the costs associated with a project. However, it can get very complex at times. And it is often difficult to figure out what exactly a firm's cost drivers are. Moreover, monitoring project activities and assigning suitable cost drivers can be a time-consuming and costly effort.

This is especially true for service industry firms that are represented by our present day IT projects companies. Such businesses may conduct hundreds of activities within a given project, on a given business day. It can be very challenging to figure out important activities and their cost drivers. In practice, most firms implementing ABC use 15 to 20 cost drivers at the most. Managers need to classify all their project activities per these cost drivers in order to compute overheads.

A close monitoring of actual costs not only helps us calculate profits and incentives in the current project, but it also helps determine the costs of similar upcoming projects. The actual costs, original estimates, and variance data are stored as the historical data in the organization. They form an important base for accurately forecasting the costs of future projects. Allocating overhead may be a big challenge for a project manager, especially in large companies. An accurate monitoring and control of actual cost is important for the project manager and team members.

Capital Expenditure (CAPEX) and Operating Expenditure (OPEX)

A capital expenditure is money spent to acquire or upgrade physical assets such as equipment or buildings. It can also be a major business transformation exercise or a major software acquisition like SAP. Usually this cost is recorded in an account classified as property or a similar category of capital. The cost (except for the cost of land) will then be charged to depreciation expense over the functional life of the asset. The cost of the expenditure in capital assets is therefore spread over the useful life of the asset. This type of outlay is made by companies to maintain or increase the scope of their operations. Oil and gas, telecom, semiconductor, power, and other utilities are among the most capital-intensive industries that require CAPEX.

Note: In the United States the tax code sometimes allows a technology purchase below a certain dollar amount to be "expensed"—written off entirely in the year of purchase—rather than depreciated over its useful life. Some managers like this because it can reduce profit and, therefore, taxes.

Operational expenditure (OPEX) is a category of regular expenditures as a result of normal business operations. Routine repairs are operational expenditures. Project management expenses and staff salaries are classified as operational expenses. Expenditures incurred in purchases or anywhere in supply chain, including warehousing and sales, also come under this category. The purchase of a laser printer involves CAPEX, but the paper, ink cartridges, power, and maintenance costs represent OPEX. For a large business, operational expenditures include the salaries of employees and facility maintenance and holding expenses such as rent and utilities. Depreciation of machines and IT infrastructure that is used in the projects and production process are also accounted under operational expenses. On an income statement, "total operating expenses" is the aggregate of a company's operating expenses over a period of time, such as a quarter or year.

As a manager, you will invariably be involved in the process of budgeting at the project level or even at the department level. If you appreciate these primary finance terms of CAPEX and OPEX, you will not only budget better but also work out better savings for your department.

Break-Even Point

It's simple and everyone talks about it. The break-even point (BEP) is where gains cover costs: the point where the gains from business equal the costs incurred. In other words, break-even point is the point at which cost or expenses and revenue or income are equal; there is no net loss or gain. At BEP, a profit or a loss has not been made, although opportunity costs have been paid, the capital is received, and the risk is adjusted. From there on one can expect profits.[4] Conceptually a business might start making profits beyond a break-even point. Once financial statements and the data are in place, we can figure out break-even using the following formula as

---

[4] Wikipedia, "Finance," http://en.wikipedia.org/wiki/Finance.

Break-Even Point = FC ÷ [1 − (VC ÷ S)]

Where:

FC = Fixed Costs

VC = Variable Costs

S = Sales

Let's assume

Sales (S) = $1,000

Cost of Goods Sold (VC) = $500

General and Admin (FC) = $100

Then VC ÷ S = 500 ÷ 1000 = 0.5

Break-Even Point = 100 ÷ (1 − 0.5) = $200 in sales

And the company operated well over the break-even point during this period: $1,000 ÷ $200 = 500% of break-even.

Break-even analysis is one of the simplest methods to use to know when you've become profitable.

Budget and Budgetary Control

A budget can be called an Budget and budgetary control organization's plan expressed in monetary terms. A budget can be prepared for an entire organization or its parts in terms of geographical territories, functional divisions, products, or significant activities like a strategic project. A budget can include capital to be employed, incomes, and expenditures. A budget is usually prepared for a definite period like a financial year or a quarter. It has to be prepared and approved in advance of the period start.

While working with budgets, the actual may vary when compared to the budgeted amounts. In such cases either actuals are corrected or the budget is modified. The aim is to have as minimum deviation as possible. This act is called Budgetary Control that aims at achieving maximum efficiencies while working with management policies. The aim of whole process is to assist the management in planning, coordination, and control. A budget may be seen as a management tool to communicate policies and targets at the operations level.

Table 9-3 shows a sample project budget sheet.

Table 9-3. Sample Budget Sheet

Project Budget Sheet for Automation of Payroll
Project ended Feb. 18, 2011 (Amounts in US $)

Budget Head	Budgeted Amount	Actual Spent at project end	Variance	Remarks
Hardware	5,000	3,500	1,500	Used existing hardware
Software tools	12,000	14,000	-2,000	Last minute upgrade to Windows 7.0
Labor	20,000	27,000	-7,000	Scope creep
Rents	5,000	2,000	3,000	Many people worked from home
Utility	2,000	1,700	300	
Travel	5,000	3,000	2,000	Used video conferencing
Contingency	3,000	1,000	2,000	
Totals	52,000	52,200	-200	Marginal overshoot within the powers of PM

Capital Budgeting (Investment) Decisions

The efficiency of financial management is judged by the success of its ability to maximize shareholder wealth. Decisions should maximize the net present value (NPV) of all expected future cash flows. NPV refers to the sum, discounted to take into account the cost of capital and, occasionally inflation, of expected net cash flows. The core principle of NPV is that a dollar, if invested elsewhere today, will earn interest. NPV is calculated as the difference between the present value of cash inflows and the present value of outflows.

In NPV calculations, the present values of all current and future cash flows (for a fixed period) are calculated taking inflation into account. One dollar scheduled to come in tomorrow may have a value of only 90 cents today. In a similar fashion, all expected future cash flows are discounted to get their present value. If the NPV of a prospective project is positive, it might be considered for acceptance; however, comparisons with other candidate projects might be required. With all other factors the same, a project with the highest NPV is chosen, as higher NPVs reflect higher profits. On the other hand, if NPV is negative, the project may be rejected since net cash flows will be negative.

Let's consider an example in which a retail business wants to purchase an existing store. It first estimates the future cash flows that the store is likely to generate. This cash flow is then discounted to get one aggregate, present value amount; let's say it's $763,000. Now if the store owner is willing to sell his business for less than $763,000, it's a good deal. NPV is positive. If the store owner wants more than $763,000, the investment presents a negative NPV, so the purchaser may turn down the offer.

The net present value method is very useful for manager for evaluating existing projects and businesses. If the NPV of a project is negative, it may be considered a candidate for elimination.

Company Valuation

How much money is a finance company worth?

Net Asset Value (NAV), or the book value of a company, can be measured by adding all assets and subtracting all liabilities. It's the most commonly used method for valuating a company. NAV thus obtained can be used in making investment decisions by comparing it with the ongoing market price of the company (net worth based on the market price). Discounted cash flows (DCF) is another commonly used method to value a company. It takes into account the current cash flows and discounted values of future cash flows (for a fixed period). DCFs are divided by the total number of outstanding shares of the company to arrive at intrinsic worth per share. Note that either method may not precisely calculate the value of the business in the real world, particularly NAV. Often you don't know what a business is worth until you put it on the market.

The valuation of high-tech companies can be more challenging than that of conventional companies. Constant innovation is a way of life in high-tech companies. They primarily own intangible assets like technology, intellectual property, and business processes that might take them to a path of high profitability. However, all these assets are not reflected in financial statements. Market data for many US companies can show a rise in their market capitalization even if their cash flow is negative for extended periods. High-tech companies need to invest a lot of capital in building up their technology assets and intellectual properties. In the initial stages, these investments show up as a negative cash flow but in the long run it's expected to generate profits for the company. High-tech companies by virtue of their competitive advantage are expected to generate higher profit margins and higher growth rates when compared to traditional companies. However, the overall game for high-tech companies is very risky. Intangible assets and uncertainty typical to high-tech companies make their valuation very difficult.

Summary

In this chapter I touched upon a variety of topics in finance and economics. Both fields are vast, making it difficult to cover them in a single chapter. By now, you might have seen how important knowledge in basic finance and economics is for practicing IT managers. There are standard texts available on the topic of finance for nonfinance managers. I strongly recommend you read one. It should explain in detail much of what I've outlined.

IT and Business Processes

It is the era of business transformation. In an attempt to reduce operating costs, companies are consolidating and streamlining their IT organizations. Efficient processes can help not just streamline IT, they streamline the business as well. Lean and efficient processes are the primary goals, whereas IT is just an implementation tool, as usual. In this chapter, I won't go deep into the mechanics of how to do business process reengineering (BPR), but I will discuss business transformation from a strategic angle that is very important for business and technology executives—and those who want to rise in the IT ranks.

As an IT manager, you may need to support the business transformation initiatives of your organization. You may participate in the design, redesign, review, and automation of business processes from both the business and IT points of view. You may also participate in transition and change management initiatives that are integral to any business transformation process.

Introduction: BPR Defined

A business process is a set of ordered activities that interrelate to produce a useful product or service, or a portion of it. The product or service can serve a particular goal or it may be for internal consumption; and it may be for a particular customer. Management and strategic processes, like product development or performance management, direct or form a framework for operations. Operational processes like production, sales, and purchasing form the day-to-day activities. Processes like HR, accounting, or help desk operations are called supporting processes because they support operations.

Frederick Taylor (1856–1915), a pioneer of industrial efficiency and scientific management, suggested that managers can discover the best practices to perform work by analyzing the process for creating goods and services. He also suggested that these processes be reengineered (redesigned or improved) every so often for optimal productivity gains. In Taylor's time, technology was not available for large companies to design processes that work in a cross-functional manner. Specialization was the mantra for efficiency gains.

In recent years, business process reengineering (BPR) has become a necessary and regular task for all organizations. Making sure that processes are as efficient as possible is a housekeeping task, but an important one. When it comes to BPR, top management must be committed in all respects. It is an uphill task, and employees, who may not like change or fear the loss of their jobs, often resist in both direct and indirect forms. During and after a BPR exercise, employee participation and commitment might weaken. Some employees may try to discourage others from participating in reengineering initiatives. Management should be prepared to deal with these obstacles by way of proper incentives and by ensuring required levels of employee participation.

Let's take an example of a mid-size company implementing ERP software like SAP. A number of the organization's business processes will be redefined or reengineered to SAP's standard processes. Because of this, there will likely be resistance from employees, and there may be some job cuts as well. Management has to provide proper incentives for staff to adapt to the new paradigm. Managers have to justify any job cuts and ensure stability to remaining staff. There should be a strong communication plan to drive management's viewpoint on "Why ERP is good for our future." Communication must explain how employees' futures will be affected and how exactly SAP, in this instance, is going to make their working life different and better.

The time between the start of BPR and the end is another important factor in its success. A BPR project regarding a complex process might take eight to twelve months. To contain any resistance, a significant amount of progress needs to be shown within a reasonable time frame. The more difficult part of a BPR exercise may be its implementation. Employees are apt to resist change when suddenly they are expected to follow a new process radically different from the old one. Management has to devise an incentive scheme and other creative ways to encourage staff to adhere to new processes. Communication is the key here—before anything else, the staff should be convinced that the new processes are an improvement over the older ones and that the new processes are meant to make their jobs easier. BPR can mean a significant cultural change for many organizations.

The benefits of BPR can be enormous. Greater efficiency is the goal. If it is achieved, the process and people connected to it become greater assets to the company. Ultimately, it adds tangible assets like cash, new facilities, and infrastructure. A well-planned change management exercise usually follows BPR to facilitate smooth change across the organization.

Concepts like Total Quality Management (TQM), ISO 9000 (a quality standard set by the International Standards Organization), and enterprise resource planning (ERP) also bring about positive changes at the organizational level. They are all well-defined and formulated vehicles designed to implement BPR. All must also be well supported by information technology, which makes processes easier to implement. With IT, the process constraints are implemented naturally. In a work flow application, for example, you can't proceed to the next step unless the previous one is complete. ERPs like SAP thus provide built-in, standard processes so that the organization need not reinvent the wheel when it comes to process design. A clear understanding and appreciation of these concepts at the grassroots level is the first and foremost condition for any successful implementation.

BPR is a strategic initiative; success in its implementation is proportional to the alignment of project objectives with the organization's goals. Therefore, it is of the highest priority to develop and effectively communicate a clear vision of the objectives before embarking on a BPR project.

The Reengineering Process

Identifying the business processes for a reengineering project is obviously a strategic decision. If you ever find yourself part of a BPR project, there are a few things you'll want to keep in mind. Instead of trying to change several processes at a time, for example, it might be advisable to first take up a few high-impact processes that will result in a quick turnaround. Quick results will be in the favor of the BPR project and act as a showcase for the other processes in the project.

The processes taken up for the BPR project should be divided into phases, with the total project duration not exceeding 12 months. Change management efforts should follow each phase. Project structure might involve a BPR leader at the organization level, process leaders, process reengineering teams, and the employees involved in or affected by the reengineering project. Getting employee input is critical because they, more than anyone, understand the original process.

For larger projects, a top-level process committee may be involved. If the BPR project is strategic, top levels of management need to drive the initiative. An external consultant, not involved in the day-to-day functioning of the organization, can be valuable in finding creative ways to design new processes.

As a part of a reengineering project, the target processes are broken down into logical and manageable sub-processes. Each subpart is measured and targets set in quantitative terms for parameters like cost, quality, and time. Each subpart is assessed for need and means of improvement. Simpler and more efficient ways to carry out the task are explored. Measurements are taken for both the existing state and the future state (improvement targets should be realistic). Quantitative and qualitative definitions of processes greatly help in overcoming criticism of BPR project skeptics.

Concepts of process prototype, process entities, process objects, and process activities, though not discussed in this book, are very important in any BPR exercise. Information technology also plays a vital role and is inseparable from today's BPR projects.

Change Management in Business Scenarios

I discussed change management in the first part of the chapter. Based on their experiences in India, some authors[1] have suggested a method for change management using BPR, as follows:

---

[1] V. Nilakant and S. Ramnarayan, *Managing Organisational Change.* (Sage Publications, 2001).

1. Establish a need for a BPR project and why it must be done. This needs to be understood at the grassroots level.

2. Make provisions for keeping the current business running and not disrupted by the BPR project.

3. Establish a change management team as an integral part of core BPR team.

4. Prepare the organization for change.

5. Establish a change team at the grassroots levels to drive the change by active employee involvement.

6. Align organizational structure, systems, and resources to support the change.

7. Identify and remove any roadblocks in the process.

8. Make sure the change (the new processes) becomes an integral part of organization culture. (This might be the most difficult to implement.)

9. Even after the BPR effort is over, adopt continuous process improvement as a daily effort.

10. Devise an incentive and rewards scheme for motivation and innovation.

11. Identify and promote people with the right mindset for enacting and embracing change.

These points emphasize the need to understand the importance of BPR and to keep the business running smoothly. Existing business may utilize all the bandwidth of the executives, so their availability to take part in BPR exercises needs to be planned realistically and carefully. Good communication and preparing the organization for change is also essential.

BPR as a "Quick Fix" Seldom Works

BPR is often used to cut costs and get back into the game by companies that are on the edge of disaster. This isn't always the best idea. Some companies sacrificed their in-house production capabilities and gained short-term profitability; later they were forced to reevaluate their strategic direction. It is better to be proactive and initiate change long before it becomes necessary.

Assessing current process capabilities, communicating effectively, managing change deftly, and aligning the objectives of a BPR exercise with the organization's business strategy are very important in achieving lasting benefits. If BPR is not used as a long-term solution, it is merely a short-term exercise for improving operational efficiencies with localized effects. BPR must be used as a strategic weapon to overhaul a process or the organization.

Business Processes and Organizational Performance

Organizations use business process reengineering as a way to bring substantial improvements to operational efficiencies and reduce the costs of day-to-day operations. A BPR exercise aims to improve organizational performance by bringing major changes in business processes and organizational structure. An organization is made up of its people, processes, and assets. A BPR exercise impacts all three for desired performance gain. If the people, processes or assets are not performing well, overall organizational performance is poor. The main thrust of BPR is renewing processes that are key to achieving the organization's business goals. Sometimes even relatively small changes can make a large difference in customer service levels and cash flows.

BPR doesn't always bring the wonders expected. Less than 25 percent of BPR projects achieve their stated objectives. All successful BPR projects have a strong leadership commitment, a solid management strategy for change and transition, and motivated and informed employees.

The Role of the Leader and Manager

To succeed, any BPR exercise must have the full commitment and support of executive management. Leaders must be capable of and willing to drive change. Managers in a company undergoing major process changes must plan and act to control employee fears, and overcome any resistance to adapt to the changed environment.

An article by Maureen Weicher, et al, points out, *"Managers in the organizations after reengineering are compared to coaches. They do not order; they guide. They do not direct the work of others; they coordinate, facilitate and empower."*[2] It's like being the coach of a soccer team before a major match. The coach needs to contain the team's anxiety while motivating them to do their best. The coach needs to analyze performance and drive his team with winning strategies—very much like a leader-manager in a BPR exercise.

Reengineering Recommendations

BPR must be escorted by strategic planning and it must take advantage of IT as a leveraging tool. The aim of any BPR exercise should be to make the organization more customer-centric. Any change must be driven by internal teams comprised of managers and those who do the work at the grassroots level. Assistance from external consultants can be useful, but consultants can't take the driver's seat. A long-term and high level of commitment is needed from executive leadership as well. Any BPR exercise should be time bound and take into account the corporate culture. Constant and effective communication across the ranks can be the single most important factor in the success of any BPR project.

Summary

Business process reengineering has been proven to help organizations achieve their overall objectives. But, it is successful only if the activities in which the processes are based are directly related to the needs and objectives of the business. BPR is often combined with other improvement philosophies, like continuous improvement, Six Sigma, and Just-in-Time to get enhanced and more lasting effectiveness.

Case Study: Business Transformation of an Applications Portfolio

It's a common story: as a company grows, custom or homegrown business applications are created and actively used to automate business processes. Different business groups within the organization develop applications to help in automation of their business processes. Many of these applications are localized and limited to the respective departments. Yet they proliferate.

---

[2] Maureen Weicher, et al., "Business Process Reengineering Analysis and Recommendations," http://www.slideshare.net/Timothy212/business-process-reengineering-3917082.

Some companies still have applications that have been running for two to three decades, and may have only upgraded them once or twice. Yet the global business scene has changed considerably during this time, and so have the most efficient business processes.

Packaged applications like ERP and supply chain management programs (SCMs) offer standardized versions of newer processes that not only reflect current business realities, but are also easy to adopt and maintain. Many companies have upgraded their processes through such programs, but mapping existing processes to packed applications is not an easy task. A well-planned business transformation or a business process reengineering exercise is needed. This case study attempts to familiarize readers with such transformation exercises faced today by business organizations across the world.

In reading through this case about a BPR/business transformation (BT) at a *Fortune* 500 company, you will understand how the theoretical framework for a business process reengineering study is developed. This case also studies enterprise application integration (EAI) and legacy transformation (LT).

The BPR team in this study integrated a portfolio of applications into an enterprise-wide ERP. Then, a set of legacy applications and processes were transformed to adopt standardized business processes through state-of-the-art technology.

Introduction

V Inc. is a leading global supplier of machinery used in the fabrication of integrated circuits. This case discusses a massive business transformation project that the company underwent. A large part of the exercise concerned the company's site service portfolio, which contained data on equipment configurations for client installations. The portfolio was an integrated repository for configuration data, contracts and warranty information, service workforce data, and service delivery data.

Business processes in the site service portfolio were overlapping, repetitive, and did not interface easily with each other. This resulted in extra work, errors, delays, and customer dissatisfaction. Older legacy systems were replaced with standardized global processes implemented on an SAP platform, spanning all company locations across the globe. The goal of the transformation was to standardize and automate low-level, repetitive, and manual transactions so that management could focus on the core business and new strategic initiatives.

Part I of this case study discusses the theoretical framework of the BT project at V Inc.

Part II describes site service applications and challenges they were posing to V Inc.'s business.

Part III discusses the actual business transformation of the applications portfolio.

Part I: The Philosophy Behind the Project

Site service applications (described in Part II) posed a number of challenges to V Inc.'s operational effectiveness and the smooth running of the business. Non-standard business processes hindered operational synergies globally and inhibited a focus on core business and new initiatives. A lot of manual intervention and paper-intervention was required in outdated business processes that caused data integrity and scalability issues. The applications were not interfaced well with each other; this resulted in inadequate sharing of information and gave rise to information islands. That in turn severely affected staff throughput.

Legacy systems in the site service portfolio were constructed on multiple technology platforms maintained by multiple vendors who severely lacked in coordination. The security and control procedures were also obsolete, posing serious security challenges. The final result was very high application support costs (up to 80 percent of the budget).

Objectives

The mandate was to standardize processes, remove redundancy, and make possible seamless operations across all functions. None of this was possible with the existing application portfolio. The most important pre-condition to the transformation project was to keep the business running at minimal cost to the organization. Objectives included implementing the following:

1. One major platform (SAP) for all core processes across the organization

2. Minimal separate applications interfacing with the SAP system

3. Global standards in all processes

4. More accurate and consistent data across the organization

5. Role-based security access with robust authorization control
6. Increased employee, customer, and vendor satisfaction

The Strategic Approach

V Inc. believed an incremental approach enabled frequent adjustments based on current business conditions, and provided time for the organization to make desired process improvements. An incremental approach provided more time and accommodated more process change iterations to reflect and anticipate rapidly changing market conditions. By making smaller incremental changes more frequently, the organization could still realize significant improvements in terms of productivity and cost savings.

Yet the company also understood that at times the organization needed to take a radical approach first, to position itself for ongoing incremental improvements.

V Inc. decided to undergo a sweeping BT exercise to overhaul its long ailing systems and then adapt to an incremental approach as it moved forward. Figure 10-1 shows some internal employee communication on the BT project.

Figure 10-1. Business process revision cycle

High-Level Output of the Process

V Inc. started the project by developing and maturing the organization's business strategy. The transformation process began with discovery and analysis to come up with recommendations for changes in the form of a road map. The tangible deliverables were

- A view of the "as is" state

- A view of the "to be" state

- The framework for BT

These outputs were generated for at least three different viewpoints: the business viewpoint, the information viewpoint, and the technical viewpoint (see Figure 10-2). The strategy (Enterprise) element was not touched for this particular transformation.

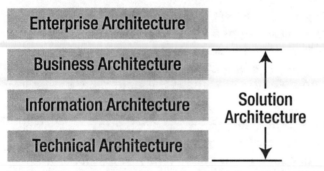

Figure 10-2. Architecture elements seen as deliverables at V Inc.

Business Leads Technology at V Inc.

V Inc. realized that an organization cannot effectively deal with the IT architecture without establishing a business viewpoint. In short, business strategy drives IT architecture, and not the other way around. The advantage of leveraging the broad use of IT to directly support the business direction is generally far greater for the enterprise than the return available from a more efficient use of technology within the IT organization.

Over the years, the company made an effort to combine business transformation and enterprise architectures to produce a concentrated focus on leverage points in which technology could improve immediate business performance. This created recommendations for specific technology products and practices to deliver the results in the most economical, yet timely, way possible. Greater business benefits were delivered faster and for less outlay. Without an overall architectural plan, the technologies and patterns chosen to implement business transformation would have been unique, short-lived, and caused incompatibilities for sharing. Without business transformation, the effective use of technology could not be effectively targeted at the greatest opportunities for business performance payoff. Done right, however, the synergy could be powerful.

Core Principles of BT

The following seven processes tell how the business transformation was to be carried out at V Inc. A large emphasis was placed on working out policy objectives. A clear-cut framework on improving the existing processes and designing new processes was provided to process designers. In order to stay focused, emphasis was on a phased approach.

1. *Determine the business context*: The business context is the articulation of the overall enterprise strategy. It can start with the desired business vision, which includes economic, competitive, technical, social, and regulatory factors, and the available resources. The outcome of the process is the enterprise strategy: how it will accomplish its goals.

2. *Determine the "as is" state*: Once the business context is in place, the next step is to look at the current state of the business processes and the functions performed. It may be useful to add the perspective of the hierarchy of business purpose.

3. *Form the future or "to be" state*: By looking at the larger business context, the future state of business processes can be imagined. The future state represents a vision of where the enterprise wants to be—in, say, two to three years—in terms of business processes and other factors.

4. *Generate broad policy directives*: This same analysis can be used to generate a series of architectural principles (that is, values and beliefs based on the business strategy), which should be observed in subsequent work.

5. *Perform a gap analysis*: Comparing the "to be" state with the current state uncovers the ground that must be covered. The results will be used as an input to the road map of the

transformation process. The goal is to lay out a proposed sequence and investment plan to create systems that support the business strategy in optimal fashion.

6. *Create guidelines to be employed by process designers*: Once the future-state vision and principles are in place, there is also a need for day-by-day design guidance to be employed by the business process designers. These guidelines are separate from the future-state vision.

7. *Determine focus*: It may not be practical to tackle all the architecture demands simultaneously. You must prioritize. The goal is to focus on high paying or competitively differentiating areas. An organization may find it valuable to capture details regarding the current-state of business model in the high-reward areas first, and then proceed to understand the implications of the information and technical architecture supporting these applications. This translates into taking a route of understanding the business first and then looking into the technological aspects of the as-is state.

Part II: Site Service Applications

V Inc.'s site service portfolio was a collection of tightly coupled applications, developed on IT platforms like J2EE, ORACLE – PL/SQL, and Lotus Notes. They were homegrown applications developed over 15 years. Nonstandard business processes caused operational burdens and made it difficult to launch new business initiatives. Obsolete technology platforms like Netscape Application Builder added to the existing skill shortages. Inadequate information and process sharing across systems were a challenge and application support costs were a major issue.

Site Service Applications: Functions, Technologies, and Limitations

Site service applications contained vital data about equipment configurations for client installations. They tracked the status of installations and revenue realization. The portfolio was an integrated mechanism for configuration repository management, contracts and warranty, service workforce management, and service delivery. The portfolio contained sophisticated reports and dashboards for service status, escalation, and issue tracking. Site service applications had interfaces with other enterprise-wide applications, like parts logistics, finance, HR, and sales.

Opportunities and orders were finalized in ORACLE Apps (sales). Then the data came to the site services applications that established the base for service management. It then went to finance for revenue and profitability calculations.

Eight Major Applications of Site Service

The site service portfolio contained the following elements:

1. *Installation Dashboard*: An integrated dashboard, accessed through Single Sign-On (SSO). This web portal integrated all process steps for installations.

   Technologies: HTML, JSP, Servlets, Oracle reports, Websphere application server, Websphere portal server, and IBM Secure Directory Server (LDAP).

   Challenges: System integration, system security and controls.

2. *Config Repo (configuration repository)*: Stored core product data and structure for all site services and product quality procedures.

   Technology: ORACLE PL/SQL.

   Challenges: Database compatibility issues between ORACLE and SAP, job scheduling.

3. *Workforce Management (WFM)*: HR system used for organization structure, self-assessment, certifications, training records, and labor demand planning.

   Technologies: SAP, HTML, Oracle Application Server, Lotus Notes, and PeopleSoft.

   Challenges: Processes overlap with HRMS, and poor user interfaces and system usability.

4. *Product Project Plan (PPP)*: New product installation, warranty- and contract-related service plans.

   Technology: ORACLE PL/SQL and others.

Challenges: Product licensing, data migration, and system security.

5. *Product Service Plan (PSP)*: PSP site and the product business unit (PBU) agreements prior to product shipment.

   Technologies: HTML, Java, and Netscape Application Server.

   Challenges: System integration.

6. *Time Track*: An effort management and performance-monitoring tool for the field staff.

   Technologies: HTML, Java, and Netscape Application Builder (NAB).

   Challenges: Complex web of interfaces, many bottleneck processes at enterprise level.

7. *Reverse logistics*: Electronic and printable paperwork for customer returns had serious safety and legal implications.

   Technologies: HTML, Java, and NAB; interfaces with SAP parts logistics and vendor payment.

   Challenges: Interfaces, system integration, and maintainability.

8. *Customer Signoff System (CSS)*: Maintaining legal customer signoff processes until completion.

   Technologies: HTML, Java, Servlets, iPlanet, Open Source for PDF generation.

   Challenges: Needed interface with CSS and SAP finance, causing serious data integrity issues.

Figure 10-3 depicts how site service applications were positioned in the larger IT context. As shown by the flow of arrows, there was a lot of interaction among them. They also interacted with systems external to the portfolio, including HRMS, Finance, Vendor Payment, Payroll, and Sales Management systems. Many of these external systems were part of ERP systems.

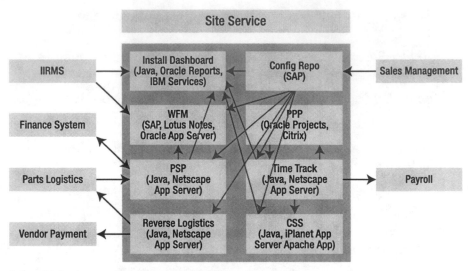

Figure 10-3. Site service applications portfolio of V Inc.

This section offered short descriptions of site service portfolio participants and their challenges. These challenges were mainly in the areas of system security and control; data related issues like integrity, migration, and compatibility; system maintainability and licensing issues; system interface issues; process bottlenecks; and overall process inefficiencies due to excessive manual interventions. The reason behind these challenges was that the systems were never developed for integration. They were each stand-alone applications purchased or created as business needs evolved. Later, when their maintenance became very tedious, a decision was made to retire and replace them with more standard SAP processes.

Part III: Implementing BT

A transformation project is a foundational investment in the systems and process architecture of a company. At V Inc., the project was divided into three phases:

Phase 1 provided finance- and services-related capability.

Phase 2 integrated the manufacturing and business units.

Phase 3 covered the remaining departments within the organization.

As discussed, the BT project impacted the workings of the entire corporation. Almost all the business processes embedded in legacy applications were affected. Older SAP systems were to be upgraded and two ERP applications were to be retired. It was a massive exercise by any standards, but this study will concentrate only the transformation of the site services portfolio.

Phase I of the project concerned the configuration repository, the service workforce, contracts and warranty, parts logistics (including reverse logistics), and service delivery. Figure 10-4 shows the schedule that the BT team created to implement the transformation. Note the activities that constituted the project.

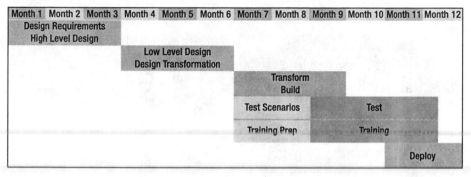

Figure 10-4. BT program management schedule

Why V Inc. Chose SAP

The majority of core applications were already on the SAP platform at V Inc., so choosing SAP for the site service portfolio was a natural choice. Many related applications also had an interface with SAP, thus making migration relatively easy and with minimal risk.

Another practical consideration was V Inc.'s high-level customization of SAP, which made any other choice for migration an extremely risky proposition. V Inc. also had a workforce skilled in SAP and enjoyed a priority relationship with SAP AG as a company. So there were multiple compelling factors that made SAP the clear choice for V.

How the BT Project Solved Challenges

The work had begun. A new application named Product Service Systems (PSS) was implemented within SAP. It provided a single source of information to facilitate decision making, service delivery, and performance evaluation. This application (along with SAP Service Order standard functionality and processes) provided a more effective way to manage costs and work efforts. The notable change for service personnel was a significant reduction in the time needed to do service-related administrative tasks.

Figure 10-5 depicts this architecture along with interfaces with other systems like finance, HRMS, vendor payment, and sales. All these systems were part of an integrated SAP-based solution for V Inc.

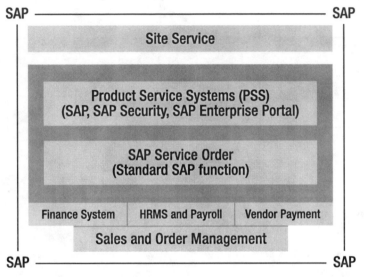

Figure 10-5. V Inc.'s site service applications portfolio after transformation

The PSS, along with the SAP Service Order, replaced the entire site services portfolio. New dashboards, equipment order status, and site nonconformance (anything not conforming to quality standards for manufacturing, installations, etc.) were added to site services. It resolved the interface and nomenclature issues. The data integrity issues caused by the existence of multiple systems were also prevented thanks to a single technology platform for all processes. Centralized, role-based security access and a better authorization control process based on job profiles were also implemented.

Apart from the changes in process, mapping some customization was required in SAP to accommodate the full spectrum of the "to be" processes of the site service portfolio.

Site Service Applications: From "As Is" to "To Be"

The implementation of Product Service Systems and SAP Service Orders transformed the site management processes. The administrative tasks performed by the site personnel were changed after implementing the transformation process.

Some of the transformation changes are shown in Table 10-1. The third column indicates the to-be state; they are the SAP module names on which as-is applications are mapped and are for information purposes only. What is important to appreciate is how the legacy systems are mapped onto the standard processes of SAP.

Table 10-1. Site Service Applications: Current vs. Future

Function	As Is	To Be (mapping)
Configuration Repository update	Config Repo	SAP Product Service Systems
Installation Planning	Product Project Plan (PPP), Product Service Plan (PSP)	SAP Product Service Systems
Effort Reporting	Install Dashboard	SAP Product Service Systems
Site Non-Conformance Reporting	Quality Website	SAP Service Order
Effort Entry	Time Track	SAP Service Order
Problem Escalation	Separate systems for each region and business units	SAP Service Order
Parts Returns	Reverse Logistics	SAP Service Order
Parts Ordering / Tracking	SAP Parts Logistics	SAP Service Order
Downs Information	Downs Dashboard	SAP Service Order
Customer Sign Off	Install Dashboard	SAP Enterprise Portal

Industry standard best practices (see Table 10-2) were used for performance measurement. Again, the performance measurements in as-is and to-be systems are mapped in the table. They are case specific and other business processes may have a different set of parameters for measuring process performances. What's important to note is that in the to-be system (SAP), there were objective measures available for each of the process performance parameters required for the site service functions. This made it easier to objectively measure the process performance.

Table 10-2. Measurement Practices: Current vs. Industry Best Practice

Performance Measurements	As Is	To Be
Cost	Total entitlement cost per fiscal period based on unplanned events	Per event and event type measured against standards for product
Cycle time per maintenance event	No systematic method No data System uptime tracked by customer	Available by event (WIP/historical) and work standards for product type and task
Quality and effectiveness	Historical Pareto/trend of part usage and spending	MTTR (mean time to repair) standard targets and repeat repairs tracking

The service orders process automated many processes that were manual and time consuming. The expected improvements to the data entry process after the transformation are provided in Table 10-3. Again, it's not important to understand the specifics, which are particular to this case. Please note the considerable process simplifications offered by the to-be state. For example, in row one, data entry was to be changed to 20 groups from an original 400 tasks.

Table 10-3. Expected Improvements of Data Entry Process After the Transformation

Data Entry Category	As Is	To Be
Data Entry	Per task (about 400 tasks)	Per group (about 20 groups)
Fault Codes	3 sources: Quality/ Service Order Status/ Knowledge Management	One source and common set (SAP Service Order)
Part Ordering / Disposition	Multiple data entry into different systems	SAP Service Order
Job Code	List of about 50 to select	Consolidated job codes of about 10

The Benefits BT Brought to Site Service

BT brings a number of benefits to site service functionality. The Service Order function of SAP that replaced most of the functionality allowed making event-based decisions to be managed through cycle time and cost. This allowed the benchmarking of processes, providing the way for continuous process improvements and comparisons with the previous year's data. The Service Order functionality of SAP was standardized to be in-line with the industry. The process also offered integrated Spare Parts management, a need long felt by the business. Staff utilization was improved as a result of standard and efficient administrative processes. Most of the challenges posed by site service legacy systems were addressed, which translated into reduced support costs.

Key Challenges Faced in the BT Project

The biggest challenge with V Inc. in the BT exercise was to keep the day-to-day business running when the staff was otherwise engaged. Another was to drive the change culture through the ranks. The staff was not experienced in undergoing that type of transformation. A process visionary in senior management addressed some of the organizational challenges associated with conflicting objectives, culture changes, and needed roles. Process-centric training at all levels helped in addressing the challenges. A BT research cell within the company facilitated the project on the process discovery, modeling, and transformational aspects.

Critical Success Factors

Any business transformation initiative requires a coordinated effort on many fronts: process, framework, governance, and application clustering. The right mix of resources, accountabilities, education, and tools are also needed. The success of the BT project at V Inc. can be attributed to the following:

- Business first—not just technology requirements

- Not mixing future and current-state requirements while constructing the initial process model

- Ensuring participation of all key stakeholders that involved users from all regions, business units, and support function units in the design and testing

- Frequent communications, dedicated website, important announcements, and dedicated team to answer queries and send communications

- A core business-led BT project team that tracked each phase of the deployment and provided ongoing management

- Including end users in developing training and test scenarios

Conclusion: The Benefits to the Business

This case study focused on the BT of the site service portfolio of V Inc. The project helped address some major challenges on the company's operations and technology fronts. Site service applications were brought on a single technology platform, giving the advantage of process standardization and reduced support costs due to integration. The resulting application agility reduced the market response time as far as new applications were concerned. The benefits of the BT project to V Inc. as an organization, including the site service portfolio, follow.

- Major process simplification was achieved for more than 500 applications, including the site service portfolio

- The organization retired 180 redundant applications

- Savings of about 25 percent of IT costs for site service business processes projected over next two years

- A business-driven, process-oriented, and continuous-improvement IT culture was adopted

- A more agile and lean IT organization was created

- A minimization of silos was achieved through a single platform for all core process

Acknowledgments: My sincere thanks to Venkat Paturi, Prabhakar Kanagarajan, Laxmi Narayan, and others on the BT team, whose continuous guidance and inspiration enabled me to present this case. It was Laxmi who helped me write some portions of this case.

IT and Business Analytics

Let's start with the basics: business intelligence (BI) is about getting usable intelligence from data. It's been around for a while. Using BI, you can provide the right information to the right people at the right time and through the right channels. Informed decision making leads to competitive advantage.

In almost every organization, information is available in abundance. Structured data accumulates over the years thanks to the variety of operational information systems that produce it. Traditional models of operations might not be able to fully utilize the new opportunities presented by this abundance of information. BI systems, created to make sense of all the data, can organize, analyze, store, and retrieve a huge amount of information. This lets us work on new, agile organizational models that are more adaptable to constant change, which, in turn, helps us beat the competition and discover new business opportunities.

Business analytics is the new kid on the block; I'll discuss it in detail shortly. Compared to traditional software sectors, business analytics and business intelligence are far less crowded career fields. They present exciting career opportunities to those who love working with data and statistical techniques. Many corporations have not yet developed their own expertise on business analytics. They need in-house experts in these areas. Most companies are using these techniques in some fashion, but may be dependent on external vendors to work it out for them.

Today, executive decision making has gone far beyond the capabilities of traditional or older in-house decision making tools. The bottom line is: every company needs analytics and intelligence techniques. A company may develop expertise in-house or seek the help of external vendors. In either case, an IT manager needs to be aware of how BI and BA works and what's taking place in these fields.

The chain of responsibility for an analytics project starts at the top: executive management needs to create the overall strategy and include information technology in it. Middle management and operations managers then design business processes and decide how information and knowledge is to be used. Business analysts are responsible for creating reports and analytics; they are the people who are responsible for providing the information and knowledge. Then there are the people responsible for data warehouses, data cleansing, and data collection. IT infrastructure people in turn are responsible for maintaining databases and technology infrastructure. However, these responsibilities can vary from organization to organization; there usually is no rigid structure.

What Is Business Analytics?

Business analytics (BA) deals with the methodologies organizations use to make optimized decisions. It rests on a foundation of complex techniques and advanced statistics. Collecting and analyzing data through BA can lead to business breakthroughs.

By applying BA, for example, it is possible to gather data on how a population reacts to certain product variations or features. This information is very useful in devising a new product line with features that are likely to maximize sales, and target as narrowly as a particular group within a particular region.

A proper analysis of data might also tell about something like recurring customer support issues, allowing proactive steps to be taken before issues grow out of proportion. Business analytics is often used by marketing people to predict and analyze consumer behavior. This is done by applying statistical analytical techniques on historical data of customer transactions. Without high-quality data and statistics, business analytics have little or no meaning to an organization.

The Difference Between BA and BI

Business analytics employs statistical methods and analysis on past business performance to develop new business insights and drive business planning. BA may use a combination of technologies, skills, practices, and applications in continuous, iterative investigations. Business intelligence, on the other hand, uses a consistent set of metrics on past data to measure performance and drive business planning. BI can employ statistical techniques like BA.

Business intelligence is more about reporting, querying, OLAP (Online Analytical Processing), and alerts. BA can be used as an input for human decisions or it can fully automate the decision-making process.

BI can answer what happened in the past, in what numbers, the frequency of occurrence, location of the problem, and what corrective actions were needed. BA can tell us why this is happening, what will happen next, what will happen if the trend continues, and how we might use the information to optimize an aspect of the organization or product/service offerings.

What You Can Do with Analytics

Analytics can answer information-oriented questions like what happened, say, in the past two years with sales in a particular region (as can BI). But it can also answer questions like, how are current product sales in each region? And, what are sales likely to be in six months? Digging deeper may provide insights regarding how and why certain things happened. Of course, answering these questions may require some mathematical modeling and/or experimental design.

Analytics can also help answer insightful questions like, what is the best action to take next? Or, what is the best or worst that can happen in this particular scenario? Analytics aim to move toward more insightful answers to the problems or questions that an organization needs to know to stay healthy and ahead of competition. It's about informed decision making rather than intuitive decision making. It's also about reducing the risks in decision making and providing managers with a potent competitive advantage. An analytics consultant can be involved in this process to suggest how a company can make their data more useful. Or an IT manager can take the role of the analyst who studies the data and statistics to churn out useful intelligence.

Today, analytics are applied almost everywhere: predicting consumer behavior or what will sell, determining a price range for a particular market, optimizing the supply chain and operations, improving logistics and finding the best routes for the transportation fleet to take, determining what factors are really driving the financial performance in a company, managing risk, making good investment decisions, issuing credit cards, maximizing sales and profits, and much more.

Caution When Using Analytics

Some decisions have to be made when there is little or no time for data collection. Think of war or play on a sports field. Those decisions need to be made using gathered expertise, intuition, and previous experience. Analytics typically play no role in such situations. Some situations are new and there is simply no available data for analytics. In some cases, like stock markets, plenty of data is available, but the data can't necessarily be relied upon for current or future actions. There are times when the experience of managers is more valuable than any kind of analysis; for example, valuing plant and machinery for insurance purposes.

Almost all results based on analytics have to be used along with human wisdom. Analytics are based on models, assumptions, and data. There is room for error with these, and blindly applying results might lead to disaster. Analytic models may first need a careful test with a controlled set of data before actual application. When results are successful and consistent under test conditions, the models can be used in real-time situations.

Pre-Conditions to Applying Analytics

An organization might have a process orientation with some degree of perfection in mind, be it Six Sigma, Lean, reengineering, or a combination. The key is to identify which attributes in the process are associated with satisfaction and value from the standpoint of the end customer. If you have a comprehensive measurement system for these process attributes, you can perform statistical analysis on your data and determine the correlations among business drivers.

The classic DELTA (Data, Enterprise, Leadership, Targets, Analysts) framework captures five conditions that are a must for any analytical initiative to succeed. Applied to process analytics, these are

- *Data*: This deals with data sufficiency and data quality requirements for the analytics process. Sufficient data should be there for experimenting, modeling, and testing as analytics demands. This category is also concerned with technology and the management of data used in the whole analytics process.

- *Enterprise*: An enterprise viewpoint is necessary for effective analytics. Without it, analytics initiatives may be localized, making it very difficult to draw any significant benefits at the enterprise level. The process under any analytics initiative should have the cross-functional or cross-boundary scope to make a difference in overall business performance.

- *Leadership*: Effective BA calls for cross-functional and capable leaders that have strong executive management support. The leadership focus covers much more than just one project. Leadership must strive to create an analytics-based culture in the organization.

- *Targets*: Metrics are necessary to track the results of analytics projects. Examples might be strong customer loyalty, increased performance in the supply chain, better hiring by matching candidates to skill set requirements, better quantitative risk management, and so on.

- *Analysts*: They must have the capabilities to build the models and derive results. They also bring an analytics culture to the organization by enabling business managers to appreciate and apply it in day-to-day decision making. A good analyst must have good reasoning and analytical skills as basics—and she must love numbers and statistics.

The readiness of processes in an organization needs to be assessed in all the areas represented by DELTA. All the gaps need to be fulfilled for any meaningful analytics project to occur.

Analytics Vendors

Prominent BI and BA tools vendors include IBM (Cognos and R and SPSS), SAP (Business Objects), and SAS Institute (SAS). These vendors periodically publish white papers that provide important updates on their respective tools. The SAS institute web site (www.sas.com) is also a good source for white papers on business analytics.

Summary

Business analytics is an emerging field that offers many opportunities for new entrants, consultants, and businesses. This field does not yet have much trained talent, so there are great growth opportunities. Today, analytics are applied in almost every part of a business. Analytics can be used to search for new trends and patterns, and make informed decisions that add to the business' bottom line.

Case Study: Spatial Analytics in the Real World

Contributed by Vijay Venkatachalam, Director, Omega Analytics, Bangalore

This section introduces geographical information systems (GIS), a branch of analytics concerned with visual maps and geographics. It covers an actual case that shows how the marriage of geography and information systems is helpful in practical business scenarios.

Basics of Geographic Information Systems

GIS is one of the fastest growing fields in the information technology arena. It has applications in banking, natural resource management, defense, utilities, and government, among many others.

Maps are fundamental tools used to depict spatial or geographic data. In GIS digital maps are used to establish patterns, linkages, or relationships in data through either a single map or multiple maps. At its simplest, GIS provides an automated version of traditional map analysis. A GIS is used to access an integrated, location-referenced database of maps that can be superimposed, combined, and analyzed per user specifications. GIS has advantages over other data management systems in its ability to present geographical relationships in a digital map form that is easy to visualize and comprehend. Creating accurate data sets for a GIS system involves exploring satellite images to identify outlines of geographical entities like roads, lakes, rivers, and other landmarks. It is then followed by a ground survey in order to capture the names of these entities.

There are four components of GIS: data, hardware, software, and users. These components must work in an integrated fashion for any usable inferences to be drawn from a GIS analysis.

Applications of Spatial Analytics in Banking

The GIS mapping of a particular branch of a bank involves defining a trade area around the branch, including socio-demographic profiles and purchase choices of customers in the area. With this information the bank can plan new products and product features accordingly.

GIS analysis can examine the interrelationships between land use, infrastructure capacities, proximities of major civic amenities, and economic growth. Banks can utilize these GIS simulations to make strategic decisions like whether to open a new branch, or to relocate or close a branch. The location dimension that is provided by GIS, along with routine data used by classical asset management systems, is very useful in asset-maintenance activities like location inspection and monitoring of a class of assets.

GIS-based solutions for the management and cash replenishment of ATMs work in real time, and they may provide effective ways to manage the cash. A GIS-based application can show the locations of ATMs on a map, along with their respective cash status. The daily cash requirements for a bank or ATM can be predicted with the help of historical cash transactions and other demographic data, such as population density and economic levels. GPS-loaded, GIS-based fleet management systems cost effectively monitor the real-time locations of the cash vans that replenish ATMs.

Drilling Down: Personal Loan Customer Analytics

The project for a multinational bank with several branches throughout the city involved integrating data from various ORACLE databases with digital maps of the city. It required the IT team to plot around 40,000 customer addresses and to analyze spatial spreads and correlations.

Case Pictorials

Figures 11-1, 11-2, and 11-3 are slides from GIS software. First, a map of the city is plotted (see Figure 11-1). It's just like any city map, indicating important landmarks, roads, and area names. Next, bank branches are plotted over the map (see Figure 11-2). The map can be used similar to Google Maps, even allowing drill down with a mouse to get directions to a particular bank branch.

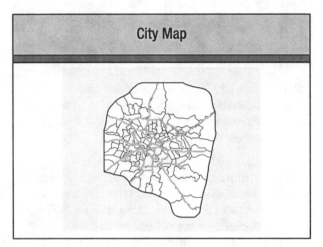

Figure 11-1. A city map on GIS software. Lines mark and separate various areas. Details like major roads are also seen.

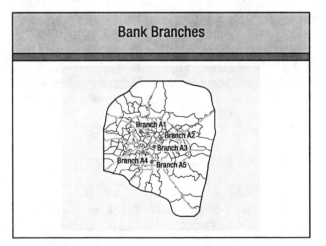

Figure 11-2. Bank branch locations are now marked on the city map.

Finally, the main component: the address of each bank loan customer is plotted in the form of dots on the city map (Figure 11-3). The distribution of loan customers is now available in pictorial form for every branch. This is important analytical data for the bank. It can be used to roll out geographically-targeted financial products or appropriate promotions at regional branches.

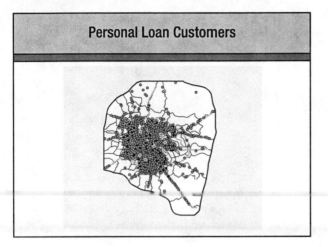

Personal Loan Customers

Figure 11-3. Geographical locations of the bank's customers are now included. This helps the bank locate customer density by area.

This case study shows how spatial analytics helped a bank to find out the distribution and density of its personal loan customers relative to its branches and city geography. The bank can utilize this information in a variety of ways, like opening new branches in dense customer areas, increasing the staff at certain branches, and so on.

IT and Operations Management

Enterprise resource planning (ERP) and supply chain management (SCM) systems now guide operations in many organizations. Where it is in use, ERP software has completely changed the way operations managers operate. After decades of development that created disparate and stand-alone IT systems, integrated ERPs have or soon will become a ground reality in most large and medium-sized organizations. And no IT manager today can survive without working knowledge of ERP and how it affects an enterprise's functioning and the development and maintenance of other IT systems.

In this chapter, I'll go through the basics of ERP and SCM, their functions, and their differences. I'll also present a detailed case study that explains ERP selection parameters and other practical aspects and ERP implementation.

Introduction

Historically, the different functions of an organization—manufacturing, planning, distribution, marketing, and purchasing—operated independently. These departments form the functions in a supply chain, the pathway that takes raw materials at one end and delivers finished products or services into customer hands at the other end. While many companies have made efforts to integrate these functions through IT, many other companies still operate departments with their own separate objectives, which may conflict with one another.

Mass manufacturing setups, for example, might operate with an aim to maximize their throughputs. While this may reduce the cost per unit, this goal may not be in line with the organization's overall goal of maintaining low inventory levels.

Thus, in many cases there is no single integrated strategic plan available for the organization. It's easy to see why this is so inefficient and why there's a need for information systems that can integrate the silo-based functions of an organization and support information-based decision making. ERP and supply chain management systems strategically support the integrated functioning of an organization and its decision making.

What ERP and SCM Mean to Line Managers

The recent advances in ERP software and SCM functionalities, combined with information technology, has provided an unprecedented tool in the hands of operations managers to efficiently handle both the demand and supply sides of an enterprise in real time. Some of the advantages that today's line manager realizes with ERP and SCM include the following:

- An uninterrupted flow of information, materials, supplies, and services across the supply chain

- Reduced inventory investments

- "What if" simulations for informed decision making

- Optimization of resource use

- Better visibility across both sides of the supply chain

- Competitive pricing and lean operations

- Efficient administration

Why Everyone Talks About ERP

ERP is the single largest software in an enterprise. It interfaces with almost all other systems in the organization. Almost everyone is affected by the ERP—be it implementation or steady state running. ERP makes it possible to view the entire organization as an integrated set of processes. This is a more dynamic view than a traditional departmental or functional perspective.

The entire organization looks to the ERP for real-time information about customers, suppliers, competition, and market changes. The real-time information provided is needed for everything from regulatory compliance to maintaining operational transparency. It doesn't just focus on granular specifics like inventory levels and sales; it allows a high-level look at the functioning of the entire enterprise. The information the ERP provides forms the basis for valuing an organization, determining supplier relationships, and assessing the quality of the company's management.

ERPs are a highly integrated network of business processes and systems that are built on a single technology platform. This makes the sharing of data and processes across departments a natural occurrence, thereby helping executives make informed decisions. Standardization, visibility, traceability, and control are made possible by a well-implemented ERP.

Major Functions of an ERP

ERPs are much more comprehensive than regular SCM products. For example, the SAP R/3 ERP covers production planning, shop floor control, business planning, sales, and logistics. On the surface, it looks like ERPs cover everything that SCM systems claim to provide. However, the difference is in the details. The reality is that a high-performance organization needs both. Therefore, we will first study the functions of an ERP in some detail and later contrast them with SCM products and how the two can work together effectively. The following list details the major functions of an ERP.

- The sales and distribution module takes care of order entry and delivery scheduling. This module checks on product availability (in inventories) to ensure timely delivery. It also checks the customer's credit line.

- The business planning function consists of demand forecasting, capacity and production planning, and the detailed work routing information that describes where (work centers) and in what order the product is made on the shop floor.

- The production and capacity plans generally get very complex in manufacturing organizations. Simulation tools are provided as part of SAP R/3. These can help managers decide on how to overcome shortages in materials, labor, or time.[1]

- Once the system completes a master production schedule (MPS), the next step is the MRP (materials requirements planning) module for further processing and order release.

- The major outputs from the MRP function are: an exception report, order proposals, and an MRP list. Situations such as rescheduling of order proposals and late delivery of materials that need a manager's attention are listed in the exception report.

- The MRP list contains the details of dispatches and receipts for every product and its components. Order proposals from the MRP module are used to order materials (purchase orders) and issue production orders.

- The next step is shop floor control. The planned orders generated by the MRP system are converted into firm production orders. Next in the order are shop floor scheduling, shipping, and job costing.

- The logistics system comes into the picture at the end, which consists of inventory and warehouse management. The sole aim of this module is timely delivery to the customer. The purchasing function is also grouped as a part of logistics.

The overall ERP process can be summarized in the following order: sales and forecasting data, production and capacity planning, production execution, and logistics. This functionality represents the basic functionality common to all major ERP vendors, including SAP and Oracle Applications.

Younger generation of ERPs, often called ERP II, may include modules like customer relationship management (CRM), human resources management systems (HRMS), supply chain management, and integrated financials. Another functionality commonly offered in the new ERP II covers project

---

[1] vsnew, "ERP vs. SCM: What's the Difference?" http://en.vsnew.com/erp-vs-scm-whats-the-difference.html, July 2009.

management (PM), knowledge management (KM), work flow management, analytics, and portal capabilities. As you can see, the newer ERP products aim to be all things to all people—provided all people have the right to see the information.

What Is SCM?

SCM is often implemented on the top of ERP implementations.

An integrated supply chain management system is a complex network of manufacturing, storage, distribution, and transportation facilities. It covers the procurement of materials, their transformation into finished and semi-finished products, and finally their distribution to customers. Supply chains exist in every industry. Their functioning and complexity differ by industry sector and organization.[2]

Some experts[3] have compared the functioning of a supply chain with a well-balanced and well-practiced Olympic relay team. The entire team needs a very high level of coordination and practice to win the race. Teams are naturally competitive and each member knows exactly how to get positioned for the hand off. Pretty much the same thing happens in the functioning of a supply chain management system: the output of one department leads to the input of another, and everything needs to occur in a well-balanced and timely manner.

Major Functions of SCM Systems

Supply chain management has four major decision areas, each one of them with strategic and operational elements: location, production, inventory, and transportation or distribution.[4]

Strategic supply chain decisions are closely associated with long-term corporate goals. They guide the design of SCM systems. Operational decisions have a relatively short-term or day-to-day focus. Once the

---

[2] Ram Ganeshan and Terry P. Harrison, "An Introduction to Supply Chain Management," http://lcm.csa.iisc.ernet.in/scm/supply_chain_intro.html.

[3] Ellaran Cooper, *On Supply Chain Management*. (SCM Research Literature, 1993).

[4] Ram Ganeshan and Terry P. Harrison, "An Introduction to Supply Chain Management," http://lcm.csa.iisc.ernet.in/scm/supply_chain_intro.html.

strategic planning of the supply chain is over, operational decisions focus on the efficient management of product flow across the functions.

Let's look at each of the four functions of SCM in detail.

SCM Location Function

The geographic positioning of production facilities and factories, warehouses, and suppliers is the very first step taken when creating a supply chain. The location of these facilities involves strategic thinking, availability of resources, and a long-term plan. The size, number, and location of these facilities determine the routes of product and supply movements from sourcing points through factories to the final consumer.

These decisions are of strategic importance to any organization since they represent the grassroots policies for accessing consumer markets, suppliers, and manufacturing facilities. Location decisions are determined by the SCM's optimization programs, which take into account the costs and limitations encountered in production and logistics for each location. Locations of facilities are of major concern in decisions made at the operational level, and they significantly contribute toward the final cost of products and services.

SCM Production Function

This function determines key strategic decisions: what products to produce, where to produce, and which distribution channels to use to get products to customer markets.

Production decisions assume the location setups (where to setup plants and inventories) are already done and that material and product flows through company facilities are already determined. Another strategic decision in production function is deciding and planning the capacities of plants. The capacity planning of production facilities has a huge impact on revenues, overall product costs, and customer service levels.

Production planning and scheduling functions, like master production schedules, plant maintenance, and shop floor control, fall under the category of operational decisions. Plant scheduling, product routing, production inventories, and quality control measures are important considerations at any production facility. These functions, along with the location functions, are an integrated part of the most basic SCM systems.

SCM Inventory Function

Supply chain inventory locations exist at practically every stage. Inventory might include raw materials, work-in-progress or semi-finished goods, and finished goods. Inventories can also be in-process or in transit between locations. The primary purpose of holding inventory is to provide a buffer against uncertainties that might arise in the supply chain. Low inventories may indicate an efficient supply chain. The concepts of Just-in-Time aim to have zero inventory in the system.

But holding inventory can be very costly—as high as 20 to 40 percent of its value. So, efficient inventory management is critical in supply chain operations. Inventory goals are strategically set by top management. However, most professionals approach the inventories from operational perspectives. Inventory deployment strategies like push versus pull, inventory control policies, economic order quantities, reorder levels, and determining safety stocks have all been traditionally determined from operational perspectives.

Here we are discussing the functions of a SCM system itself. All the inventory functions described in this section come bundled as a feature of any basic supply chain management software system.

SCM Transportation Function

Transportation decisions are very much dependent upon inventory and location decisions. There is often a tradeoff between the direct costs of using a mode of transport (like air or surface) and the indirect costs of inventories associated with that mode. Air shipments are fast, reliable, and require fewer safety stocks (a buffer maintained against uncertainties in material supply), but the costs may be prohibitive.

Transportation costs form more than 30 percent of total logistics expenses, so achieving good operational efficiencies is desirable. Routing, scheduling, and lot-sizing policies play an important role in effective transportation management. Shipping lot sizes may be based upon the production batch size or upon quantities that are most economical to ship. Again, the transportation function features come bundled with any basic SCM software system.

Evolution of SCM Systems and Technologies

IT has played a key role in each stage of the evolution of today's SCM systems. Figure 12-1 is a block diagram that shows the evolution of SCM systems as it started from materials requirements planning (MRP).

Figure 12-1. The evolution of SCM

- *MRP*: MRP had BOM (bills of material), quantity per assembly, order quantity, BOM explosion (calculating component quantities based on the BOM). The output was end raw material quantities and the approximate timing for placing production and purchase orders.

The roles of IT in MRP systems were to process enormous amounts of data and reduce processing time. (But even then, processing still took 12 to 20 hours). IT was depended upon for consistency, speed, and accuracy.

- *MRP II*: MRP II went further into production planning, capacity planning, costing, answering what-if questions, demand and sales-order entry, work in process, and shop floor control. MRP integrated everything and allowed traceability to customer or planned orders.

At this point, the focus of IT worldwide changed to management information systems (MIS), and creating information systems with a modular structure.

- *ERP and E-ERP (Extended ERP)*: MRP II systems were further integrated into other systems and functionalities such as accounts payable, HR, field systems, and so on, within and outside the organization. The major focus was high-level planning. E-ERP was an extension of ERP to other systems of the organization.

The IT focus was a high level of system integration, planning capabilities, integration with external entities like vendors and financial institutions, real-time data availability across the functions around the globe, preliminary data warehousing, and business intelligence.

It's clear from the evolution pattern that the later systems were more integrated and their spread wider than their predecessors. Like any other information system, the use of ERP and SCM demand a very high level of discipline (especially for integrated systems like ERPs). Since everything is integrated and interdependent, spurious data entered in one transaction may impact hundreds of other transactions down the line. This is discussed in the following sections.

SCM vs. ERP

While ERP has been around for some time, SCM is relatively recent entry to industry. SCM is more focused in terms of functionality. It offers many specialized ways to optimize important results, like inventory for safety stock, order quintiles, routes for transportation at minimum cost, and so forth. It also offers simulation capabilities, like determining the effects of shipment and production order delays. SCM also features a state-of-the-art graphical user interface. However, the demarcation line between SCM and ERP programs is getting increasingly blurred.

You Need Both ERP and SCM

We already discussed ERP and SCM as individual entities; we now note their differences, as well as the latest trends in both the technologies. The major vendors in ERP are SAP R/3, Baan (now owned by Infor Global), PeopleSoft, and ORACLE Apps. The big names in SCM are i2 and Manugistics.

ERPs like SAP R/3 seem to provide most of the functionality that is offered by SCM vendors like i2 and Manugistics. The following list details some differences between ERP and SCM.

- There are studies that tell large corporations with complex supply chains that they need to install SCM systems along side their main ERP; otherwise, they may incur 10 percent higher costs due to expediting, shouldering inventory imbalances, and experiencing low order fill rates.[5]

- ERP systems are great at planning capabilities, but they separately consider the material, capacity, and demand constraints in relative isolation of each other.

---

[5] Gartner research data on ERP and Supply Chain Management.

- Some leading SCM products are able to assess all relevant constraints simultaneously, and do real-time simulations of modifications in these constraints.

- ERP systems are vast in functionality and cover much more than SCM, but they are more transaction focused.

- SCM systems are focused and specialized so they can answer the questions related to their functionality in no time, but the same answers from ERP systems may take much longer.

- SCM products generally provide many other specialized enhancements that can add immense value to the day-to-day functioning of a line manager. This may include visual maps of the entire supply chain that highlights any problem areas. Manugistics, for example, provides a state-of-the art intuitive graphical user interface (GUI) that easily takes users through the mass of supply chain information most companies accumulate. This GUI gives you the visibility into the entire working of supply chain, including demand, supply, production, scheduling, and transportation. SAP has also added similar functions to its products.

ERP and SCM Integration

ERP addresses a larger function and SCM provides a quicker, more specialized service. SCM applications generally sit on the top of an ERP set up. ERP and SCM systems depend heavily on each other in terms of sharing processes and data. Emerging software applications can handle collaboration between ERP and SCM systems. One such program is by Cross Worlds Inc. It integrates the process and data sharing between the ERP and SCM systems of different vendors, and requires almost no programming. With applications like this, and no doubt others to come, the differentiating line between ERP and SCM systems is thinning and may one day disappear.

Today, almost all the ERP vendors are adding more SCM functionality to their standard product offerings. SAP and Oracle, the top two ERP market share leaders, have both added SCM functionalities recently. Baan and PeopleSoft both are bringing SCM functionalities into future releases of their ERP products. SCM vendors are also expanding their offerings to include functions traditionally part of ERP products.

Large ERP vendors are making swift moves into smaller market segments with new products featuring SCM, pushing some small and mid-sized ERP and SCM vendors to close their shops. With these developments, implementations may become simpler, faster, and less expensive for corporations.

As we discussed, SCM products work in conjunction with ERP products, making collaboration a must. Suppose a line manager wants to know the effect of a delayed shipment on his ability to keep a particular order delivery date. If he has ERP alone, it's a possibility that he may not get an accurate answer. ERP plans demand, capacity, production, logistics etc. in relative isolation from each other while SCM software plans everything in an integrated fashion. So SCM software can give better answers to real time changes in constraints, but SCM depends upon ERP for many things, including master data and basic transactions. So they must collaborate.

Data Warehouses and Data Mining

Now that we have seen the basic functioning of both ERP and SCM, we also know both have huge databases. The data consists of thousands of transactions created and accumulated weekly. This enormous amount of data may bring useful intelligence information to the company in terms of trends and patterns.

A data warehouse (DWH) is a single, complete, and consistent store of data integrated across various applications in the organization. A DWH provides users faster, easier, and direct access to corporate data. Companies have made use of their ERP/SCM data warehouses to increase their revenue and cut the costs. Next are two brief cases on how companies took advantage of implementation of a DWH in their supply chain management software.

Case 1: A retail finance company consolidated individual client data by household. Doing this they were able to get a better picture of services and products used by individual households (instead of individuals). This helped the company to tailor its offerings, and individuals became more likely to buy products and services customized to their family's needs.

Case 2: An auto component manufacturer extracted and analyzed all its demand data from past years. It then tried to understand the demand pattern and forecast for the current and coming years. The manufacturer found its demand pattern was periodic with regular spikes (like seasonal demands), but also unpredictable with random spikes.

It was relatively easy to plan the SCM system for periodic demand and predictable spikes, but unpredictable and random spikes in demand were a nightmare for the manufacturer to fulfill. So it decided to make a policy correction by offering a 5 percent discount for large orders placed 15 days in advance. Unpredictable spikes were prevented, saving a lot of money compared to the other alternative—maintaining high inventory in anticipation of sudden demand spikes.

Collaboration and Integration in SCM

Wal-Mart, the most successful retail chain in the world, offers the lowest rates in the industry while providing an amazing variety to choose from. They share specific real-time sales and consumer demand information with their vendors. This made the whole supply chain market driven, which was traditionally made-to-stock. Wal-Mart Information Systems is an excellent example of collaborative supply chain and very high levels of integration throughout, which has given rise to the company's amazing business results.

Challenges/Issues with SCM Systems

Like any other application, there are some limitations to today's IT-based SCM systems. Challenges, when not tackled in a proper manner, become issues. The following lists a combination of challenges and issues.

- Selecting the right package

- Selecting the right implementation partners

- Time to implement

- Discipline

- Algorithms complexity may require skilled manpower for handling inputs and interpreting results

- Data accuracy

- Handling of disturbances (planning and execution) in real time and readjusting accordingly

- Maintaining a knowledge base for all operating countries in terms of regulations, duties, procedures, and other location-dependent factors that can have an effect on the global supply chain

- Customization and upgrades
- Legacy interfaces
- Infrastructure planning
- The bull whip effect: demand based on local economic factors farther down the supply chain get amplified in the form of exaggerated orders

The Myth Around SCM Systems

There is a strong belief that implementing an IT-based SCM systems solution always creates benefits, but that's not true in all cases. Each supply chain has its own inherent complexities in terms of the interdependency of processes, people, and systems between the supply chain partners. Technology can't do wonders unless the fit is first evaluated very carefully. A sizable percentage of SCM implementations are failures, as the following case explains. A careful technology evaluation and ROI (return on investment) analysis is needed before investing in any solution.

SCM in the Iron and Steel Industry

This case starts when the SCM systems were relatively new in the market. There was a lot of enthusiasm around SCM installations. Many corporations implemented them just because they were the trend. The iron and steel industry was no different in following this trend. Many corporations within the industry shelled out millions of dollars to implement these technologies with only a partial understanding of the pros and cons. SCM systems in many corporations were behaving badly because they were allowed to get out of control. The reason: the much-required discipline was not maintained from the beginning. Lots of junk transactions found their way inside the SCM data stores.

The decisions made based upon the SCM data were not very meaningful to the line managers. They were still banking upon the older legacy system for support. Years after their installation, the SCM systems could not achieve the required maturity levels. Executives could manage the business operations with reasonably good efficiency by supplementing SCM systems with their old legacy systems.

With the current state of operations, it was very difficult to realize profits in proportion to increased revenue. Unrealized receivables, inefficient production lines and supply chains, and poorly managed inventories and logistics were major issues. The conditions would have been better if the SCM and other information systems were able to support the operations per expectations.

Many companies in the industry were in this situation. The information managers were struggling to make SCM systems efficient enough to cope with the increased demands posed by a booming economy. Proactive measures were required to predict the probable bottlenecks in the supply chain. All analysis efforts were focused on when and where bottlenecks could occur, and how much time and resources it would take to bring systems on track. Even this was not easy as the information systems were in bad shape and the available data was not reliable.

Inefficiencies had built up over the years and suddenly everything was expected to turn around within months. But there was no choice. If proper systems were not in place soon, profitability was bound to take a hit. Eating into the bottom line would be increased customer penalties for missing shipping deadlines, excess freight costs, more costs in procurements, and labor overtime across the supply chains.

Executive management wanted a clear picture of the total demand coming from different sources, like regular market orders, spare parts, and export markets. Demand forecasts for spare parts and replacement components were required separately, as they were managed differently. Management also wanted a big picture of overall capacity, which included in-house manufacturing and the capacities of vendors down the supply line.

The information that executive wanted is a natural output of SCM systems—if they are working as expected. But they weren't. Given the case, as an information systems manager, how would you deal the situation?

The answer is not easy and straightforward. There are two angles to it. First what could have been done to get the desired output from the SCM system systems? And second, in the current situation of chaotic information systems, what should management do?

Well, in the first situation, the answer resides in the case. The company needed discipline while using the system. It should have required that all transactions be carried out only through it. It should have created better awareness and devised a better incentive program to work with the improved processes offered by SCM systems. They could have maintained the quality of data that was going into the SCM systems. None of this was done, or it was done partially at best.

As for the second question, the answer looks relatively straightforward. The company needed to devise ways to work even if the SCM system failed. It had to be prepared to fall back to older systems of spreadsheets and legacy systems till the SCM systems were cured. Not as easy as it looks. But there was no option; the show must go on.

Implementing or improving SCM systems may take a long time. It can be months or even a year. The companies in our case study were struggling for quite sometime to bring their SCM systems back on track. Improving systems can sometimes be more painful than implementing new ones. All these companies suffered losses in operating efficiencies, and probably profits too, until they had their systems fully on track.

Summary

This chapter covered ERPs and SCMs, complementary software applications that serve the operations management needs of organizations through integrated, real-time planning. Several cases were presented to substantiate the theory and to enhance your understanding. ERP and SCM are vast topics and the fields are evolving. It's an exciting time to be an IT manager!

Case Study: Single ERP Choice and Implementation

This case study covers Enterprise Application Integration (EAI). We have seen that large corporations literally have hundreds of applications, even if they employ ERPs in key operational areas. These applications sometimes form silos, or information islands where information is accumulated but is not easily available to other applications or a wider audience. There are many strategies to integrate these applications. Service-Oriented Architecture (SOA) or choosing only one ERP (Single ERP) are two strategies that already discussed in this book. This case study takes you through the strategy of a Single ERP for EAI and describes how to adopt it as a main integration strategy.

ERPs were discussed in this chapter, so it will be appropriate to cover their selection and implementation too.

Overview

EAI is a current trend across IT organizations. Numerous monolithic applications with traditional architecture have been built over the years in almost every large organization. There is often little or no communication between these applications, which creates data inconsistency problems. In some cases, interfaces between applications exist but are unmanageable due to volume and complexity. The web of interfaces gets increasingly complex over time, giving rise to data integrity challenges. This system of stand-alone applications and their complex interfaces often proves to be the biggest obstacle to quickly respond to dynamically changing business needs. This scenario also creates data duplication, which increases the costs of data storage and the need to secure sensitive data.

This case is about a large semiconductor manufacturing company, Z Inc., considering various alternatives for system integrations that will bring improvements in operational efficiency. Z Inc. ultimately chose to implement a Single ERP, replacing many homegrown enterprise applications.

Introduction: Current IT/Business Scenario

The IT and business organizations in this large corporation are misaligned. The IT organization is frequently cited as an impediment to business change. Many information systems (and the supporting infrastructure) were built using rigid legacy systems and approaches, or were implemented hastily and/or parsimoniously. The key value proposition of enterprise architecture is aligning IT and business processes with the organization's objectives and strategies. Because businesses and IT organizations speak different languages and have different temporal perspectives, a primary goal of enterprise architecture is to bridge that gap, largely by examining the business strategy and corresponding requirements, and by translating business intent into action.

During the past few years (prior to the recession at least), many organizations have undertaken transformational initiatives, and they have increased IT spending for improving operational efficiencies. Because many previous initiatives did not deliver promised results, companies regard this renewed activity carefully. Leading organizations have adopted portfolio management techniques to balance risk and return on these investments. A portfolio approach to project funding and management also identifies the interdependencies between these investments.

Project completion, however, does not mark the end of the technology investment lifecycle. Completed projects generally create operational systems, applications, and a technology infrastructure that generates value, but costs money to maintain. Most organizations have complex environments and excessive operational expenses. In many cases, the cost of supporting existing IT systems crosses 80 percent of the total IT budget. Therefore, enterprise architecture teams are always tasked with optimizing the application and infrastructure portfolios.

Enterprise architecture includes an organization's strategies, business processes, applications, information, technology, and infrastructure, along with perceptions of its desired future state. It also includes the steps, standards, and guidelines on how to achieve the future state that best supports the company's business strategy. Enterprise architecture is tasked with the planning and discipline to ensure that investments in process improvement and information technology support the organization's strategic goals.

Z Inc. knew it needed to improve its architecture and so called in expert help.

The Business Case

Z Inc. is undergoing IT infrastructure transformation for lower operational costs and consistency of data and business processes across the organization. It currently has more than 300 applications, which include stand-alone web-based applications, and enterprise applications like SAP and ORACLE Apps. All of these applications are interdependent and communicate with one another. The technology landscape is diverse. It includes C/C++, Lotus Notes, J2EE, .Net, SAP, ORACLE Apps, Netscape, Web Methods, COBOL, and CICS. These applications are established on more than 175 independent databases.

Many of these applications are mission critical to the operation of the company and require 24/7 support. The operational costs are high, as the company must maintain a huge IT department. Due to diverse technological platforms, there is very little cross-application functioning among IT staff. These traditional architectures have led to a number of issues stemming from overlapping (and often conflicting) data and application logic. These problems are exacerbated by point-to-point integration, and result in

- High operational and development costs
- Slow time to market for new or modified processes, partners, products, or services

- Transactional latency (the time required to execute a transaction) because of antiquated workflows, trade exceptions, and failures

- Resource-consuming reconciliation processes across disparate systems

- Increased risks and missed opportunities

Efficiencies that could be enabled through newer technologies, such as SOA, are not realized because of difficulties in introducing architectural change, and identifying and implementing shared services/modified work flows. These difficulties are worsened by the lack of standardization in business procedures and policies. For example, commercial terms may be set by the portfolio managers and they may differ from individual plan (project) sponsors. This is likely to make centralized administration (and automation) problematic.

Figure 12-2 shows traditional application architecture at corporations with several gigantic stand-alone applications, each employing a complete set of data and processes. There was very little collaboration with other applications. Z Inc. is represented in this application architecture before it began implementation of a Single ERP.

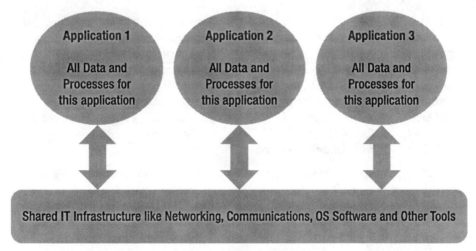

Figure 12-2. Traditional split architecture with gigantic applications

The IT organizations within companies like Z Inc. are focusing on developing and managing robust and flexible infrastructures to reduce costs, realize operational efficiencies, and more readily respond to changing business requirements and market conditions. Historically, attempts to reduce costs and achieve efficiencies through automation, while successful in the short term, contributed to high costs and inefficiencies.

Achieving a flexible and robust infrastructure requires major changes in traditional approaches to architectural design, business governance, and technology architecture. To reduce costs while improving operational efficiency and quality service levels, the business organization must adopt architectures that facilitate intelligent integration across disparate processes within their transactional and business environments.

Architecture Choices for Integration

Two enterprise architectural styles were considered to eliminate the redundancies, improve efficiencies, and simplify operations and IT resources. The following list provides details.

1. A *Single ERP approach*, wherein all the critical monolithic applications would be re-written in mySAP. The salient features of this approach would be to provide

   * A single technology platform throughout the organization
   * A single application and database supporting all business processes of the organization
   * Operational efficiency and reduced operational costs in long term
   * Easy technology upgrades

2. *Service orientation* to promote consistency and sharing of resources. The salient points of service orientation (see Figure 12-3) were listed as follows:

   * A service-oriented architecture (SOA) is suited for request-and-reply interactions that can be used to implement business processes.
   * Services promote sharing of resources by enabling multiple end points to use the same processes, datasets, and rules.
   * In addition to cost savings from the elimination of redundant data and processes, an SOA introduces consistency across disparate applications.

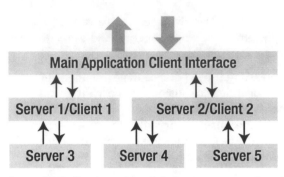

Figure 12-3. Service-oriented design to promote shared data and processes

The Choice Between Two Approaches

The strong manufacturing process orientation of mySAP secured the deal in favor of Single ERP. Z Inc. cited the following business advantages of mySAP over the SOA approach.

- *Reduced costs*: Decreasing operating costs by converting time-consuming, manual processes into streamlined, online functions. Benefits include matching supply with demand, and improving overall enterprise planning.

- *Strong manufacturing orientation*: Utilizing existing functions and reducing order cycle times to improve manufacturing resource utilization, reduce excess inventories, and adapt to shifts in customer demand.

- *Out-of-the-box planning functions*: Reducing planning cycles and lead times, enabling faster response to opportunities, and continuous process improvements.

- *Plant and equipment functions*: Optimally maintaining plants and equipment, deploying them to support appropriate projects, and complying with safety and regulatory standards.

- *Rapid, cost-effective time to market*: Improving internal and external collaboration and project management, accelerating the product development cycle to develop, and maintaining a competitive edge while responding to changing marketplace demands.

- *Reduced risk exposure*: Lesser exposure to PLC (product/ project life cycle), compared to the SOA approach, may ensure that project meets stringent quality requirements.

- *Lower total cost of ownership*: Possible integration of existing IT infrastructure with other mySAP Business Suite software and product development tools, including CAD products.

The Existing Architecture

As evident in Figure 12-4, a large number of homegrown monolithic applications were clustered around three enterprise applications, which in turn talked to homegrown data warehousing applications. This resulted in an equally large number of technology platforms to maintain. It made overall IT operations difficult and relatively expensive and keeping pace with evolving technology for each platform was almost impossible. This resulted in some of the applications running on a development environment more than a decade old.

For some of these platforms, support was no longer available from the original vendors. Windows NT and Netscape Application Server were two such examples. This made maintenance of applications built on these platforms/operating systems difficult and expensive. And Z Inc. carried a huge risk of having its business processes on obsolete technologies.

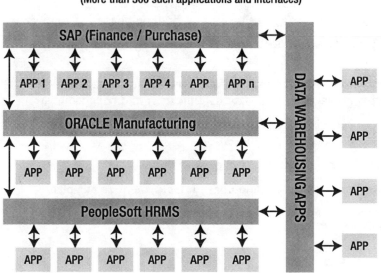

Figure 12-4. Z Inc.'s current IT infrastructure

As evident in Figure 12-5, the majority of the organization's applications were to be transferred onto mySAP architecture and standard functionalities. SAP R/3 offered core business functionality while peripheral modules like HR, SCM, CRM, and BI replaced many standalone applications.[6]

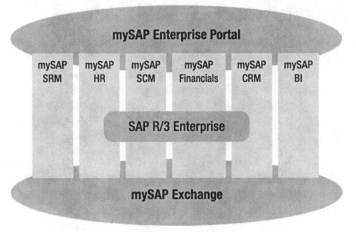

Figure 12-5. The target enterprise architecture at Z Inc.

Z Inc. decided to put its entire suite of homegrown applications, interfaces and other enterprise applications (ORACLE Apps and People Soft) to a Single ERP, mySAP. This was a huge task to be done in phases, as follows:

Phase I: Identify, validate, and document all the existing business process across the organization.

Phase II: Wherever required, reengineer and streamline the existing processes, with an objective of operational efficiency and reduced costs.

Phase III: Map the reengineered processes to mySAP and develop the specifications for the areas of customization.

Phase IV: Detailed planning, costing, and organization.

Phase V: Construction, validation, and phased deployment as per plan.

Phase VI: Maintenance and production support of commissioned functionalities.

---

[6] Jose A. Hernandez, *Roadmap to mySAP.com*. (Premier Press, 2002).

Implementation Steps Followed

Many organizations have suffered ERP project failures because of unplanned or under-planned implementations. A key component of the planning required to avoid such failures is the development of a reliable estimate of implementation project costs and duration. This process must go beyond simple "rule of thumb" metrics and vendor cost promises.

The mySAP implementation for all the business processes across Z Inc.'s organization was a mammoth task. The implementation could be seen in four major categories.

1. Mapping existing finance, spare parts, and services process from SAP Ver 4.x to mySAP.

2. Mapping manufacturing, order management, and inventory from ORACLE Apps to mySAP.

3. Mapping of all the business processes from numerous homegrown applications (more than 150) to mySAP.

4. Mapping and data migration to mySAP from various databases (more than 175) across the organization. The existing databases were on various versions of ORACLE.

Implementation Task Checklist

The following process checklist helped achieve dependable cost estimates of and timelines for the ERP implementation project. A range of critical activities were associated with the implementation, many of which are often overlooked in estimation efforts.

1. Appreciate the project, its challenges, and importance.

2. Define the scope of the project with as much precision and detail as possible.

3. Emphasize strategic planning.

   - Analyze existing business processes and information flow.
   - Devise new processes wherever required.
   - Work out the gap analysis with ERP functionality. Gap analysis is a method to find out the gap between existing processes and those offered by ERP as standard processes.

- Do the functional mapping and plan for customization of ERP as required.
- Plan for other system interface development and deployment efforts.
- Plan for external interfaces, including design construction and deployment.
- Work out the scalability, performance, and other hidden requirements.
- Do the technology plan including physical infrastructure.
- Reexamine and reset project objectives as required.
- Work out resource estimates and other financial transactions, including travel and contingency.
- Plan with the project end in the mind.
- Develop a detailed project plan with schedule and resource allocation.
- Ensure right resources are assigned to implement and support each function.

4. Develop a plan for transition and change management.

5. Schedule an implementation process review and actual implementation starts.

6. Plan for data collection, cleansing, and migration.

7. Schedule and test database set up.

8. Provide functional and technical trainings for process mapping and customization.

9. Develop process customization and mapping on ERP.

10. Fully embrace integration with internal and external systems.

11. Implement user acceptance testing for final customer buy in.

12. Develop a final go-live checklist.

13. Go live evaluation and count down functions.

14. Implement go-live checklist.

15. Keep production environment under observation.

16. Execute the transition and change management plan.

17. Constantly take feedback and evaluate the effectiveness of change. management plan including the people factor that may be the most important of all.

Before the project starts it is desirable that the processes are documented and transformed into more logical and simple steps per business needs (see Figure 12-6). All the legacy systems are studied and their scope defined for inclusion in the ERP project.

A few quick success stories help build the confidence of stakeholders and a few best practices should be mentioned.

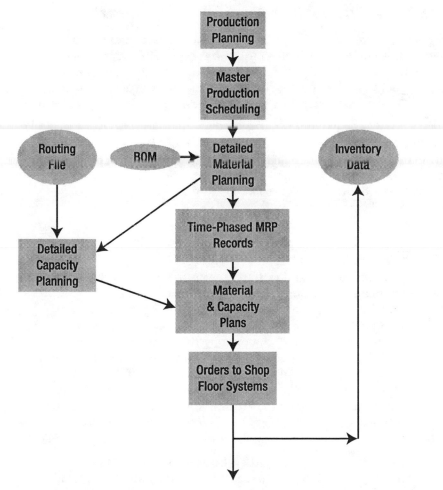

Figure 12-6. Example of process documentation: generic production order process

Include All Costs

While working out estimates, it's important that all possible cost points are taken into account. These include technical, functional, quality assurance, project management, testing, training, database support, and infrastructure staff. Staff salaries, bonus and awards, and contingencies may also be taken into account. ERP projects are much more comprehensive than simple IT projects, so the estimation process may be more elaborate and detailed. It should consider the 17 points mentioned in the checklist.

Write New Code After Careful Consideration

Existing legacy systems, interfaces of ERP with internal and external application, and coding for process customization in ERP systems are important aspects in any ERP implementation that requires custom code writing. Sometimes it may be desired to map the functionality of existing legacy systems on ERP systems by writing custom code. Similarly, custom code may be required for interfacing with internal and external applications.

Writing custom code is a very delicate part of any ERP project. It helps if the business processes are simplified and standardized so that automation is feasible now and easy to maintain later. Adopt the standard functionality of the ERP. Many custom functions and code may create challenges in ERP upgrades.

Cleanse the Data

Data preparation, cleansing, and migration may take considerable efforts and energy. Legacy system data can't be used "as is" with the new implementation. Process and application duplication in the company may leave a lot of redundant and inconsistent data. So, new data sets need to be collected and a lot of cleansing of the existing data may be required. The amount of historical data that needs to be migrated will also determine the efforts under this head. What will matter is the amount of data to be transformed, the number of tables to be populated, the quality of data in legacy applications, the amount and nature of new data that needs to be collected, and the mechanism of migration. After the migration, the new database needs to be tested for completeness and correctness.

Finally, you need to have a structured evaluation and audit plan for continuous feedback on the whole process. This may prove important to achieve success.

ERP Testing

Contributed by Diptesh Dasgupta

Enterprise Resource Planning is software that automates and integrates the entire business functioning of an enterprise. Major vendors include SAP, ORACLE Apps, JD Edwards, and PeopleSoft. This section only discusses SAP testing.

ERP software is designed to handle most business processes, but it needs to be customized to cater to the specific process. Each enterprise is different. This process is called *customization.* There are several organization-specific business processes, however, that cannot be customized and must go through an explicit development process. These development projects are often classified as reports, interfaces, conversions, enhancements, and work flows and forms.

Because ERP software becomes an integral part of the enterprise, testing is critical. Imagine if the system delivers the wrong goods to its customers or the wrong salary to the employees or the wrong tax to the federal government. This testing needs to be methodic and rigorous.

Testing Teams. There are three predominant teams for implementing and testing an ERP. The team that understands the business processes and has the power to get the ERP implemented is known as the business team or the functional team. The team that implements the ERP is known as the project team, and the team that independently validates the implementation is called the testing team.

SAP Testing. SAP is a widely used ERP package common in mid- to large-scale businesses around the world. The following sections take you through the SAP testing process. SAP suggests that customers follow the Accelerated SAP Methodology for implementation, commonly known as ASAP Methodology.

Implementation Phases. There are five phases in the implementation of SAP:

1. *Project preparation:* The beginning of the project where the organization creates a project charter, and conducts an "as is" study.

2. *Business blueprint:* The company creates the "to be" vision and documentation.

3. *Realization:* Implementation of the "to be" process.

4. *Final preparation:* Integration of the units developed and testing the whole solution.

5. *Go live and support:* Final cutover to the new system and production support.

Testing starts in the blueprinting phase. The testing team gets engaged and starts working with the project/business team to come up with the testing strategy, resource plan, and test schedule. During the realization phase, the testing team is being advised by both the business team and project team about needs and wants. It begins to prepare a solution.

The project team meanwhile conducts the technical and functional unit testing for the configuration and development activities. The testing team starts developing the test cases based on the business scenario provided by the business team. The project team also provides blueprint, functional, and technical specifications used to create the test data sheet for the test cases. During the next phase, the final preparation, the testing team starts testing and simultaneously creating an automation test script. The testing is generally divided into three phases: System Integration Testing (SIT), Performance Testing (PT), and User Acceptance Testing (UAT).

SIT—System Integration Testing. SIT is conducted to see if the solution provided by the project team works perfectly and in harmony with the other applications that provide input or receive output from the solution. The test cases developed by the testing team should assess the requirements in three ways: positive, negative, and exception. The testing is generally executed in two cycles, SIT-1 and SIT-2. In some implementations, there could also be SIT-3.

PT— Performance Testing. PT is the load and stress test of the system. It looks for the break point in terms of stress, or in other words, it looks for the stress limit the system can take before it breaks. Performance testing also looks for the duration it takes to complete a transaction. The analysis of data can reveal the bottleneck that causes performance issues. Next comes "performance tuning," which is done to bring the application to the performance benchmarks. Performance testing is generally automated; the most commonly used tool is HP Roadrunner.

UAT—User Acceptance Test. This is a test done by the business team to verify that the solution provided by the project team meets the current business process requirements. Hence a set of test cases are made that contain all the possible business scenarios in SAP terms. These scenarios are provided to the business team after being trained in the SAP system. Once they are satisfied with the results, they sign off.

One major part of testing is catching defects or bugs. These are defined as the inability of the system to perform the task as required. Defects are of various types and are mainly due to the following three reasons.

- *Customization defects*: Defects in the system because the customization has not been done properly.

- *Technical defects*: Development not done properly.

- *Security defects*: The system does not allow the user to perform a process because it has not provided the proper authorization to the user/tester, or there's a question about whether the data or host system is safe.

In each phase of testing, the goal is to eliminate all defects.

The testing process closes with the completion of UAT, the business sign off, and test team sign off. Then the project can go live. In most cases, there is post go-live support by the testing team. The team continues to resolve defects and retest when necessary.

Testing Effectiveness Metric. One of the key performance indicators is testing effectiveness, measured in this way:

System Integration Testing Defects ÷ (SIT Defect + UAT Defects + Post Production Defects)

Testing effectiveness is 100 percent if UAT and post production defects are nil.

Conclusions

The problem discussed in this presentation represents a typical IT scenario common in large organizations. Over time, many monolithic applications on a variety of platforms get developed to automate various business processes across the organization. These applications may or may not communicate. These traditional architectures lead to a number of issues stemming from overlapping (and often conflicting) data and application logic.

The current industry trend is integration. The two architectural alternatives discussed here are SOA and Single ERP. Depending upon the organization needs and the budget, any one of them or a combination of both may be a right solution. Unfortunately neither of the approaches ensures technology independence and vendor independence. A large enterprise may have a variety of applications. For limited-scope applications and those with a short life, the business logic is not likely to change during the useful span of the application. Also, the possibility of reusing code or business logic is diminished. In such cases SOA doesn't make a lot of sense. SOA is also not a good solution in one-way messaging applications. In such cases the loose coupling of SOA doesn't offer any tangible benefits.

Z Inc. being a manufacturing company, taking the Single ERP approach by implementing mySAP may prove the right choice. MySAP offers many manufacturing functionality features, which form a major chunk of the company's business processes. However customizing mySAP to accommodate the business functionalities of more than 150 homegrown applications may be a major challenge and risk.

A project of this scope takes two to three years to complete depending upon the size of organization. In the case of Z Inc., the job was just completed at the time of this writing. As a result of the project, the organization expects operational efficiency, reduced operational costs, and quick response to dynamically changing business needs. The IT organization will undergo a sea change in its operations, with only one single application and technology platform across the organization to support and maintain. Isn't this sufficient reason to undertake this uphill task?

Acknowledgments: My sincere thanks to Venkat Paturi and Ravi Anadanam, whose continuous guidance and inspiration enabled us to present this case.

Corporate Governance in IT Companies

The importance of corporate governance became very clear in 2002 after a series of corporate meltdowns and frauds caused the loss of billions of dollars in shareholder investments as well thousands of jobs. Many companies filed for bankruptcy, and criminal investigations were initiated against many corporate executives. Enron Corporation, Tyco International, and WorldCom were among the names in headlines on a daily basis. Suddenly, everyone started showing an interest in corporate governance. New legislation was passed by the US Congress. The New York Stock Exchange (NYSE) and NASDAQ introduced new standards demanding that companies improve their corporate governance to maintain their listings.

Corporate governance is related to creating wealth for shareholders in both the near and long term. It requires a complex system of checks and balances. There are three key actors on the screen of corporate governance: shareholders, management, and the board of directors. The aim of corporate governance is to ensure that corporations follow the law and regulations. In addition, there is a public relations benefit to being a good corporate citizen. At a more micro level, governance is all about making sure that the organization delivers on its promises to both employees and customers and that both groups end up satisfied.

What follows is a broad overview of governance issues. It's not meant to be comprehensive, nor provide legal guidance. Laws vary from jurisdiction to jurisdiction.

The Corporation and Its Control

A *corporation* is a formal legal entity that is publicly registered for doing business. The privileges and liabilities of a corporation are separate from those of its members. There are many forms of corporations, and most are created to do business. They are governed by corporate law, which is designed to protect the interests of management, employees, and shareholders.

Under the law, corporations are afforded limited liability. In the case of bankruptcy, for example, shareholders may lose their investments and employees may lose their jobs. But neither will be personally liable to company creditors except in rare cases. Like human beings, corporations have rights and responsibilities under the legal system. They can be booked for criminal offenses such as fraud. Corporate shares are also are freely transferable. A corporation can exist beyond the lifetime of its investors and shareholders. This feature provides corporations much required stability, as well as the capability of accumulating wealth and doing mega projects. Such features make corporations a very attractive business entity.

A corporation can have voting and nonvoting members. The company is usually controlled by a centralized management under a board of directors elected by the shareholders. The chief executive officer (CEO), president, chief financial officer (CFO) and other top officers are usually appointed by the board of directors to manage the strategic and operational affairs of the corporation. While shareholders naturally have some influence—some say not enough in publicly held companies—big creditors such as banks and other financial institutions can also have a control over the affairs of corporations. In some cases, these creditors may have one or more members on the board, which can influence the decision making. When the board makes a decision to liquidate or dissolve a for-profit corporation, shareholders get whatever is left over after paying off creditors and other parties that may have interests in the corporation.

In the case of liability, shareholders benefit from the limited liability provisions of the law. Publicly traded corporations are required to publish an annual report and other financial data for the protection of investors and creditors. In many cases of poor corporate governance, the published annual reports and financial data were seriously flawed. There are many standards, such as Generally Accepted Accounting Principles (GAAP) in the United States, that have stringent guidelines for accounting as well as publishing annual financial statements and other data.

The structure of the corporation is continuously evolving in response to new government regulations and market conditions. In the case of irregularities, deciding who is responsible, shareholders or management, becomes a big challenge. Different jurisdictions vary significantly on this topic.

Board of Directors

Board members are elected or appointed by the shareholders, as stated earlier. They oversee the activities of a corporation. They appoint members of the executive management; they make and approve strategic decisions. The powers, duties, and responsibilities of the board are determined by company bylaws. The bylaws also indicate the number of directors there should be on the board, election procedures, and frequency of their meetings.

The board of directors is the highest management decision-making body in a corporation. It is accountable to shareholders for the performance of the corporation. Directors establish high-level policies and direction for the organization, and they ensure adequate financial resources for operations. The board approves the corporation's annual budget. As board members, they also have some legal responsibilities. They appoint the members of executive management including the CEO and CFO. The whole of executive management is answerable to the board of directors. It takes more of a supervisory role, and day-to-day management is left to key executive team members.

In theory, the control of the company is divided between the board of directors (or governors in some countries) and the shareholders, as played out in the annual meeting of share holders. (An annual meeting is also known as a general body meeting in many countries other than the United States.) In practice, control varies from company to company. Boards of directors in large public corporations tend to have more de facto power. The board can encompass a voting alliance that is difficult to overcome. One reason is that some institutional shareholders such as pension funds and banks grant their voting rights (proxies) to the board at annual meetings.

Members of the board may come from both inside and outside the company. Insiders are usually senior members of the executive management team, such as senior vice presidents of large business departments. Board members who are insiders from executive management are generally not paid anything extra for serving on the board. External members may be eminent business and social personalities who are compensated for being on the board. Company laws require that a certain percentage of board members are external. Directors other than owners or managers are often called *independent directors, disinterested directors, outside directors,* or *nonexecutive directors.* External board members may, and often do, serve on the board of several companies simultaneously as long there are no conflicts of interest. Board members are expected to be ethical and honor the laws and practices with respect to conflict of interest, corporate property, opportunity, and information. They are expected to work without undue pressure and to always vote only for what aligns with their conscience, knowledge, and belief.

Powers and Obligations of Board of Directors

The board of directors is given the power to ensure that the company is managed properly. Most of the time, the board exercises its power in meetings. Legally sufficient notice must be given to the board members for these meetings. Meetings without sufficient notice may still be valid provided all the members attend.

The board of directors, in most cases, has power when the board acts as a whole and not individually. There can be exceptions to this rule, though. The board of directors can appoint any of its members or any other employee as its representative and delegate any or all power to that person to be exercised jointly or singly. The board also has the power to appoint the managing director (CEO) and other executive members of management.

Directors exercise full control over the management policies of the company, but the company is run for the benefit of its shareholders. Laws therefore impose strict controls over the board in relation to exercising its powers. Directors at all times must act honestly and in good faith. All their powers must be exercised for proper purposes and may not be misused. While taking other positions, directors can't place themselves where their duties and interests conflict with their current position. If a director enters into a transaction with another company, and his own interests conflict with the company, he needs to ensure that the company gets the maximum out of that transaction and that his own interests are not given preference. A director can't use the company property, opportunity, and information for his gain without the written consent of the company. A director may not serve on the board of other, directly competitive companies. A director must disclose his shareholdings and notify the stock exchange of this information. Directors may be held liable if an act of negligence is proved on their part.

The powers and liabilities of the board of directors vary in every jurisdiction, but general provisions to safeguard the interests of shareholders and customers remain the same.

Powers and Obligations of Shareholders

By registering a company as a corporation, one must accept certain legal responsibilities that are imposed by the underlying laws. These laws operate to protect the interests of the company as well as shareholders, society, and creditors. If a company fails, shareholder liability is limited to the amounts they have invested in the company. If directors and officers of a company provide personal loan guarantees, they may, however, lose personal assets in the case of a loan default. Shareholder powers include changing shareholder rights, hiring and dismissing members of the board, approving mergers and acquisitions, and approving major financial transactions and decisions related to liquidation of the company. A company can, further, adopt a constitution for corporate governance.

As mentioned, a company may continue to exist even if its shareholders, officials, and directors die, leave, or sell their shares. A company's assets belong to the company as a separate legal entity. At the same time, it is shareholders who own the company. They can pass ordinary or special resolutions that can affect the company. These resolutions must be in accordance with the company constitution. Special resolutions can affect the company as a whole, or the interests of some or all of its investors. Appointing and removing directors is generally done by an ordinary resolution that is simply a majority vote. A special resolution may require a 75 percent majority or higher. Shareholders are most active at annual meetings that are conducted to adopt financial reports, appoint auditors, elect directors, and conduct other business that requires such general body resolutions. Special general body meetings can be called anytime on an as-needed basis.

Shareholders are required to inform the company if their shareholding exceeds a certain percentage of the company's share capital. In some cases, for example, if the shareholding exceeds 2 percent of the company's share capital, the shareholder must inform the company within 15 days.

Why Corporate Governance?

Governance always relates to an area of responsibility. Effective management, processes, policies, and decisions are required to supervise expectations, power, and performance. At the department level, governance might involve implementing these policies. At the corporate level, governance might take the form of developing policies on investment, use of information, staffing, and so on. Governance is basically a process through which decisions are made and implemented in an area of one's responsibility.

Governance can be defined at different levels—for example, corporate governance, project governance, and information technology governance. This chapter is mainly concerned with corporate governance.

At its core, good governance is all about good corporate leadership. To help in achieving its goal, every organization makes strategic and operational plans that are in line with the vision set at the top level. Good governance continuously steers the organization toward the set vision through strategic and operational plans. It makes sure that the day-to-day operations are always aligned with the vision, thus creating a strong future for the organization.

The board of directors and the members of executive management have the main responsibility of driving good governance practices across the ranks. An effective board will make sure shareholder assets and funds are used wisely and appropriately to maximize wealth and profits while maintaining all the social responsibilities of the organization. Good governance will reduce the risks of financial failure and greatly reduce the legal hassles while steering the organization toward a total all-round success.

There is increasing evidence that companies with good corporate governance practices have higher market valuations. Improved corporate governance structures and superior business processes help ensure quality decision-making and smooth and effective succession planning. They also contribute positively to the long-term success of companies—regardless of the industry segment and its sources of finance.

Corporate Governance Codes

Corporate governance is a priority for many corporations because it provides a way to manage risks and add value for shareholders and customers. Improved corporate governance gives corporations a way to reduce their own internal organizational risks and, as a result, improve their ability to operate in high-risk business environments. It's a general conclusion that the existence of good governance practices could have avoided the worst part of many recent financial failures.

Poor standards of corporate governance, particularly in the area of transparency and disclosure, can hamper the growth of companies and even make them unstable. Poor corporate governance practices led to the dramatic failure of many corporations in the United States, Western Europe, and India (Enron and Satyam Computers, for example). In many cases, investor pressures for performance are fierce, and management sometimes takes undue risks or violates compliance rules, acts that are simply not in the long-term interest of the organization.

Governance still looks voluntary in practice, even if it's strictly enforced by the law. The responsibility of directors is almost unlimited compared to the time they can spend in overseeing business. In many cases, the quality and rigor of internal audits may be questionable because internal auditors are not independent and report to the same business managers that are being reviewed. There is also too much dependence on external audits, which may be a cause of worry sometimes, as the amount of time external auditors spend in auditing a corporation may not justify the mammoth size and volume of the problem being audited. In any case, the board is largely dependent on executive management to do the right thing. Board members have to rely on the data and information that is supplied to them. In this regard, boards must be given total control to oversee and implement the code of corporate governance.

For information purposes, I am listing the requirements of some major corporate governance codes.[1] There are multiple codes provided by European and US agencies. The following are some important points culled from various sources, just to give you a flavor of the nature of corporate governance in various countries and industries. Not all apply in all situations, nor do all carry the force of law. I encourage you to refer to the reference in the preceding footnote if you are interested in more details.

---

[1] Richard Anderson & Associates, "Risk Management & Corporate Governance," www.oecd.org/dataoecd/29/4/42670210.pdf.

- Codes suggest either a majority of nonexecutive directors on the board or a balance of nonexecutive and executive directors.

- Codes suggest that nonexecutive directors meet alone occasionally without the presence of executive directors.

- Codes insist on a transparent process for appointing directors that is not under the sole control of executive management.

- Codes suggest a compensation or remuneration committee to decide on the remunerations of board members, including executive members and other members of executive management.

- Codes require an audit committee.

- Codes require corporations to conduct annual internal audits overseen by the audit committee.

- All codes envisage the need for conducting performance audits of individual board members, the board itself, and its committees.

- Codes suggest the board needs to approve the equity compensation plans of the directors and executive members of management.

- Codes say corporations must develop and publish an appropriate code of business ethics and conduct. The board must certify that the code is being followed.

- Codes suggest that the roles of chairman and CEO must be separated. It's the chairman who will provide the directors with necessary pieces of information about the affairs of the company that may be required for their effective functioning.

- In European codes, directors are subject to periodic elections and required to report certain information, such as the buying and selling of stock, to the markets.

- Codes often also discuss the role of institutional investors and how they can help maintain good corporate governance.

- A French code requires that the directors represent all the investors rather than small interest groups. Independent directors are to fulfill that role.

- It's the job of the CEO and senior management to assess and manage the risk exposure of the organization. An audit committee will see only the guidelines and processes that are used to handle the risks.

- Every company must be equipped with reliable procedures to assess the organization's risks and commitments, including off-balance sheet risks.

- The board should maintain a system of controls to safeguard shareholders' interests. Risk management and internal control are treated as two separate streams. Risk management related to financial reporting processes is further differentiated from the preceding two.

- Common observations regarding risk include the following:
  - Risks are frequently not linked to strategy.
  - Risk definitions are often poorly expressed.
  - The organization must develop intelligent responses to risks.
  - Risk analysis must take into account stakeholders.

How to Implement Corporate Governance

Effective corporate governance demands proper internal controls. *Internal controls* are policies and procedures put in place by management to ensure that important goals and objectives will be met while following the principles of good corporate governance. Internal controls promote operational efficiencies and effectiveness while ensuring adherence to prescribed policies and other regulations. They also help provide reliable financial information and protect relevant records and assets.

In Chapter 4 we discussed how overall IT governance helps in achieving desired service levels. It's the effectiveness of internal controls implemented within the overall governance framework that determines the levels of operational efficiency.

It's management, and not the auditors, who set and exercise internal controls. Internal controls should provide an assurance that financial reports and data are reliable and accurate enough for business and regulatory requirements. Internal controls are applicable to manual as well as computerized systems. Internal controls must ensure the timeliness and validity of transactions. All transactions must be properly recorded, authorized, valued, classified, and reconciled to relevant subsidiary records.

Any internal control system is a complex environment. At the top level, it starts with the basic management philosophy and operating style of an organization. Then there are management structures such as separation of duties and lines of reporting. It's important that each person in the hierarchy understands his or her authority and responsibility. Personnel need to be trained with the latest updates in trade, regulations, and organizational policies and procedures. Communication and information systems play an important role in implementing internal audit controls. They need to be foolproof and comply with the control requirements. A competent internal audit function is important as well.

For the effective design of an internal control system, the first step is to perform a comprehensive risk assessment. It may cover the corporation's mission, transactions, compliance, and assets. Risk management and controls must be in line with organizational objectives and strategies. An internal control system is designed to manage risks and may involve strategies for risk avoidance, risk transfer, risk mitigation, and risk acceptance. All the control points are identified, and potential exposures are analyzed. Technology, processes, and organizational structure must be linked in order to design effective internal controls.

Internal controls start by deploying the proper personnel, policies, and procedures to manage the identified risks. Independent checks are maintained along with rigorous records and documentation. Physical controls are placed over assets and records. Policies and procedures are relevant, complete, and well documented at any given point in time. Ensuring consistency in policy compliance is equally important. Good controls ensure a smooth flow of financial information and overall coordination in a decentralized environment. Proper escalation and problem resolution processes are set in place. Setting up of accountabilities may be the single most important element in any internal control system. Whistleblowers and monitoring systems tend to play an important role in effectively functioning internal controls.

Internal audits are important tools to ensure and implement corporate governance. They represent a systematic approach to evaluating and improving the effectiveness of governance processes and risk management. Company insiders act as internal auditors, who are given proper power and authority to carry out their work independently. The scope of internal audits may cover operations, finance, fraud analysis, detection and prevention, asset management, and compliance with laws and regulations. Internal auditing involves measuring compliance with the company's policies and procedures, and auditors may advise executive management and the board of directors on better executing their responsibilities. But the audit doesn't cover execution of the organization's activities. Publicly held companies generally have an internal audit department led by a chief audit executive who reports to an audit committee of the board.

Besides conducting audits, internal auditors also have a role in risk management and implementing corporate governance. In internal audits, the charter is to measure efficacy of operations, reliability of financial reports, and compliance with professional standards and laws of the land. In the risk management process, internal audits need to chart how the organization identifies, analyzes, and responds to risks. They need to ensure the effectiveness of the overall risk management process. Internal auditors are often quoted as being the fourth pillar of corporate governance (the other three being management, external auditors, and the board of directors). Internal auditors help the audit committee perform its duties effectively. Internal auditors inform the board's audit committee on the effectiveness of internal controls, set the agenda for meetings, identify capabilities of key managers, and ensure that the audit committee receives reliable information. Internal auditors also coordinate external audits.

Consulting auditors, who are seasoned corporate professionals, can also help management to implement corporate governance. Their level of independence is in between internal and external auditors. Consulting auditors are used if a company lacks sufficient expertise in auditing certain areas. They are also sometimes used to augment an existing internal auditing staff. Consulting auditors can work independently or can team up with internal auditors for their work.

External auditors are also used to independently assess the effectiveness of corporate governance within a company.

External Audits

An external auditor's report is considered an important legal financial document for any business. Auditors certify the information in financial statements that can be used to attract investors and obtain financial loans. So it's in the interest of the business to get a clean audit report from external auditors.

The auditor's report is only an opinion (and not an evaluation) on whether the information presented is correct and free of material misstatements. Everything else is left for users to decide. Actual journal entries may not be evaluated by the auditors.

Unqualified audit reports are issued by auditors when they think the entries are free from any material misstatements and entries are prepared fairly in accordance with GAAP. To a user, this would mean that the company's financial position and state of business affairs are represented fairly in the report. This is the best report a business can get from an auditor. A *qualified report* is issued when a couple of situations in financial statements don't comply with GAAP but largely follow the principles of GAAP. A *disclaimer* is issued when the auditors are unable to form any opinion on the financial statements and as a result refuse to issue any opinion. This may occur when auditors start work on an entity but can't complete it for various reasons. Auditors can also comment on the state of internal controls for a public company. These types of opinions—called Committee of Sponsoring Organizations, or COSO, opinions—are now required along with the opinion on financial statements. COSO is an organization widely known for providing guidance on crucial aspects of organizational governance, internal controls, business ethics, fraud, enterprise risk management, and financial reporting.

Sarbanes-Oxley

The *Sarbanes-Oxley Act* (SOX) is a US law passed in 2002 to reinforce the practices of corporate governance and regain investor confidence that had been shaken due to major corporate and accounting scandals. SOX was sponsored by US Senator Paul Sarbanes and US Representative Michael Oxley. SOX legislation has wide implications, as it establishes new or enhanced standards for all US publicly listed company boards, executive management, and public accounting firms. It contains eleven titles, or sections, that legislate additional responsibilities for corporate boards and mandate criminal penalties for certain infractions. The law requires the US Securities and Exchange Commission (SEC) to make sure companies comply with the requirements of the new legislation.

SOX broadly covers the following topics:

- Defines new standards and guidelines for corporate boards and audit committees.

- Provides new guidelines for accountability standards and also sets criminal penalties for the mismanagement of corporations.

- Defines new independent standards and guidelines for external auditors.

- Introduces a new Public Company Accounting Oversight Board (PCAOB) to work under the SEC. The PCAOB oversees public accounting firms and also works on accounting standards.

Generally Accepted Accounting Principles

Here's what Investopedia[2] says about *Generally Accepted Accounting Principles (GAAP)*:

> *The common set of accounting principles, standards, and procedures that companies use to compile their financial statements. GAAP are a combination of authoritative standards (set by policy boards) and simply the commonly accepted ways of recording and reporting accounting information. GAAP are imposed on companies so that investors have a minimum level of consistency in the financial statements they use when analyzing companies for investment purposes.*

The United States has its own version of GAAP that is called *American GAAP*. Either way, GAAP is a standard, providing guidelines that companies are expected to follow while compiling their financial statements. Still, there is a lot of opportunity for those who want to play with data for their own advantage. So even if accounts are maintained as per GAAP, auditors can't assume anything. Even financial statements prepared as per GAAP may need close scrutiny and professional review by the auditors.

More recently, GAAP is slowly getting phased out and is giving way to the International Accounting Standards (more precisely, International Financial Reporting Standards, or IFRS) as global business becomes more widespread. IFRS is established and maintained by the International Accounting Standards Board. In some parts of the world, local accounting standards are applied to small companies, but all publicly listed or large corporations must comply with the more comprehensive IFRS. This way, statutory financial reporting is compatible internationally, across jurisdictions.

---

[2] Investopedia, "Generally Accepted Accounting Principles – GAAP," www.investopedia.com/terms/g/gaap.asp.

Information Technology Governance

IT governance focuses on risk management and performance of IT systems. This type of governance is needed for greater accountability in decision making regarding IT systems that is in the best interest of shareholders. Investments in IT systems are increasing day by day, something that has long-term implications for investors. IT governance forms a system in which all relevant stakeholders, including board members, senior managers, clients, and employees are responsible for their part in the decision making that affects IT. This makes decision making regarding IT issues more accountable as each decision is judged on its alignment with the organization's strategic objectives. While managing risk and ensuring the right compliance levels are essentials of good governance, it is sometimes more important to focus on delivering value and measuring performance.

There are many supporting references for the implementation of IT governance. Some of them are as follows:

- *AS8015-2005*: In 2008, this Australian standard was approved as ISO/IEC 38500.

- *COBIT*: Control Objectives for Information and related Technology (COBIT) is taken as the world's leading framework for IT governance and control.

- *ITIL*: The IT Infrastructure Library (ITIL) is mainly used in service delivery management.

- *ISO 27001*: This standard focuses mainly on IT security.

- *CMM*: The Capability Maturity Model (CMM) has a focus on software engineering. It's from the Software Engineering Institute (SEI).

- *TickIT*: This certification program is for quality management of software development.

Corporate Governance vs. IT Governance

Corporate governance is a way to control and manage a corporate entity. It consists of a set of policies, processes, customs and traditions, laws, business practices, and institutional practices that are applicable to or adopted by the entity. Corporate governance helps an organization to meet its goals in the most effective and efficient manner possible. It's a strategy that allows a corporate entity to manage all aspects of its business so that it can meet its goals while complying with all applicable laws and a code of business ethics.

IT governance is a subset discipline of corporate governance that deals with risk management and performance of IT systems. The aim of IT governance is to ensure that the investments in IT organization are in line with business strategies and generate desired business value while keeping associated risks under control. This is done by implementing a well-defined IT organizational structure that clearly assigns the roles and responsibilities that are related to information systems, data, business processes, and associated IT infrastructure.

Summary

Corporate governance can be defined in many ways. One such definition, used in this chapter, is this: governance is basically a process of making good decisions and implementing those decisions in an area of one's responsibility. The management and staff of an organization are making and implementing the decisions. We can have hundreds of checks and balances in place as a part of internal control systems. But after all, it is humans who must intend to follow them. Controls can be bypassed or overruled, as typically happens in high-growth phases of the business. Corporate governance can be implemented only by leading through example. When the top management is serious about it and practices governance to the core, only then can the staff be expected to follow.

Society at large has a big role in making corporations follow corporate governance principles. Internal auditors are the paid employees of any corporation. So there is a limit to how much they can go against the will of executive management in implementing corporate governance. In an infamous case from India that made the headlines the world over in 2008, external auditors signed inflated and overstated accounts for seven years in a row. Fake certificates of bank deposits were used by top management that showed a cash reserve of over 1 billion dollars. Actually, the company had only a few million. This was in spite of a full-fledged internal audit department and reasonably good information systems. The computer systems were tampered with to the point that the final financial statements were taken out for the review of auditors. So it's the intention to implement corporate governance that comes first in any system of internal or external controls. Corporations are a section of society, and in case after case we see that it is the moral and ethical standards of society at large that will make any system of corporate governance work in the true sense.

IT in Modern Vehicle Development Programs

Guest chapter by Shailesh Kadre

A considerable portion of IT efforts in any manufacturing organization goes toward supporting and carrying out engineering activities. IT for engineering is a different world altogether from the one most IT people are used to. Middle-level managers in IT departments need to appreciate the engineering aspect of IT because they are responsible for supporting it as well. In this chapter, you will look at a vehicle development program as an example of the use of IT in engineering. You will learn about the role of IT in rolling out a car, from the initial concept to the dealer's place.

If you don't understand some of the specific engineering details, don't worry. Focus on getting a feel for the overall process, because you may one day be part of just such an effort.

Computer-Aided Design Software in Vehicle Development Programs

During the early days of product development, designers used drawing boards for designing and drafting purposes. In the old days, it required a lot of time to create two-dimensional (2D) drawings and then, by drawing different views, to create a three-dimensional (3D) shape of the object.

Computer-aided design (CAD) software makes the job much easier now. The use of computers has simplified the design process. It has also reduced the drafting effort required of designers. With advances in mathematical modeling for complex curves and surface generations, it is now possible to generate real-life complex structures on computers. Working with CAD software may require some knowledge of programming languages, however.

Fast-track growth in the field of computer graphics has further improved the situation. Before making actual prototypes and finalizing design concepts, designers now have a lot of options to try. Usually, designers start with a simple concept design, and then afterward—depending on the functionality and other design considerations—add various features to it. With various 2D and 3D features readily available in CAD software, they end up with a final design in a 3D format. Nowadays, designers spend most of their time creating 3D models. CAD tools generate 2D drawings automatically as necessary.

CAD programs can also easily make *parametric designs*—those that change some aspect of the design if one or more of the parameters (like the diameter of a pulley) changes. That makes it easy to regenerate the design by changing only the affected portion. All other dependent parameters automatically get updated.

These inherent features of CAD tools have reduced the overall product-development cycle drastically. They also give designers more time to think creatively about the various functional and aesthetic aspects of the product design. This improvement can be easily seen if we compare the shapes and styling of automobiles from the 1950s to those we have today.

Computer-Aided Manufacturing in the Production of Automobiles

Any manufacturing process that is controlled by a dedicated centralized computer or computers is known as *computer-aided manufacturing* (CAM).

Until recently, most manufacturing was done without computers. Conventional machine tools such as lathes and milling machines, for example, are operated manually. But the quality of parts produced by these machines totally depends on the skill and experience of the individual machine operator. With the development of computers and information technology in manufacturing processes, it is now possible to control various manufacturing operations by dedicated computers. This ensures parts and operations that are of uniform quality.

In machining processes, two types of machines are used. For repetitive jobs, *numerical control* (NC) machines are used. These are hardwired and have a fixed program for the various machining sequences required to do a job. Only machining parameters can be changed. They are suitable for repetitive jobs in which not much job variation is expected. Another type, known as a *computer numerical control* (CNC) machine, uses a dedicated computer. These machines are soft-wired and can handle a large variety of machining jobs. They have their own programming language. All the stages of the machining operation can be defined in the program sequence, from the point when the machine is started to when the job is finished. Before actually machining any of the components, one can simulate and visualize the total machining operation on the computer screen. This helps the operator arrive at optimized machining parameters such as speed, feed, type of tool, actual machining time, and so forth, at the planning stage itself. Once the programming is finalized, the process is fully automated. The operator's job is to just observe the whole process and troubleshoot on the rare occasions when the machine or program malfunctions. Before running the job on actual material, a CNC machine program is usually tested on softer materials such as special wood or foam.

For processes such as the manufacturing of casted parts, in which extremely high temperatures of molten metal are involved, computer-aided automation helps. With the use of material-handling equipment such as robotic arms, high-temperature parts can be conveniently removed from the furnace. The dedicated computer provided on these machines makes the work of the operators a lot easier by handling the changes in various manufacturing variables such as different shapes, sizes, and operational parameters.

CAM operates in very close interaction with CAD. Nowadays, CAD software has the capacity to generate the program for CAM operation. For any complex part generated by CAD designers, the CAM programs are automatically generated by the CAD tool itself. With the development of multi-axis milling machines, almost any complex 3D shapes can be generated, just as they were originally produced by a CAD designer using software tools.

It is a dream of all designers to quickly build prototypes of their design. CAD and CAM help product designers visualize how their designs look in real space. Rapid prototype development machines are also developed for this purpose.

Computer-Aided Engineering in Automobile Design

The biggest challenge of any structural engineer is to predict the structural adequacy of real-world, engineered structures. *Structural adequacy* means that the structure should perform its intended function. For example, in the event of a car crash, the design of a car body should be such that the occupants in the car remain safe; the car's upper body should absorb all the energy generated during vehicle impact, without causing any damage to its occupants inside. Another example is the foundation of a very tall building. The foundation should be strong enough not only to support the entire weight of the structure but also to take care of additional loads that may come in the event of earthquake. These structures are complex and pose the biggest challenge to engineers at the time of designing.

It is not always possible to determine the analytical mathematical solutions that ensure structural adequacy. An *analytical solution*, also known as a *closed-form solution*, is a mathematical expression that gives the values of certain engineering variables (like the width of a frame) at any location of a body. This unknown quantity can indicate deformations and stress levels generated at any predetermined location in the structure, due to external loading. Such analysis is a classical approach to solving engineering problems and may provide very accurate results. This approach has limitations, however. It is applicable only to very simple structures with simplified loading conditions.

In the absence of reliable analytical solutions for complex engineering problems, in some cases it is possible to build prototypes and to test them under actual operating conditions. This approach is commonly used in the automotive industry. Normally this is an expensive and time-consuming process, which might not be suitable for applications requiring multiple design iterations. The reliability of this method depends on building three to four prototypes per test. If the structure is large, a lot of approximations are used in building these prototypes in order to come up with reliable results.

Because of the limitations in analytical and experimental methods, smart people developed numerical methods. *Numerical methods* involve developing mathematical expressions that nonetheless use some approximations, unlike closed-form solutions. These approximations are based on some assumptions, but the final accuracy of the solutions is within tolerable limits. Numerical methods require a lot of number crunching, usually more than closed-form methods. This comes easier, thanks to advances in computer technology in recent years. Today, such numerical methods have evolved as an effective tool for solving complex engineering problems. In the initial design phases, numerical analysis techniques are applied regardless of whether the design prototypes are available or not. These techniques are fully exploited commercially and are widely available in the form of off-the-shelf software tools.

Apart from these numerical techniques, a knowledge base has been developed in the form of computer software for the design and manufacturing of vehicles. The software is used to do virtually everything in the construction of cars. High-end computers are used for the design of vehicle bodies, including its styling and contours. They are also used for planning of vehicle manufacturing in the factory. In a modern vehicle factory, everything from conceptualization to the final rollout is done with the help of computers. And as an IT manager, you need to provide hardware and software support at every stage.

Finite Element Analysis

Once CAD models are ready, *finite element analysis* (FEA) techniques are applied to analyze the patterns of stress and deformation in a structure. This information is used to redesign the component until it is safe for use under actual operating conditions.

In finite element analysis, the CAD model or the structure is represented by a collection of subdivisions that are called *finite elements*. These elements are joined together by *nodes*. Simple mathematical functions represent the distribution of actual displacements over the entire element. The displacements at nodal points are unknown. The final solution gives the approximate displacements at these nodal points. This requires large amounts of numerical computations. The displacements calculated at nodal points are used to determine the stress distribution all over the structure. This is a very short description of a rather long subject.

FEA has a great role to play in vehicle design. It is specifically used for the design and redesign of vehicle components before they are moved into production. FEA models are prepared for full vehicles and simulate real-life loading conditions. A good finite element analysis gives the vehicle designer an indication of where the component is likely to fail. Accordingly, the component can be redesigned. At the end of this chapter, you'll find a real time example on the use of FEA software.

Case Study: A Complete Design Cycle for the Development of Automotive Systems

You have read about the role of concepts such as CAD, CAM, and CAE in the design and manufacturing of vehicles. Today's vehicle factories are highly automated and use IT at every step. And that's why they need huge IT support to keep going. Enterprise resource planning (ERP) and supply chain management (SCM) software also have a major role to play; they are integrated with engineering and product life cycle software in these factories. Other experts can handle the day-to-day workings of these engineering applications, but as an IT manager you must have a general understanding of their functioning—maybe from 1,000 feet above.

Here's a case that will help give you that view. This case explains the manufacturing cycle, from conceptualization to sale, for a sports utility vehicle (SUV).

T Inc. is a US-based tier-1 automotive supplier providing manufacturing and engineering services related to automotive systems. It has manufacturing, design, and development offices in many countries all over the world, with sales revenue running into millions of dollars from engineering services alone. The engineering services of this company cater to the design and analysis requirements of a leading European automotive company, XYZ Company.

T Inc. has received a request from XYZ to design the frame ladder and other subsystems for a new SUV to be launched in the European market. T Inc. also has the capacity to manufacture these systems required by the client. Therefore, T Inc. receives the full contract, from design to manufacture, for the required components. The company is also responsible for the warranty-related issues that occur on these parts in the field during the normal operation of the vehicles.

In the initial phases of any analysis, the design department needs to clearly understand the requirements of the proposed vehicle from the marketing department of XYZ Company. This includes the operating conditions of the roads and the environment in which the vehicle will be operating for most of its life. The total warranty miles of the vehicle are decided based on the type of vehicle and operating conditions. What follows is an explanation of how T Inc. goes about fulfilling the contract—or any similar contract.

Road Load Data Acquisition

T Inc.'s design cycle starts with the *Road Load Data Acquisition* (RLDA) activity. On the basis of an initial study performed by XYZ's marketing people, a benchmarking vehicle, which closely resembles the proposed configuration, is identified. The design cycle starts with the study of this vehicle, which is instrumented with accelerometers (instruments to indirectly measure the force on vehicle components) and load cells at various predetermined locations on its systems. The output of the accelerometers and load cells is stored on a centralized computer system fitted on the vehicle itself. This produces a huge amount of real-time data— way too much for human beings to handle. But specialized software is available at T Inc. to handle multiple signals at a time. This newly instrumented vehicle is then operated on predetermined roads in the region. The RLDA activity may take months. The output is the accelerations and loads at various locations (components) of the vehicle. This data is then utilized for generating loads and boundary conditions (the extreme conditions to which the vehicle will be subjected) for a virtual simulation at the later stages of the design and validation.

Another approach, also used by T Inc. and based solely on information technology, is to create virtual loads from road profiles generated in virtual simulation. Initial models of the vehicle are created in a computer by using multi-body dynamics (MBD). The virtual model is then tested on the virtual roads. Designers determine the loads at full vehicle and subsystem levels, which are subsequently used for the further analysis of the main components. Ride and comfort level can also be studied in this approach. This approach is cheaper and faster compared to the physical design but requires a highly skilled staff to do the job.

In parallel with the RLDA, the design department also builds a 3D CAD model of the full vehicle. This process is complex and required the integration of many interdependent disciplines of T Inc. and XYZ Company, including marketing, design, industrial design, electrical, engine and power train, and so on.

The total design cycle at T Inc. is divided into two major parts. First, some vehicle systems and subsystems are designed in-house. These include the vehicle frame, subframes, main body, and engine. The design process at this early stage is relatively flexible, and major design changes at this point can be handled effectively. Second, for standard systems such as vehicle suspensions, transmissions, or electronic items including batteries, the design department has to depend on outside suppliers. When designing a vehicle, therefore, space must be left to accommodate these standard items.

All the vehicle parts are recorded in a master list called the *bill of material* (BOM). This is an important document; a controlled copy is stored in a central location on a T Inc.'s information systems. The BOM is assessed not only by the designers but also by other vehicle departments and vendors. The correctness of the BOM ensures that all the parts conform to the latest design version. All this is possible only with the help of ERP software such as SAP. This way, even vendors can also access the latest information regarding design changes.

The parts are designed by T Inc. on the basis of functionality and packaging constraints, and then these initial designs are finalized. Standard software packages are used for this purpose. Two major design criteria exist for any component or subsystem design: design for durability and design for safety.

The loads obtained by the RLDA activity and predicted by the designer for the components and assembly are used in the analysis of the various components. With the use of commercially available software such as Nastran and ANSYS, designers at T Inc. can simulate the behavior of the components under service loads. Yet the designer must thoroughly understand the physical system. A slight mistake in assumptions while performing analysis can lead to wrong results. It is the responsibility of the analyst using CAE tools to arrive at a physically realizable solution that accurately simulates the actual system. The output of the analysis can be the prediction of deformations of the components. Another output may be the stress distribution on the components under various operating loads. These deformations and contour plots help designers predict the structural performance and also identify the weak regions of the components at which failure may occur during vehicle operation or field testing.

The Development Cycle at T Inc.

The total vehicle development cycle is roughly divided into four to five stages. In some companies, these are known as *gates*. You start from the initial design concept of the vehicle and proceed through engineering sign-off. The names of these gates, or levels, may vary from company to company. In the design office, models are developed corresponding to these gates. Normally, the target dates at each level of vehicle development are stringent and strictly driven by an aggressively scheduled vehicle launch. At the end of each stage, the performance of components is observed and a failure analysis performed. The learning from each of the previous stages is applied to ensure design improvements in the next stage. This also gives the designers a chance to identify any critical systems that underperform during testing or analysis.

As stated earlier, the main objective of the vehicle design is to ensure not only the durability of its components but also the safety of its occupants in the event of a crash. With the increasing speed of modern automobiles, occupant safety has become an important aspect of any vehicle design. During a crash, occupants are subjected to severe shocks that can be fatal. CAE tools such as LS-DYNA can perform detailed crash analysis of the full vehicle and subsystems. Everywhere in the world, strict norms and standards have been developed to ensure that vehicles and their components are designed with safety in mind. Before launching any vehicle in the market, the manufacturer has to satisfy these norms by testing full-scale prototypes. This testing is a very costly affair. So at the design stage, engineers evaluate the crashworthiness of these vehicles at the full vehicle and subsystem level. It is just not possible to predict the behavior of these complex systems by hand calculations. For this purpose, high-end computational tools such as FEA software are developed and used in the automotive industry as standard analysis tools.

Manufacturability of components is also taken into account during the design phase. Dedicated software programs take care of various issues involved in manufacturing processes, including bending, forming, casting, and molding. Specialized computer software programs such as Altair HyperForm, LS-DYNA, and many others are there to validate the manufacturing processes.

While loading, various components may come in contact with each other. This can also be simulated by using various contact algorithms in commercially available software. They can exactly predict the behavior of the components under operating conditions. Once the components meet both performance and manufacturing criteria, drawings are released formally for manufacturing and given to the tooling department, which has state-of-the-art computer-aided manufacturing facilities.

Stages in Design and Development Summarized

The key aspects of the design and development cycle for the major components of the new SUV manufactured by T Inc. are summarized here.

XYZ's marketing department first performs the initial market survey to determine the need for a new vehicle to be launched. After careful consideration of market and company needs, the correct configuration of the vehicle is identified. Marketing specifies the required warranty miles of the vehicle. Detailed studies are made to determine the operating conditions in which the vehicle is supposed to operate during its warranty miles. Detailed routes are chalked down for the vehicle to be tested for the definite number of miles. Marketing and the vehicle program management team then establish a vehicle-level development program with important milestones, deliverables, and dates. The program manager keeps a strict eye on these milestones.

The complete cycle at T Inc., which is designing and manufacturing key components, is divided into the following distinct stages:

- Mule building
- Virtual prototype building
- Engineering prototype 1
- Engineering prototypes 2, 3, and 4

The first stage is *mule building*. The *mule* is a makeshift arrangement of the actual vehicle to be tested. It is a vehicle that is made from an already available, closely resembling vehicle. Required changes are done in order to closely match the proposed vehicle. This vehicle is instrumented with accelerometers, as discussed earlier. The mule is then tested on the various routes developed initially. After exhaustive testing, detailed data is gathered for the road load accelerations. This data is used for further analysis.

In the design office, workers start a design activity known as the *virtual prototype building stage, described earlier*. At this stage, all the initial designs of all the main vehicle systems and subsystems are created on the basis of functionality and packaging constraints with respect to other subsystems.

The initial road load data obtained from the mule testing is used to validate the design concepts. If the designs are inadequate for performance, design iterations are carried out to meet the target performance within the scheduled timelines. This is called a *virtual prototype*, because only CAD designers and FEA analysts are working on the model. The initial BOM is also frozen at this stage. To build the CAD model, a tool such as NX Unigraphics software is used. Simultaneously with the virtual prototype stage of the model building, engineers complete virtual validations.

The next step is to build *engineering prototype stage 1* (EP-1). By creating some makeshift tooling arrangements, engineers make physical engineering prototypes. They are sure to use the latest versions per the BOM. This is an important stage, because the tooling department and design office come to know the actual problems that may be encountered during mass production of the vehicle.

The next steps can be called *engineering prototype stages 2, 3, and 4*, in which the steps already described are repeated. After the vehicle systems and subsystems perform as per their expected level, designs are finalized, and the design department officially releases all the drawings for manufacturing.

After various trials are taken, the tooling department at T Inc. makes production tools, to be used for the final manufacturing of the vehicle. The preceding process can take two to three years.

So the next time you take your car on a highway, keep in mind all the work that went into it!

Summary

A major portion of IT efforts in any engineering company goes into product design and manufacturing. This chapter is meant to create an awareness of the topic. There are many software products for product life cycle management, design, manufacturing, testing and so on. As an IT manager, awareness and general knowledge of these is key, even if you are not an engineer.

Following are some illustrations and analysis for readers who are more engineering oriented and want to get a feel for FEA software and how it compares with closed-form solutions, or hand calculations as they are called in some cases.

Chapter Appendix

FEA: Software Validations for OptiStruct and Nastran

In this section, you'll take a look at a typical, simple mechanical problem to be solved by using finite element analysis (FEA). This example is included in this chapter to give a better feel for engineering software to those interested.

As you can see in Figure 14-1, we have a cantilevered beam fixed at one end (shown by triangles), with the load applied at the other end (indicated by vertical arrows). The beam is 15 mm wide, 2 mm deep, and 50 mm long. It has been divided into finite elements by quadrilateral elements. This is known as a *mesh* in FEA terminology.

This is just a simplified example to show the power of FEA software. In reality, the structural components are much more complicated, and *meshing* requires a lot of effort.

FE Model of Cantilever Beam

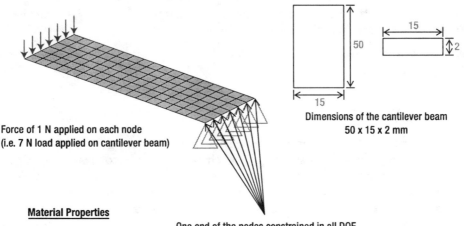

Force of 1 N applied on each node
(i.e. 7 N load applied on cantilever beam)

Dimensions of the cantilever beam
50 x 15 x 2 mm

Material Properties

One end of the nodes constrained in all DOF

Steel
Young's Modulus E [MPa] – 2.1E + 5
Poisson's Ratio-0.3
Density Rho [tons/mm³] – 7.86E – 09

Figure 14-1. FEA model of a simple cantilever beam

This is a simple mechanical problem for which the closed-form analytical solution is available using simple strength-of-material formulas. The deflection of this cantilever beam can be determined by using the hand calculations shown in Table 14-1. (This is just an example to show the hand calculations, and you may ignore the mathematical terms.)

Table 14-1. Hand Calculations to Solve Stress and Displacements (Analytical Solution)

Hand Calculations

Parameter	Symbol	Formula	Unit	
Width	b		15	mm
Length	L		50	mm
Thickness	t		2	mm
Force	F		7	N
Modulus of elasticity	E		2.10E + 05	N/mm^2
Poisson's ratio	nu		0.3	
Area moment	I	=bd^3 / 12	10	mm^4
Deflstance of farthest fiber	y	=t / 2	1	mm
Moment	M	=F * L	350	N – mm
Stress	Sigma	=My / I	35.0	N / mm^2
Defl		=FL^3 / 3EI	1.39E – 01	mm

OptiStruct is an FE solver that is available in Altair HyperWorks software. Similarly, Nastran is also a FE solver developed by MSC Software. Both of these FE solvers are commonly used in the automotive industry. The preceding example of a simple cantilever beam can be solved by using both OptiStruct and Nastran FE solvers. Figure 14-2, Figure 14-3, Figure 14-4, and Figure 14-5 use these FE solvers to display the typical stress and deformation patterns for the cantilever beam.

Static Analysis Results in OptiStruct Solver

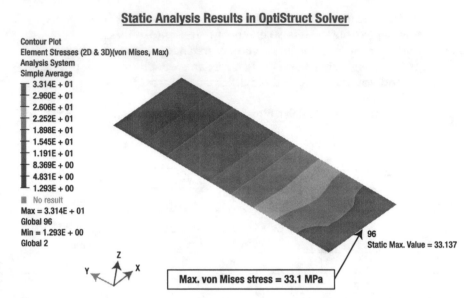

Contour Plot
Element Stresses (2D & 3D)(von Mises, Max)
Analysis System
Simple Average
- 3.314E + 01
- 2.960E + 01
- 2.606E + 01
- 2.252E + 01
- 1.898E + 01
- 1.545E + 01
- 1.191E + 01
- 8.369E + 00
- 4.831E + 00
- 1.293E + 00
- No result
Max = 3.314E + 01
Global 96
Min = 1.293E + 00
Global 2

96
Static Max. Value = 33.137

Max. von Mises stress = 33.1 MPa

Figure 14-2. Stress analysis of a simple cantilever beam using OptiStruct software. The arrow at the end shows a highly stressed region.

Static Analysis Results in OptiStruct Solver

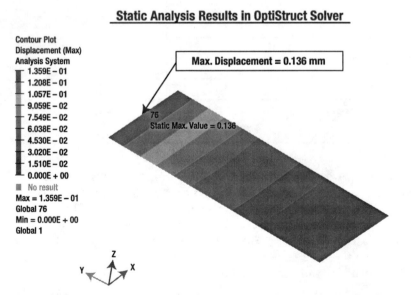

Contour Plot
Displacement (Max)
Analysis System
- 1.359E – 01
- 1.208E – 01
- 1.057E – 01
- 9.059E – 02
- 7.549E – 02
- 6.038E – 02
- 4.530E – 02
- 3.020E – 02
- 1.510E – 02
- 0.000E + 00
- No result
Max = 1.359E – 01
Global 76
Min = 0.000E + 00
Global 1

Max. Displacement = 0.136 mm

76
Static Max. Value = 0.136

Figure 14-3. Displacement analysis of a simple cantilever beam using OptiStruct software. The arrow at the end shows maximum displacement.

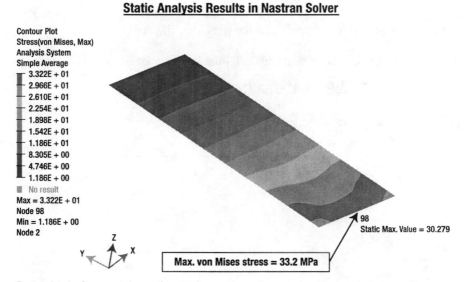

Figure 14-4. Stress analysis of a simple cantilever beam using Nastran software. The arrow at the end shows a highly stressed region.

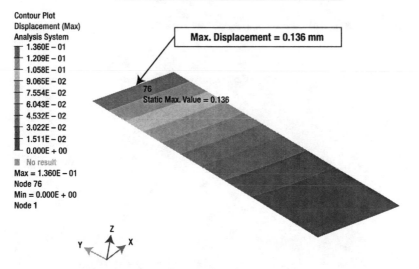

Figure 14-5. Displacement analysis of a simple cantilever beam using Nastran software. The arrow at the end shows maximum displacement.

Table 14-2 compares the displacement obtained by FEA and by the analytical approach. There is a marginal difference between the results.

Table 14-2. Comparisons of Nastran and OptiStruct Results with Hand Calculations

Static Analysis Results Summary

Analytical Stress	Analytical Displacement	OptiStruct Result	Nastran Result	% Accuracy for Stress	% Accuracy for Displacement
35 MPa	0.139 mm	33.13 MPa	33.2 MPa	95	98.5
		0.136 mm	0.136 mm	95	98.5

Streamlining IT Using Service-Oriented Architecture

This chapter covers the topic of Enterprise Application Integration (EAI) through the route of Service-Oriented Architecture (SOA). The objective of this chapter is to cover the different aspects of SOA implementations. You will learn about some of the myths about SOA and its various business benefits. Real-world case studies are presented to demonstrate how SOA helps to dynamically create business processes and provide companies with the flexibility to change.

Large corporations may have literally hundreds of applications, even if they employ ERPs to work in key operational areas. These applications sometimes form silos, or information islands, as information is accumulated but is not easily available to other applications or wide audiences. There can be many strategies for integrating these applications. SOA and Single ERP are two. This chapter takes you though SOA and then shows you what it takes to perform EAI by using SOA as the main integration strategy.

In most large corporations, a whole lot of legacy system inventory has developed over the past few decades. Many of these applications are silo based and not in line with business objectives. Using EAI is becoming a trend in helping corporations employ leaner business operations and respond swiftly to fast-changing market needs. As an IT manager, you must be familiar with the options available for working out required legacy integrations. SOA is one such proven EAI strategy. It has been adopted by many organizations across the globe.

Both SOA and ERP can be used for application integration. You have studied Single ERP as an application integration strategy in earlier chapters. In this chapter, you will look at SOA's integration capabilities. In later sections, you will compare SOA and ERP as integration strategies.

Software has evolved from mainframes to present day personal computers, and client-server systems to internet-based applications. Service orientation is a comparatively newer trend. Service-Oriented Architecture and Service-Oriented Enterprise Architecture or Applications (SOEAs) represent the newer models or trends in systems development. The majority of IT organizations are converting their gigantic software applications into more-flexible and agile SOEAs. SOA, in coordination with event-driven system architecture, brings out a newer generation of business component driven architecture that can enable business agility.

Understanding Service-Oriented Architecture

Service-Oriented Architecture is a best-practice model for the systematic design of request/reply applications. Its primary purpose is to enable business-level software modularity and rapid, nonintrusive reuse of business software in new runtime contexts. According to Gartner:

> *Service-oriented architecture (SOA) is a client/server software design approach in which an application consists of software services and*

software service consumers (also known as clients or service requesters).
SOA differs from the more general client/server model in its definitive
emphasis on loose coupling between software components, and in its use
of separately standing interfaces, which are the design essence of SOA.
Loose coupling differentiates SOA from basic software modularity.[1]

Web Services Description Language (WSDL) is the proposed standard used
to define the service interface in a majority of new development tools. At
system runtime, a service interface is delivered as a pair of programs: the
service interface stub and the *service interface proxy*. When SOAP (Simple
Object Access Protocol) is used in service-stub and service-proxy
communications, it is called a *web service*.

Comparing SOA and ERP as Integration Strategies

EAI can increase an organization's ability to share real-time information
quickly and cost-effectively. An integrated application network delivers
much more business value than a set of isolated applications that have a
limited ability to talk to each other. EAI can be achieved via various
strategies, including XML, asynchronous messaging, integration through
schemas, and application transformation through SOA and ERP
customizations. Application integration through interfaces can be challenging
because the number of different interfaces can be enormous.

EAI may be needed as a result of ERP implementations, e-business projects,
mergers and acquisitions, or data warehouse implementations. Choosing an
EAI strategy will depend on your stakeholders' needs. No one strategy can
be said to suit all. An organization needs to educate itself on different EAI
options, and the chosen option should be scalable as a minimum
requirement. SOA can be adopted as one EAI strategy, and ERP can also be
used to integrate applications. So what is the difference?

As discussed earlier, ERP is integrated software that can be used to
perform a vast majority of an organization's processes. It uses a single
database and a common set of user interfaces across business processes.
An SOA, on the other hand, may be used to integrate the existing set of
legacy systems across the organization. These legacy applications originally
exist as relatively isolated applications. Once integrated through SOA,

---

[1] Gartner, "Definitions on SOA," www.gartner.com.

legacy applications may be able to freely talk to each other. But in the future, the legacy applications may still need support and maintenance as they tend to rely on the same older business processes and technologies. Integrating through an ERP, in contrast, requires a single maintenance expense for one application and technology. The number of technical skills that are needed in support may also be reduced drastically when an ERP is used to integrate the business processes. Investments in ERP may be seen as channeled toward optimizing the use of systems instead of spending IT budgets for the maintenance of the same old legacy applications that are integrated using SOA.

In some setups, ERP's standard functionality may fulfill most of the business needs, and so little customization to accommodate non-ERP-supported functionalities may be required. Application integration (integration of business processes, to be more precise) through ERP will be a natural choice for these situations. However, in other organizations, custom processes can offer much more than the standard functionalities offered by ERP. The heavy customization of ERP that would be required in such cases might not make sense from a maintenance point of view. Future upgrades of heavily customized ERP software can be challenging and tedious. In such cases, integrating existing legacy applications through SOA may be the right choice.

Using SOA to Streamline IT

IT organizations are focused on developing and managing robust and flexible infrastructures to reduce costs, realize operational efficiencies, and respond more readily to changing business requirements and market conditions. Historically, attempts to reduce costs and achieve efficiencies through automation, while successful in the short term, have contributed to high costs and inefficiencies.

These attempts have been characterized by the application of automation to work flows and processes previously designed around manual constraints. The underlying business processes, work flows, and organizational structures have not been altered as part of these primarily IT initiatives, usually a mistake.

These traditional architectures, shown in Figure 15-1, have led to a number of issues stemming from overlapping (and often conflicting) data and application logic. The problems are exacerbated by point-to-point integration of applications that results in a tangled mess (of interfaces) that is difficult to maintain. This results in high operational, maintenance and development costs; slow turnaround time for new or modified applications and processes (time to market); poor application and transaction performance because of obsolete work flows; increased risks and missed opportunities in terms of data integrity (and process) issues; and lost business as a result of slower turnaround time.

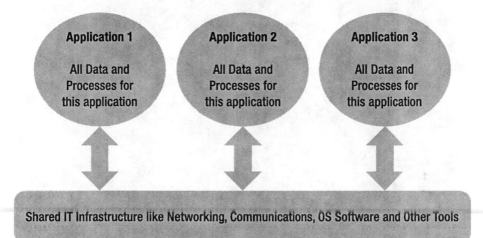

Figure 15-1. Traditional fragmented architecture with gigantic stand-alone applications

Achieving a flexible and robust infrastructure requires business organizations to make major changes in traditional approaches to architectural design, and in the governance of business and technical architectures. The lack of standardization in business procedures and policies makes it difficult to adapt to newer and efficient technologies such as web services. Difficulties in introducing architectural changes, identifying shared services, and modifying work flows further worsen the situation.

The SOA Motivation

Organizations must adopt architectures that facilitate smart integration across disparate processes throughout the business. An SOA is suited for request and reply interactions that can be used to implement business processes while promoting cost savings, consistency, and sharing of resources. SOA promotes sharing of resources by enabling multiple end points to use the same set of data and processes. SOA promotes consistency across enterprise applications by eliminating redundant data and processes. A single server program with a given set of data and services can be utilized by many client applications (Figure 15-2), thus eliminating data redundancy and coding the same process at multiple places.

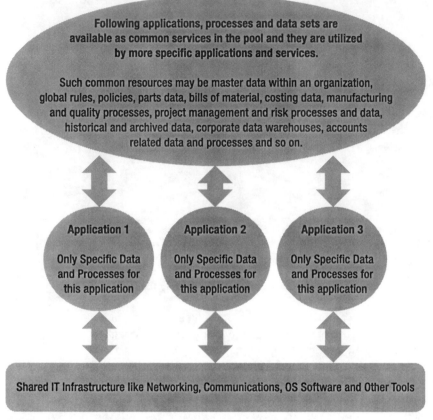

Following applications, processes and data sets are available as common services in the pool and they are utilized by more specific applications and services.

Such common resources may be master data within an organization, global rules, policies, parts data, bills of material, costing data, manufacturing and quality processes, project management and risk processes and data, historical and archived data, corporate data warehouses, accounts related data and processes and so on.

| Application 1 | Application 2 | Application 3 |
| Only Specific Data and Processes for this application | Only Specific Data and Processes for this application | Only Specific Data and Processes for this application |

Shared IT Infrastructure like Networking, Communications, OS Software and Other Tools

Figure 15-2. SOA designs to promote shared data and processes

Misconceptions About SODA and SOA

Service-Oriented Development of Applications (SODA) is the development structure behind applications under SOA Model. This new approach is used to construct applications from a set of loosely coupled processes. It's an approach that uses service as a primary unit for imparting modularity to the applications. It is an assembly-based approach compared to conventional, coding-based approaches. In the SODA paradigm, the code, platform, and underlying program logic are hidden from the consumers (of services) behind service interfaces.

In an SOA development approach, applications are delivered as packets of software services and not as monolithic modules of software. SOA applications have a process orientation and a flexibility that is not common in conventional application suites.

Following are the common myths surrounding SOA. A detailed treatment of these myths is beyond the scope of this presentation. But one thing is common: none of the statements can be taken at face value, and we can say that they have no logical base.

- Services and components are the same thing.

- You can trust that everyone who calls uses your service.

- Any use of services is SOA.

- Services make a system more agile.

- Traditional development methodologies can handle SODA with little or no change in approach.

- The use of .NET or J2EE automatically results in an SOA.

- SOA requires SOAP or, in opposition, the use of SOAP results in SOA.

Summary

SOA, though a good practice for software design, is not the answer to all IT challenges. It can provide low-cost alternatives in Enterprise Application Integration through reused and loosely coupled applications across the organization. SOA is useful as a systematic system development model, especially in cases where request/reply is the preferred relationship pattern. SOA needs considerable technical skills for middleware coupling requirements and significant effort in terms of architecture, design (and sometimes redesign of existing applications), and development. Limited-scope applications and those intended for a short life may not benefit from SOA designs based on reuse; embedded business logic is not intended to be reused or changed. SOA is request/response-driven, two-way architecture, so it may not add any value to message-driven asynchronous applications that are mainly engaged in one-way communication.

Case Study: Integration through SOA

This section provides a case study that demonstrates the benefits of application integration through SOA.

AEZ Inc. is a retail chain with interests in the entire North America region. They successfully implemented an SOA-based IT infrastructure. The SOA-based information and event-driven system (Figure 15-3) now supports a variety of requirements.

The company discovered that it was duplicating applications developed in different departments. In addition, a lot of new development effort was going into already developed functions and sub-programs. For example, the operations department had duplicated the application logic and calculations related to inventory and stock positions at many places. The company also recognized that it was using some very old code; much of it created in the 1970s. The company wanted to adopt an SOA-based model that would require very high levels of discipline and reuse. However, getting its developers to reuse code wasn't easy. The developers needed to move away from their "build only" mentality. The company took on this challenge by providing training, an incentive program, and a strong campaign in supporting the reuse of SOA.

Using SOA paradigm, they were able to reuse a lot of code from legacy systems. Through SOA, the company implemented Asynchronous connectivity, message transformation functions and a common database access to a corporate data warehouse. SOA was also useful to bring in much wanted integrity of various legacy applications that were scattered across various departments. This had a positive effect towards improving operational efficiency.

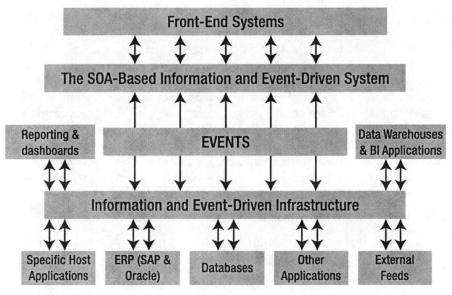

Figure 15 3. Customer's integration infrastructure

Following are the benefits that were achieved through this Event Driven Infrastructure (EDI) that is a platform used to realize SOA.

- Improved quality of business processes that resulted in reduced operations costs.

- Less time to integrate silo based legacy application as compared to any other development model.

- Event notification and database updates occur in near-real time (for example, transaction updates now happen as soon as they occur, instead of a batch process).

- Less network bandwidth is required for data transfer because only updates are propagated now.

- Interfaces are easier to maintain as formal message types have been defined, and standardized.

Finally, SOA-based adoptions saved thousands of dollars in development effort and millions of dollars in the budget. With these encouraging results, the span of the program was extended to vendor applications that were J2EE and .NET based.

Critical Success Factors and Lessons Learned

This section lists some of the lessons learned and best practices adopted from the previous cases. Many of them are common to those in the business transformation exercise discussed in Chapter 10. Both business transformation (BT) and implementation of SOA at an organizational level are mammoth tasks. Both need strategic alignment with the organization's business goals and a very high level of participation from executive management. A good IT portfolio analysis at the corporate level would be of immense help. As with BT, here you also are required to demonstrate some quick success stories. In fact, implementing SOA at the organizational level may involve some amount of business transformation.

Lessons learned from the preceding case studies include the following:

- Like any other transformation exercise, this also needs to be in line with the organization's strategic goals to ensure high levels of commitment from top management.

- A high level of participation from business is also needed. It can't be handled by the IT department alone.

- There's a need for the team to demonstrate some tangible results quickly. Demonstrating some quick results might build confidence among stakeholders.

- A planned application portfolio analysis can, to a great extent, determine redundant functionalities and reusable assets.

- The company needs to adopt standardization (both in design and construction) and reviews at every stage to ensure that newly developed functions are of high quality.

- In the case of SOA development that is based on the reuse of applications, what really counts is the streamlining of IT infrastructure and huge savings in development efforts and. Any cost-benefit analysis should take this into consideration.

- The developers should be able to clearly see the advantages that SOA brings to the table.

- A well-planned incentive and recognition program can give a real boost to the amount of reuse.

- It may be wise to explore different SOA development paradigms and find out which best suits the company.

- You must retain the momentum gained in this exercise by introducing incremental developments and making reuse a part of company culture.

Realized Benefits

As you have seen, SOA promotes a high level of reuse and integration among existing legacy applications. Integration is also achieved in SOA by the loose coupling of applications. Following are some of the direct benefits that are realized by the companies working on an SOA paradigm:

- Huge savings compared to any other mode of application integration

- Loosely coupled applications in the IT infrastructure

- Easy and low-cost integration of new business applications

- Streamlining and integration of overall IT infrastructure with heterogeneous applications

- High level of reuse in software assets

- Incremental development and deployment of business components

- Easy maintenance of application inventories and their interrelationships

SOA Is Not a Cure-All

As is true with any software development paradigm, SOA is not the solution to all your integration problems. Furthermore, there are some misconceptions about SOA. The following are some points of caution you should consider before adopting SOA for large-scale integration:

- There can be better architectures and paradigms for software development than SOA. Choices can differ from organization to organization.

- SOA is not a simple software engineering or development model.

- SOA doesn't provide technology or vendor independence.
- SOA doesn't bring free integration or free interoperability.

Strategic Thinking and the Evolution of Information Systems

Top-level strategic thinking governs information technology decisions. In this chapter, you'll learn about a medium-sized business that is striving to improve its bottom line. An organization's strategy and finance, naturally, are closely related. The chapter will gradually take you through various business situations to demonstrate top management's strategic thinking.

The main text in this chapter focuses on the company's business strategy, depicted through SWOT (strengths, weaknesses, opportunities, and threats) tables. In addition, notes appearing throughout the text indicate how this evolving business strategy affects the company's IT systems.

Understanding the Case Study

The business presented in this chapter is a foundry. Foundries have come a long way in terms of technology, product development, and operations. In the past, they could easily get a critical mass of orders required for profitable operations. This particular foundry has focused mostly on automobile original equipment manufacturing (OEM, used interchangeably with OE). However, after the global economic downturn of 2008–2009, component manufacturers such as this one had no choice but to explore other options. The company has been going through a bad patch; its main source of orders from the auto industry has been slowly drying up and, as a result, the company needs to search for alternatives.

As you review this case, you will be able to see the strategic choices being made by the company's project management team, which is aiming to reduce the company's dependencies on OEM customers, open streams of more-profitable businesses, and consider trade-offs in order to develop a sustainable advantage. You'll also see how IT systems for this foundry evolve as it becomes more market oriented.

The objective of this case study is to point out strengths, weaknesses, opportunities, and threats to the business as well as the company's critical success factors. An equally important objective is to suggest strategic options to sustain and improve the company's eroding bottom line.

Introducing the Challenges at X Ltd.

X Ltd. is ferrous foundry business that caters primarily to the auto industry. Factors typical to this business are high volume, thin margins, and heavy dependency on OEM. A large number of people are employed worldwide by auto ancillary or auto component industries. X Ltd. caters to the heavy commercial vehicle OEM sector and has more than a thousand employees.

IT Track: Because X Ltd. is solely dependent on a single customer, IT systems related to scheduling, production, and purchasing are not demand driven. The demand management component is absent. Also there are no market-facing IT systems because no marketing department exists.

X Ltd. has long been dependent on a single customer for most of its orders. With the global recession, the company has seen OEM orders rapidly going down and inventories building up. Employee morale reached a low as the company started layoffs. For the next couple of years, unfortunately, the auto industry's prospects are expected to remain the same.

X Ltd. has no option but to look for alternatives in new areas to make up for losses of revenues. The plan is to adapt the business to customer requirements rather than wait for orders to come in. This will be challenging, because it goes against the current mindset and company culture. The company has been stalled in a high state of inertia yet has to face this problem. Top management is well aware of the challenges. Yet the message down the line has not been very clear. New business development activities that promised higher margins have not been considered as important as OEM jobs in progress and those of similar orders anticipated to come. In addition, the OEM customer has been routinely loading X Ltd. with the development of components without any business commitments. The company has had to absorb these development costs, putting heavy pressure on margins.

IT Track: In its current setup, X Ltd. is mainly a component supplier and so has much lighter assemblies compared to any other auto manufacturer. The production planning is simpler, and bills of material have fewer levels. Order scheduling and inventory control is easy and straightforward. The company has firm orders from only the OEM and no planned orders are required. It has only one customer, so no stocking points or warehouses are required. As a result, the company doesn't feel the need to maintain integrated software such as ERP for its operations.

Forming a Corporate Response

Responding to this crisis situation, corporate executives initiated a project to analyze the company's current state in order to create a model for reviving the business. Project team members soon realized that they had to start thinking strategically to sustain the business for a longer time frame and to develop options for the company's resources, makeup, competencies, and strategies. One possibility is to diversify the business to reduce dependence on OEM. Following are the key goals identified for the project team:

- Provide strategic recommendations for improving revenue and profitability based on systematic studies

- Bring the company back to the old levels of profitability in a fixed time frame

- Comply strictly to the company's existing ethical and value systems

Stage 1: Initiating a Study

The team initiates a study to evaluate the company's strengths, weaknesses, opportunities, and threats—a *SWOT study*. (In this chapter, it'll mostly be called a TOWS study—Threats, Opportunities Weaknesses and Strengths.) At the first stage, only a limited amount of information is available, and it is largely based on the current economic conditions at the company. The company is largely owner-managed, and all the key positions are occupied by family members. The company does not have any experience with professional managers and has no wish to bring in outside managers or consultants.

As mentioned, the company mostly serves a single customer, a large commercial vehicle manufacturer with a worldwide customer base. The economic downturn has greatly reduced the sale of commercial vehicles. The direct effect of this has been felt as a steep drop in auto component orders, something the company did not anticipate. X Ltd. has no mitigation plans to fight the unexpected situation. Instead, the company is in firefighting mode. Already, the profit margins with OEM are smaller, and the returns to shareholders are very low. Because they are so dependent on a single OEM for orders, their competitiveness and willpower to fight their way out of the problem is also limited.

On the positive side, the company has a strong ethics and value system. They comply with industry standards and regulations imposed by the government.

Table 16-1 presents the team's first attempt at gathering information for the SWOT study. The table reflects the foregoing analysis. It also reflects a superficial view of the problem; the team knows it will have to drill down further to get answers.

Note: In business strategy parlance, the preferred sequence is threats (T) first, and then opportunities (O), followed by weaknesses (W) and then strengths (S)—TOWS instead of SWOT. In this way, the company first looks outward to determine Ts and Os and then looks internally to align those findings with Ws and Ss.

Table 16-1. TOWS Information at the Start of the Analysis

Threats	Opportunities
—	—
Weaknesses	**Strengths**
1. Low return to shareholders 2. Professional management not welcome	1. Ethics and value system: Strong on compliance, contribution, and consequences, but not competitive enough

IT Track for Stage 1: In the current setup, X Ltd. has a couple of stand-alone software programs to maintain its inventories. Payroll is also automated. And it has a stand-alone system for billing. All other functions, including purchasing, are automated but not interconnected. X also uses e-mail extensively for internal and customer communication. Apart from this, the company is using of spreadsheets for analysis, costing, time tracking, and so on.

Stage 2A: Conducting the Industry Analysis

At X Ltd., the culture, ethics, and value system of the major customer has a large impact. About 75 percent of the shares are held by their biggest single customer. Naturally, the customer/owner has a major say in the company, including the code of conduct and business practices. Though one customer has a controlling stake in the company, that customer wants the company to stay profitable on its own and not depend too much on in-house orders. The management at X Ltd. has the freedom to devise its own ways of staying afloat and competitive.

For the project team, though, it is imperative to take up a broader perspective of the auto component industry. They need to expand their horizons beyond the company tradition of servicing a single customer, something it has done since its inception.

Following are the focus areas identified by the study team. It derives its philosophy for this exercise from Michael E. Porter's work in strategic analysis.[1]

Existing Competition

Following are some factors that are considered while analyzing the impact of existing competition.

- *Industry growth rate*: Harsh economic conditions have been driving the industry toward negative growth rates. The OEMs have many vendors willing to supply margins thinner than ever before. So X Ltd. has many competitors now that are willing to supply components to the OEM (customer) at competitive rates.

- *Business practices in the industry*: The business of auto components is a high-volume game with thin margins. The supplier typically has to absorb all design and development costs. Vendors can make a difference mainly by virtue of their size and ability to make large investments in the technology used for the production of these precision parts. The competitive price is the only differentiator.

- *Switching suppliers*: When the customer (OEM) is on a high-growth path, it tends to spare less capital for investments at the supplier's end for technology, quality control, and so on. In this growth phase, the OEM gets a higher return if it invests in its own business. In such cases, OEMs tend to stick with their suppliers, because they can't spare the capital needed to switch. (The OEM needs to invest while switching suppliers because it needs to put

---

[1] Michael E. Porter ,"What is Strategy," *Harvard Business Review,* Nov.–Dec. 1996.

capital in joint component development, training, testing, and perfecting the production.) On the other hand, in downturns, OEMs may not have sufficient business but still have surplus capital. In good times, they might have invested in their own business as the expected profitability was good. In downturns, this surplus capital may find ways in nice-to-have (but not so essential) things like developing more suppliers or switching suppliers. OEMs may have their own reasons to do this. So in downturns, OEMs are likely to switch suppliers more often because they can spare the capital needed for such supplier switch-overs. This typical OEM tendency is applicable in the case of X Ltd.

Threats from New Entrants

Entry barriers and economy of scale are seen as two significant threats from new players entering the market. The following bullets explain them in brief.

- *Entry barriers*: Foundry technology is considered dicey, so established players such as X Ltd. take a lot of time and resources in maturing production processes. Changing the product mix and switching to new variants can be challenging in terms of process changes and new capital requirements. So it's difficult for new entrants to compete on price with existing suppliers. Existing suppliers have already recovered the tooling and learning curve costs because they have been supplying those components in large volumes for quite some time now. X is an old and established player in this regard.

- *Economy of scale*: X Ltd. has the advantage of depreciated plants. But the sheer volumes offered by OEMs make the market lucrative even for new entrants (especially in downturns, when getting business is the most important thing and profits may take a back seat). In the current poor economic conditions, new entrants are considered less of a risk because the customer (OEM) is not placing any orders that require new designs and tooling. And X Ltd.'s pricing is very competitive in existing components. X Ltd. has even deployed a high-pressure molding line to increase the throughput. The long commissioning time, however, weakens the potential benefits and increases the vulnerability to external threats.

Backward Integration and Technology

These two factors are important in completing the industry analysis, because they significantly affect the vendor's capabilities to add desired value at competitive rates.

- *Backward integration*: To save on high machining costs from vendors, X Ltd. performs backward integration (purchase of its own suppliers to reduce dependency) and starts offering machined casting. The value addition of this venture is encouraging and makes overall business sense, as the customer gets one-stop-shop operations. But more competition is expected, because some machine shops are also planning to add foundry facilities.

- *Technology*: OEMs offer improved technologies to existing vendor companies so vendors have a chance to upgrade—if they are financially sound. X Ltd. already has the latest technology needed in ferrous foundries for auto component manufacturing, so it isn't worried about others who have yet to catch up.

Stage 2B: Determining SWOT Progress

With the data from the industry analysis, we can update our TOWS analysis, as shown in Table 16-2.

Table 16-2. Stage 2 TOWS Analysis

Threats	Opportunities
1. OEM policies drastically change as a result of demand variations. 2. In a growth period, additional suppliers step in, which may pose a threat in lean periods. 3. Possibilities of supplier switch over 4. Established machining services suppliers are planning backward integration (adding foundry facilities).	1. Gaining competitive advantages by upgrading to high-pressure casting technology. 2. Claiming potential savings by perfecting technologies that are already in use in the company. 3. Cashing in on newly added machining shop. 4. Exploiting the global boom in foundry products with low operational costs.

Weaknesses	Strengths
1. Low return to shareholders.	1. Ethics and value system: Strong on compliance, contribution, and consequences, but this is not a direct competitive advantage.
2. Professional management is not welcome.	
3. Design costs have to be absorbed.	2. Having casting and machining under one roof gives an edge in terms of quality and convenience to the customer.
4. Technology limitations exist as far as throughput is concerned.	

At this stage, the Threats cell has four entries. Now, with demand lower, the OEM may switch vendors for ferrous parts, as noted earlier (point 3 in the Threats cell). With X Ltd. dependent on one customer, this is the biggest threat to the organization. In growth periods, when volumes are high, the OEM may add additional suppliers that then become a threat in lean periods. OEM pricing and other purchase policies may also change drastically when the demand for vehicles is lower in the market. This is also seen as a significant threat to X Ltd.'s survival. Just as X Ltd. planned backward integration by offering machining services, many existing machining suppliers are planning to build foundries in their operations. This would increase the number of competitors in the market with machining and foundry capabilities, another threat.

The Opportunities cell in Table 16-2 also has four entries based on the industry analysis. The newly added high-pressure casting line and machining capabilities are seen as strategic advantages. For many existing components of OEM, X Ltd. already has running production lines that perfect the design and production processes. This is seen as an advantage that will enable X Ltd. to offer lower prices compared to any new entrant. X Ltd. identifies one more big opportunity in the world markets: good demand for ferrous castings at competitive prices. This could provide X Ltd. with the alternative market it is looking for.

The Weaknesses cell in Table 16-2 has two new entries. X Ltd. has not been able to negotiate with the OEM regarding the sharing of design and development costs. This is eroding the bottom line at X Ltd. by a significant amount and is seen as a major weakness by the executive management. X Ltd. also has some technological limitations regarding production capacity (the number of parts per hour it can put through). This is limiting the company's capability to get the benefits of economies of scale to some extent.

In the Strengths cell, the capability of the company to offer quality castings and machining under the same roof is seen as a big strategic plus.

IT Track for Stage 2: Now X Ltd. is expanding its operations through backward integration. It is also offering machining services along with its existing ferrous component casting practice. It may need MRP, MRP II, and logistics software, as discussed in Chapter 12. The company has started looking outward by offering foundry products in global markets. It may need to add software related to sales and distribution to the IT portfolio. Further, production will be based on both forecasted demand and firm orders. Demand management, materials planning, production, inventory, and purchasing systems need to be integrated now for efficient and cost-effective operations. Everything needs to be integrated with demand management, sales, and distribution.

Stage 3A: Conducting an Analysis of the Core Business

People, technology, design costs, and export markets are the factors considered important in the analysis of the company's core business. These factors could affect product costs and overall marketing revenue for the company. Here are some results from the next analysis, on the core business.

1. The company has developed a balanced portfolio of core competencies with key person(s) responsible for delivery at every part of the value chain. Its key people are well networked in the industry.

2. One peculiarity of business at X Ltd. is that technology and equipment have a short lifespan. Ferrous foundries are tough on equipment. Even the patterns and match-plates need to be redone for every product modification. The company is not able to take full advantage of the maturity stage of the learning curve. The company also needs to adopt more-efficient business processes.

3. The product designs developed by X Ltd. for the OEM (not billable to OEM) are often transferred by OEMs to other suppliers in an attempt to create an unfair price competition. X Ltd. loses business based on its own designs and intellectual property as a result of grossly unethical practices adopted by some OEMs. The

company now has ventured into decorative castings in overseas markets with fully functional design and marketing arms, though many activities of marketing, core competency, and products-related portfolio analyses are yet to be developed. Some marketing functions are not as developed or competent as they should be. The reason: There was no need for marketing because X Ltd. has been dependent on a single customer.

4. X Ltd. is now a local player with global ambitions. Foundry operations all over developed nations are becoming prohibitively expensive, thus giving companies such as X Ltd., with lean operations, better prospects.

Stage 3B: Determining SWOT with Core Business Inputs

Now equipped with the analysis of company's core business, we can take the TOWS table to the next stage, shown in Table 16-3.

Table 16-3. Stage 3 TOWS with Analysis of Core Competencies

Threats	Opportunities
1. OEM policies drastically change as a result of demand variations.	1. Gaining competitive advantages by upgrading to high-pressure casting technology.
2. In a growth period, additional suppliers step in, which may pose a threat in lean periods.	2. Claiming the potential savings by perfecting technologies that are already in use in the company.
3. Possibility of supplier switch over	3. Cashing in on newly added machining shop.
4. Established machining services suppliers are planning backward integration (adding foundry facilities).	4. Exploiting the global boom in foundry products with low operational costs.
5. OEM products are replicable by any other supplier.	5. Exploiting technology upgrades of a cokeless cupola, which is an edge over the competition.
	6. Venturing into decorative casting and away from OEM business: *The first sign of independence by the company.*

Weaknesses	Strengths
1. Low return to shareholders.	1. Ethics and value system: Strong on compliance, contribution and consequences, but this is not a direct competitive advantage.
2. Professional management is not welcome.	
3. Design costs have to be absorbed.	2. Having casting and machining under one roof gives an edge in terms of quality and convenience to the customer.
4. Technology limitations exist as far as throughput is concerned.	
5. Business processes are not efficient and do not reflect industry standards.	3. Core competencies: Key persons, competent on every part of the value chain, are well networked with customers and suppliers.
	4. Foray into independent businesses such as decorative castings in the export market.

In Table 16-3, the Threats cell has one new entry that was revealed as a result of the core business analysis. Designs and drawings developed by X Ltd. are transferred by the OEM to other suppliers as a result of grossly unethical business practices. X Ltd. is not able to do anything, because that OEM is their only big customer.

X Ltd. has ventured into a business of decorative castings that have good demand in international markets. This is also a measure of reducing dependence on OEM. This venture finds a place in the Opportunities cell. X Ltd. has also upgraded to cokeless cupola technology for better quality in its castings. (*Cokeless cupolas* are gas-fired furnaces, typically used to preheat iron ingots.) Now it needs to fully exploit the opportunities opened up by this technology upgrade.

The Weaknesses cell has added one more entry. As a result of the analysis of its core business, X Ltd. has discovered that its business processes are not efficient compared to global standards. Maybe the company needs an ERP.

The core executive management team at X Ltd. is very competent and well networked in the industry. This point gets a place in the Strengths cell. The TOWS is now taking shape and is ready for the final shot.

IT Track for Stage 3 Analysis: As the project team ventures into stage 3 of its analysis, it is becoming clear that X Ltd. may need massive business process reengineering (BPR) and business transformation (BT) exercises to support its global ambitions while maintaining a cost advantage. In the near future, X Ltd. will need strong IT support for planned lean operations. It may also need strong IT support for developing marketing needs and international business. All this needs to be integrated with logistics, production, inventory, and demand management functions. X Ltd. may want to achieve this in stages; a single-shot implementation may be risky and capital intensive. X Ltd. could consider a medium-scale ERP and SCM system to suit the business. There are many integrated enterprise software programs available for business processes peculiar to a multilocation foundry business.

Stage 4: Creating a Final SWOT Summary for X Ltd.

In this stage, an analysis of X Ltd.'s external business environment helped discover the possible threats and opportunities, while internal environment factors helped identify the weaknesses and strengths of the company and competitors as well. After stage 3, a series of SWOT analyses were undertaken by the team. The results are summarized in Table 16-4. The final content has been refined and varies significantly from the stage 3 SWOT data. The table shows considerable improvement over stages 1, 2, and 3.

Table 16-4. Final TOWS for X Ltd.

Threats	Opportunities
1. Competitors' entry in foreign markets with low-cost production solution	1. Ability to serve additional customer groups, new markets, and new segments
2. Slower market growth	2. Ways to expand product lines to meet broader customer needs
3. Vulnerability to recession and business cycles	3. Ability to transfer skills or technological know-how
4. Growing bargaining powers of buyers	4. Integrating vertically: Must improve probability of succeeding at integration
5. Costly regulatory requirements	5. Falling trade barriers in attractive foreign markets

Threats	Opportunities
	6. Ability to grow rapidly to cope with strong increase in demand
	7. Emerging new technologies

Weaknesses	Strengths
1. Need to improve on machining after casting	1. Process innovation capability
2. Lack of access to adequate supply of skilled labor force for machining	2. Expertise in foundry and mold making
3. Need to improve machining productivity	3. Culture for risk taking: To further delegate to lower levels
4. Needs to establish broader product lines to offer a wider selection	4. Low-cost production capability including scale economy and learning curve rate (depreciated assets)
5. Branding: Efforts required	5. Ability to utilize fixed assets: To further improve in foundry
6. No clear strategic direction	6. Low-cost location of facilities
7. Failing behind in R&D	7. High level of productivity and throughput for foundry
	8. Low distribution costs
	9. Strong marketing skills
	10. Superior talent
	11. QC know-how for moving toward zero defects
	12. Process design using software
	13. Expertise in assembly process development
	14. Ability to quickly develop product to meet customer requirements
	15. Superior information systems for decision making
	16. Ability to respond quickly to changing market conditions
	17. Experienced and capable top and middle line
	18. Good reputation in auto: Can improve good contacts with players in capital markets, such as banks (cash position)

In the Threats section, five entries are listed. The most important threats are increased competition as X Ltd. enters foreign markets, a recession, and growing bargaining power of OEM as a result of an increased number of players.

In the Opportunities section, the most important factors are venturing into foreign markets, vertical integration (backward integration), and an ability to cope with new designs.

The major weaknesses are a lack of strategic direction, a narrow product line, a lack of branding, and a need for productivity improvements in machining operations.

The list of strengths is more than double than that of weaknesses or threats—a point to get cheered up about at X Ltd. Innovation, risk-taking capabilities of management, strong expertise in ferrous products, strong marketing skills, faster development of new products, and a good reputation in the industry are identified as some of the strong points.

IT Track for Final SWOT: X Ltd. is mainly a manufacturing-oriented company. The trend from all this analysis is clear; doing more business with the OEM is not as profitable as desired. So X Ltd. must diversify into global markets. Also, X Ltd. must consider providing more value-added services such as machined castings for better margins. On the IT front, the company needs an ERP and supporting software that can take care of growing operations in manufacturing and marketing. As discussed earlier, the company has been in a downturn and struggling to maintain its existing profit levels. Implementing information systems would be possible only in phases. How much capital a company wants to spare for IT is a business decision. Ideally, it should be anything between 5 percent to 10 percent of its global sales revenue.

Considering Strategy Choices for X Ltd.

The following strategy discussion is again based on the contributions of Porter. I have taken the five major strategy headings defined by Porter in his paper, "What Is Strategy?"[2] and compared them with choices at X Ltd. Dynamic operational improvements result in short-term profits but fail to translate into sustainable profitability. Operational effectiveness is important

---

[2] Michael E. Porter, "What is Strategy," *Harvard Business Review*, Nov.-Dec., 1996.

for improving performance, but this alone is not sufficient. The techniques used in achieving operational effectiveness may be easy to reproduce. I will restrict our discussion to the five-strategy mantra, as suggested by Porter.

1. Operational Effectiveness Is Not Strategy

Operational effectiveness, according to Porter, is necessary but not sufficient. Organizations such as X Ltd. have become more effective by following the methodologies suggested by international standards such as ISO. These standards are necessary to keep all levels of management charged up and in competition, but they fail to miss an important aspect of strategy. The root cause of the problem lies in the failure to differentiate between operational efficiency and strategy. Steady progress in improving operational efficiency is needed to achieve better profitability; however, it alone is not sufficient. Companies staying ahead of rivals on the basis of operational effectiveness run continuously to gain a full pace, and thereafter staying ahead gets harder day by day. This is due to rapid diffusion of best practices. This may lead to a zero-sum competition, increasingly static or falling prices, and pressure on costs. Ultimately, this may hamper a company's ability to stand market pressures and stay invested in the business for the long run.

2. Strategy Rests on Unique Activities

This part of Porter's view has two main points. First, choose a competitive strategy involving product differentiation and cost leadership. Then choose your market segmentation with your competitive strategy. Both are described here in terms of X Ltd.

Competitive Strategy

A competitive strategy is all about being different from the competition. This means intentionally choosing a different set of activities to bring in an exclusive mix of value. X Ltd. chose decorative casting as an alternative.

Table 16-5 shows how X Ltd.'s choice of decorative casting provides an exclusive value to the organization. It also indicates how the activities compare between OE components and decorative castings. Parameters such as product specifications, technology, functional needs, visual requirements, testing setup, and variety all bring in a unique set of values to the organization for decorative castings. This product differentiation as compared to competitors makes X Ltd. more competitive in the market.

Table 16-5. OE Business vs. Decorative Castings

Parameters	OE Component (Auto Industry)	Decorative Castings for Homes, Hotels, Malls, etc.
Product specifications	Definite, similar, intricate	Intricate but very creative
Technology options	Technology intensive	Flexible
Functional and performance needs	Needs functional stability	Flexible
Aesthetic and visual requirements	Low, as parts are machined later	Needs utmost attention
Testing setup	Heavy setup needed	Moderate
Variety-based positioning possible?	Not possible	Can be attempted by leveraging tool costs

Market Segmentation

The chosen market segment can describe strategic positioning—for example, in OE, domestic decorative, industry machines, and so forth. But as Porter says, "The essence of strategy is in the activities—choosing to perform activities differently or to perform different activities than rivals." X Ltd. either chooses a low-cost mass segment, or seeks high-cost differentiation through decorative castings. With OE, if one enjoys single sourcing and not all operational details are known to the customer, the first option looks good. But that is not the case with X Ltd. It can have three options for positioning:

- *Variety-based positioning*: Serve different customers with a variety of products

- *Need-based positioning*: X Ltd.'s present position, to supply the needs of OE

- *Access-based positioning*: Translates to international marketing, to cater to the casting needs of European countries

3. A Sustainable Strategic Position Requires Trade-Offs

For X Ltd., making trade-offs means cutting those features and activities that no longer gel with its overall strategy and products.

4. Fit Drives Both Competitive Advantage and Sustainability

Rather than looking at the company as a whole, managers are trying to look into core competencies, key success factors, and critical resources. The concept of fit is far more important to competitive advantage than most people think. Fit is an important concept that relates to positioning choices for a company. Positioning choices determine which activities a company will perform and how these activities will relate to one another.

Based on activities, there are three types of fit:

First-order fit: This is simple consistency between each activity and the overall strategy. This will make sure the competitive advantages of different activities supplement each other (add up) instead of undercutting or canceling themselves out. It also makes the communication and implementation of a strategy easier, involving all stakeholders, such as clients, staff, and shareholders. This consistency between activities and strategy also brings in much required single-mindedness in the corporation, which is crucial to the success of such implementations.

Second-order fit: When activities are reinforcing, the first-order fit becomes strengthened.

Third-order fit: In this type of fit, X Ltd. may optimize efforts in designing its strategies while ensuring the first and second orders of fit are in place. This will then become prohibitively difficult for competitors to imitate.

X Ltd. has demonstrated its capability to quickly develop new products and achieve volumes to meet customer demand. So it can always look for new product development and for products with a shorter life cycle.

5. Rediscovering Strategy

Finally, X Ltd. needs to choose its strategy. The company needs to explore more strategic options to reduce OEM dependency and gain control over its future.

Following are the suggested strategic options for X Ltd., based on the SWOT analysis done earlier:

- Explore overseas markets, both auto and nonauto, with an emphasis on heavy engineering

- Increase investments in household products such as decorative castings

- Develop specialized foundry components for nuclear and aerospace industry

- Explore the area of railway castings

- Explore the area of castings used in ship building

- Explore the area of castings for the machine-tool industry

- Explore possibilities on investment casting products

Presenting Strategy Recommendations for X Ltd.

You have examined the challenges and strategic choices for X Ltd. in light of the strategy framework suggested by Porter. By venturing into decorative casting and backward integration of machining activities, X Ltd. is going in the right direction. Following are the recommendations that may help X Ltd. to achieve its goal of higher profitability and reduced dependence on OEM. In this list, I have deliberately repeated conclusions from the earlier sections for the sake of completeness and easy reference.

1. *Develop a positioning strategy*: Uniqueness in activities comes from a positioning strategy. For OEM, X Ltd. could have need-based positioning. For lifestyle products such as decorative castings, X Ltd. could attempt variety-based positioning to develop a distinct set of activities that could serve a spectrum of customers.

2. *Work on business process reengineering*: X needs to work on business transformation and optimizing processes at the organizational level in order to align business with new strategies.

3. *Group processes*: X Ltd. should group similar and complementary processes to achieve a competitive advantage. I have seen two separate organizations run by one of the directors of X Ltd. in the stainless steel and copper wire drawing industries, respectively. Both companies are aiming for completely different market segments. Stainless steel wire is 100 percent export oriented, whereas a copper wire drawing plant is meant for OEM. Both companies are doing well as separate entities and have been for many years now. Similarly, for different market segments, X can also consider different divisions with specialized activities. Activities such as molding and casting can be shared across these divisions. Each division may have a specialized team with a dedicated mindset.

4. *Graduate to higher levels of fit*: For achieving a stability level in terms of profitability and operations, X Ltd. can graduate to higher levels of fit, as discussed earlier.

IT Track for Recommendations: X Ltd. needs superior information systems, including one ERP to support its global marketing and manufacturing functions.

Summary

This study has reviewed X Ltd.'s various strategic and IT options with the help of a SWOT analysis that may lead to understanding the company's strategic management. These analyses may be helpful for the company to evaluate, correct, and reposition itself in the market. Various strategic options for the company were also considered. Management has yet to make a final decision. However, it is largely agreed by management that the company needs to explore more strategic possibilities and choices and to work out a systematic actionable plan based on Porter's strategy guidelines on uniqueness, trade-offs, and fit.

IT Track Conclusion: You have seen how a midsized manufacturing business, X Ltd., plans to gradually change its operations and marketing strategies. On the marketing front, X Ltd. wants to play globally—a drastic change over its previous status as a captive manufacturing unit to an OEM. On the operations front, X Ltd. wants to expand through backward integration. So these are the changes on the strategic front for X Ltd. You have also seen how information systems must evolve to keep pace with changing business needs. It's always like this—IT has to keep up with business, and not the other way around. For the IT department of X Ltd., it's a sea change that may take at least two years to evolve to the desired stage. But once completed, it will be worth it, and then IT could be utilized as a real strategic advantage.

Acknowledgments: This chapter is based on the work of Yogesh Jain; my friend, a serial entrepreneur, and a management consultant. My sincere thanks to him. I sincerely thank the executive management and ground staff of X Ltd. for their cooperation throughout the course of this study.

What Managers Are Discussing

There are numerous professional forums available on the Internet where managers can interact and discuss problems they are facing in their day-to-day functioning. If you are a member of such forums, you can share your experiences and learn from the experiences of others. You can get suggestions for how to address problems you encounter as a manager. LinkedIn groups, for example, provide you with such a platform. For the benefit of readers, I have selected some relevant questions from a couple of such forums, where I was a member and participating in those discussions. The answers are my contributions.

The questions and answers not only provide value, but they give you an idea of what concerns IT managers these days.

How do I deal with pessimistic team members who are engaged in spreading rumors and negativity?

This is a practical problem. Project managers face it many times during their careers. How you address this problem depends on whether the team member is upset about present circumstances or is terminally pessimistic:

- *The team member spreading negativity and rumors is upset about something within the project or company.* This attitude may be temporary. You may be able to get the team member on track again if you listen carefully to her grievance, understand what she is upset about, and address the problem satisfactorily. But you must find the root cause. For example, the team member might be unhappy about how the project team is treating or utilizing her. She might be a recognized achiever on other projects, but here she might be working on a trivial task, making her feel like no one appreciates her talent or simply that what she is doing currently is not the best use of her skills. (In IT, this often happens on maintenance and support projects.) Consequently, she might be looking for a change in project or even a change in job. She might even be close to getting a new job, giving her a negative attitude toward the current assignment.

  In some cases, team leaders discriminate against team members based on ethnicity, language, geography, or age, for example. In such cases, talented team members feel frustrated and form a negative attitude. Sometimes, there is unfairness when allocating pay hikes, incentives, foreign postings, good assignments, and so forth. This also disgruntles team members.

  There can be many such reasons for employee dissatisfaction, so your job (as a PM) is to find out the precise reason and try to remediate the problem to the maximum extent possible. A fair and free work environment helps a lot. If team members have confidence that your dealings are ethical and fair, they will reveal their true concerns, which makes your job easier. If the work environment is not based on mutual trust and respect, things can be much more challenging.

- *The team member spreading negativity and rumors is a habitual pessimist with a core negative attitude related to personality type.* In such a case, you need to take action based upon the extent of negativity, or how much negativity is tolerable in the current state of the project. If the attitude is not completely poisonous, you can give the team member individual assignments. You can stay on top of the team member through frequent reviews. If the case is beyond something you can or should handle, bring HR into the loop. Harsher decisions may be required.

In any case, a degree of discipline must be maintained within project teams. The message should be loud and clear: negative attitudes, rumors, or any other kind of sabotage will be dealt with through strict disciplinary action. Proactive steps by a PM, like outdoor team-building exercises, frequent team communication, one-on-one meetings, frequent incentives for good performance, and so forth, might help a lot. For large teams, a PM has to ensure open and free communication by making team members feel free to talk to the PM anytime about problems. It's important to head off problems, especially with certain employees who may take advantage of you and the team.

So, dealing with team members engaged in spreading rumors and negativity requires understanding, proactive actions, isolation, administrative wisdom, and an environment of trust working all together. In most cases, identify, understand, isolate, and act should work.

Based on your experience as a leader or project manager, is business leadership earned or learned?

Business leadership requires a combination of emotional intelligence (EQ) and intellectual intelligence (IQ). A person's IQ changes very little over time, but EQ, which is more relevant to business leadership, can be developed to any extent through proper training, education, and experience, a combination of earning and learning. Given a decent IQ at birth, a person can become a great business leader through hard work. Engaging in team sports, social activities, and community projects is also very helpful to becoming a great business leader.

What is your process for capturing lessons learned?

In theory, capturing "lessons learned" at the end of a project sounds like a great idea. Who wouldn't want to reflect on what was done right, what could be done better, and then apply those lessons to the next project?

In practice, though, it is sometimes a different story.

Capturing lessons learned is usually difficult. At the end of every logical step in the project, or at major milestones, we have a meeting with all team members, who bring their project notebooks. The team members glance through their respective notebooks and come up with contributions on-the-fly. Both good and not-so-good lessons learned surface because the events are fresh and everyone contributes fairly openly. We also encourage case study competitions at the department level, with emphasis on learning, so team members don't hesitate to contribute even the bitter lessons as a way to help the organization grow.

Which should I obtain, a PMP or an MBA?

The PMP (Project Management Professional) certification can in no way replace a good MBA. You will need both. Pursuing a general MBA is useful (but not a must) to get strong training and grounding for business, whereas pursing a PMP is useful for more concentrated knowledge on project management. If you want to get into project management, PMP is well recognized, but if you have earned an MBA, your chances of success as a business leader increase greatly.

Of the following four options, which one would you recommend as a PM for a large project?

- A hands-on, experienced project manager
- A hands-on, experienced project manager and certified PMP
- A project manager with academic credentials for project management
- A certified project manager, such as a PMP, with some experience

I would recommend a hands-on, experienced project manager with PMP credentials. In large projects, for the post of a senior project manager, the first choice is a possibility if the PM in question has a great deal of experience, is mature, understands the process well, and grasps company dynamics.

What motivates you and how do you motivate others to achieve great results?

Achieving great results itself can be one's motto in life, and by consistently achieving great results, your success is ensured. If you get consistently good results, it's a psychological boost and provides the courage to do even better in upcoming projects. For successful people, consistently achieving great results becomes a habit and constantly motivates them to achieve excellence in everything they do.

Promoting people with quality results and a good attitude can set an example for others in the group. Leading by example can be the best motivator for your team members to achieve excellence. Rewards and recognition, and a transparent and ethical work environment, can also motivate an average performer toward excellence. Leaders have to make sure that excellence becomes a habit and a way of life in the group—be it customer management, dress and behavior codes, presentations, or whatever you do. Consistent great results can be achieved only by a quality design and never by chance.

What causes failure in projects?

There are many factors that can make a project successful, and many others that can make it a failure. In my experience, the major causes of failure of projects are

- Improper scope management

- Not managing stakeholder expectations well

- Lack of skills in the team

- Dramatic changes in the client's business environment

What's your view of "Brand India"?

A few decades back, Japanese companies shied away from putting a "Made in Japan" tag on their products exported to the western world. Even Sony did the same in its initial days. Brand India still needs a lot of image uplift in the international arena. Hopefully, in the near future India will also be one of the most sought-after brands, like Japan (maybe in services first, then in products).

What is the greatest challenge that project managers as a class face?

It's a great question. I think the greatest challenge to project management, as an art or science, is getting recognition for the value we provide. Measuring a project manager's contribution to success may not always be possible in quantitative terms. Most of the time, the contribution is vital, but services are provided in soft form, by the way of soft skills, techniques, and methodologies, which don't form part of direct client deliverables. In many projects, a technical lead typically tends to get the most credit.

Project managers not only contribute with their PM knowledge (tools and methodologies) and experience, but also contribute a lot of value in terms of interpersonal skills, creating the right work environment, managing the expectations of stakeholders, managing clients, and much more. In total, such skills make any project a success. But PMs may not get the credit due them because such skills are not direct revenue earners in the same way a piece of code is.

Good senior managers understand the role PMs play in a project's success. Perhaps in the future there will be a way to quantify the impact you bring to a project. But in the meantime, you may need to simply feel the satisfaction of what you know is a job well done. Bringing a project in on time and on budget is a quantifiable benefit.

How do you compare confidence to arrogance

In behavioral mathematics,

Confidence − (Politeness + Courtesy) = Arrogance

Most of the time, arrogance or disrespect toward others can always be related to the lack of confidence in that individual. I wonder sometimes if there is anything a person can achieve with arrogance. Even if a person is already in a power seat, arrogance will facilitate a sure path to self-destruction. I believe a person displays arrogance only when he doesn't know the right way, has lost control, needs some professional help, or, in the worst cases, suffers a combination of all three. A good and well-rounded education should result in a humble attitude. And this humility can alone get you places. In job interviews, after clearing the technical round, humility is one of the important criteria to determine whether a candidate fits in with the company.

What defines a successful business?

- It can be leveraged
- The revenue is predictable to some extent
- It's expandable or scalable

The universal measure of success is, of course, how much money you are able to make and whether it is clearly worth your time. The opportunity cost (of your time and the resources you are investing) should always be considerably less than the value you are able to create through business. Also, any successful business should always be scalable.

Of course, many people start their own business as a way to earn their daily bread through their most compelling passions. The satisfaction and joy they earn from it is the only way they define their success. I can't argue with that approach either.

Do we need project managers? Do they add value? Why?

A definite YES! Project managers bring in a lot of value and wisdom earned over years of experience. Their soft skills and overall management skills also provide lots of savings in terms of completion on time, quality, and customer satisfaction. However, a PM may prove a costly proposition in small setups, where a tech lead can easily double as a manager.

Thus, this question can be answered best by the project owners, sponsors, and department heads who employ PMs.

What are the desired functions in PMO tools?

The Project Management Office (PMO) must have the following capabilities:

- Project and program specific metrics computing (dashboard).

- Value-added reports for decision-support systems, to be used by the PMO and management. These reports may give the status of time, budget, and quality parameters, or they may simply indicate which project(s) to scrap because it is no longer relevant to the overall business goals.

- Proactive alarms based on some preset conditions (qualitative parameters). You want the alarm to sound when things like schedule or costs exceed limits. You need these at both the project and program level.

- Collaborative work flow, based on software tools.

- Costs rollups—calculating costs of projects starting from the bottom-most activities and adding them to the project level.

- Capability to create custom work flows.

- Integration with bug/issue tracking systems at project level.

The total functionality defined here may be difficult to get in a single tool, so the PMO may have to make compromises based on the available functionalities in tools licensed by the organization. Or, some custom development may be required.

Fundamentals of project management: What does a PM need to know?

As far as fundamentals, a practicing PM must know all the principles that are basic to this profession. Fortunately, most of them can be found in one place: PMBOK (*Project Management Body of Knowledge*, a guide from the Project Management Institute). Equally important is the personal side— understanding concepts like integrity, transparency, ethics, and sensitivity toward fellow team members, interpersonal skills, giving due credit to others, self-respect, and respect for others is equally or sometimes *more* important for a PM and for the profession as a whole. And where do you get training in these areas? Much has to do with upbringing, schooling, lessons learned in sports and the arts, and so on. In the United States, some swear by Dale Carnegie training.

Glory or gold—which works better as a motivator?

It depends, but in many cases it's glory first along with a reasonable amount of gold. A great deal of gold can work if the glory component is less. But the first case always works better. In the latter case, a person will stay for a brief period, make his share of gold, and return to the first case to lead a stable life.

As a positive thinker, how do you handle negativity or the negative people in your life?

Most of us have some negative people in our lives. Personally, I surround myself with positive people as much as I possibly can. However, there are some important relationships that we want to keep even if the other person's negativity is very difficult to tolerate. We can say that the mind has two memory stores. One stores positive memories and the other stores negative memories. If your mind gets a positive thought, it actuates or brings forward all positive memories from the past. On the other hand, a negative thought brings forward negativity. So it's important to avoid negative thoughts and negative people. Avoidance can be an immediate fix. You may need other ways to handle negative people if they are in your team and you can't avoid them.

How do you select high-quality PMs?

I have personally come across the following elaborate process used by companies that are ultra-conscious about the skills and quality of recruits at the PM level and higher.

First, a one-hour personality test helps to chart a candidate's personality. Based on these findings, an interview can be conducted to validate the results and develop a good understanding of the softer people skills that are so important in a PM. The next round of interview(s) can assess the knowledge and experience related to project management practices. Multiple interviews at this stage by internal or external experts may provide an error-free assessment. Some of the highly specialized companies conduct as many as seven rounds of face-to-face interviews, and a couple of telephone interviews in the beginning. All these rounds are conducted by different people to assess the core skills (project management in this case). Typically, the process takes up to two months, but this ensures that everybody agrees about the quality of the person coming in and also helps in building consensus about potential recruits even before they report for work. Equally important are the references from past employers and detailed background checks.

Independent testers—required or not?

Independent testers—those who, say, validate code—can add a lot of value in terms of quality and usability. But in many situations, you can't afford them either due to budget constraints or because you're in a start-up with limited funds. In those cases, the developers themselves double as testers. There is a catch here: they must be very quality conscious. Later in such cases, if the organization grows, it may be wiser to have independent testing teams. There's also the potential for conflict of interest in having the developers test their own code. Separation of duties addresses that issue.

Is a manager a good leader or is a leader a good manager?

It's an age-old question.

Neither is necessarily true, but both good managers and good leaders are necessary for an organization to be successful. I think almost everyone agrees: the leader is a superset that may contain all the qualities of a manager.

As noted by many, managers and leaders are remarkably different. A good leader may be a good manager in the majority of cases, but a good manager may not necessarily be a good leader. If one has to choose, it's clear that a good leader is necessary for a successful company. But you need good managers to implement or sustain, operationally, the vision and drive of great leaders. And if everybody is a leader, things might be little difficult. So you need both. You need more managers to support a small group of great leaders in an organization.

To me, the difference is this: a manager discharges the work efficiently, while a leader takes the motivational route, keeping the staff cheerful and creating more leaders down the line. A company also needs a leader who has a vision of where the company can go and how to get there.

Even if we have great policies and strategies in place, we need a good leader who will display a great sense of ownership, something that helps sustain the organization and helps managers take care of the day-to-day affairs. And leaders are indispensable in crisis situations.

How do you manage communications in an onsite/offshore team?

Onsite/offshore teams are a very common phenomenon in the IT industry. You have some members of the team at the client's site or at a stateside home base, and some members of the team performing grunt work or back-office operations in a place like Bangalore. Communication is the biggest challenge. Here are some thoughts and tips (the examples assume a scenario in which the core of the team is onsite in New York City and the rest of the team is offshore in Bangalore):

- The onsite team members and offshore team members can have a few hours of overlap by adjusting their working hours a bit (typically in India). If your onsite team is on the West Coast, communications with India are tougher. If you're lucky, you have some night owls on the staff.

- You need to have a good, workable communication plan and team structure in place.

- A web-based source code/document control system is helpful because everyone has to pick up the latest data from the server.

- The offshore team members should not leave until they have a daily "handshake" from the onsite team members.

- Maintaining a work log in the web-based source code/document control system will help. Before leaving the office, the offshore team members provide a summary of the day's activity and the instructions for the onsite team members taking over. The onsite team members do the same for the offshore team members with a status update on activities marked for them.

- Maintain an internal and client-issue log and make the latest version available in a centralized documentation system.

- In the initial days, daily calls should take place between the onsite team members and offshore team members (perhaps from home for the latter). These calls should be strictly preplanned and agenda/minutes of meetings (MoM) should be maintained religiously.

- Plan weekly status and other informal calls to apprise all stakeholders of progress and challenges.

- Everything in the project, including requirements, design, code, test results, and so on, has to be documented in a structured manner and the latest made available in a centralized source code/document control system like SharePoint.

- Any work done should be reviewed, validated, and tested against standards and requirements to avoid any last-minute surprises.

- It's a great help if the onsite PM takes a short trip to the offshore site after, say, one month of the project start (this depends).

- Rotating team members onsite and offshore will also help a great deal in appraising both sides of mutual expectations.

- Build verification tests (smoke tests) that are performed daily. The offshore team members should make reports available to the onsite team members before leaving the office, and vice versa.

- The PM should be mentally prepared for some late-night calls and actions.

What is the most challenging part of being a PM?

Project managers face a wide variety of challenges on any given project. For each project, the list of challenges will be different. Many of the challenges are not apparent initially and thus are not given due consideration in the planning phase. Here's a short list of speed bumps that can challenge the best PM:

- Changing performance and scalability requirements

- Lack of skill availability

- Diversion of resources to other projects

- Too much or too little executive management

- Lack of commitment

- Poor support

- Inadequate stakeholder analysis

- Poor overall fit of project objectives to the company's strategic blueprint

- No buy-in from end users

- Lack of accountability from team members

- Inadequate skill levels on the team

Many of these factors are beyond the control of a PM, so by knowing where the potholes are, the better you can plan to manage them with the active involvement from higher management and the PMO.

You can also expect to encounter more routine challenges, like unrealistic deadlines; scope volatility; tight budget constraints; attrition; inadequate communications planning; risks and challenges being ignored or underestimated; lack of project management skills; teams losing interest in projects with long durations; lack of detail in project plans and requirements; shifting organizational priorities; inadequate planning for change management; documentation requirements being ignored or underestimated; stakeholder expectation management; and so on.

The challenge list for a project manager is practically endless, because the responsibility of a PM is end-to-end as far as project delivery is concerned. A PM can expect a successful sail only with continuous proactive thinking, detailed planning and feedback mechanisms, validated risk-management plans, leveraging the company's history of similar projects, employing a participative style of leadership, and encouraging the team to seek constant innovation and continuous improvement. It helps to have a strong process orientation ingrained in the company, and a strong rewards-for-performance system in place. A seasoned external advisor to the PM can do wonders. In my experience, the single most important factor contributing to success is to conduct a review at every level of the project life cycle. A little luck always helps, too.

Can a bad person be a good manager?

Good character and strong skills are necessary to be a great manager. Sometimes soft skills take precedence. Processes, methodologies, tools, and so forth make the job of a manager repeatable, systematic, and easier, but I strongly believe that if you are not a good person, you can never be an effective leader or manager.

What is the PMO's authority for project performance?

In theory, the senior managers from the PMO should assist, make suggestions to, and facilitate a PM on project performance. They should be in the same boat as the PM. But in practice, it depends upon the organization and what kinds of powers are given to the PMO. To some extent, it may also depend upon who comprises the PMO. And the word PMO itself is interpreted differently by different organizations. I have come across at least a dozen such interpretations, and each such interpretation inspires a different answer to your question.

In your case, it may help if you, as a PM, the PMO, the project sponsor, and some higher authority like the VP or the department head (meaning all the major stakeholders that matter) sit in a meeting and delineate the scope of authority of the PMO and on what terms it can review your project.

The PMO is expected to lead in a participative style. In my current organization, all PMs report to the PMO, which is a centralized project management service to the organization. Team members are drawn from different verticals for specific projects. So a PM reports to the line manager as well as the PMO. We can find many more variants to this practice in the industry.

What are the success factors for representatives of the PMO?

Following are several factors that help representatives of the PMO to succeed:

- Very clear understanding of PM basics
- Personal integrity
- People skills
- Experience as a PM
- Stakeholder identification and expectation management
- Thorough understanding of the company environment
- Clear thoughts on what's expected

A web-based scheduling and risk management tool can make a large difference in the success of the PMO members.

How do we align team goals and corporate goals?

We all know that if employees/teams are aligned to the corporate strategic direction, things run smoother. This is much easier said than done, yet it must be at the top of the to-do list of a PM before starting a project.

For any relatively large project, it may be wise to involve the key team members right from the inception stage in drafting the project charter and objectives. This requires almost no extra effort, yet it aligns the team. Executives must act genuinely and with transparency toward the team at this stage when explaining the objectives and incentives for meeting those objectives. Active involvement and communication from executive management is key at this stage. A transparent and ethical work environment will ensure team involvement and alignment to corporate goals to a greater degree. A creative communication campaign and team outings at the initial stage may help a lot. In the execution stage, almost everything, including team morale, will depend upon the PM, who has to exercise a high degree of professionalism and leadership skills. The PM has to find creative ways to keep the team focused and aligned to stated goals.

When attempting to align team goals and corporate goals, the people factor matters most. How well it is employed will determine the degree to which teams are committed to corporate goals. Executive management will have to provide a nice work environment and follow through with a very high standard of professional ethics and integrity. Any compromise here will have a multifold, negative effect on the team's morale. The losses will be heavy and potentially beyond repair.

A sustained but creative communication campaign highlighting corporate goals, and road maps, may help a lot. The related literature, like strategy presentations and business road maps, must be easy to reach on the intranet and in physical form so that they are accessible by the managers when required. Regular internal quizzes and other promotions, including recognition schemes, will help maintain the excitement.

Even having a couple of new and promising members on board (of a project governing committee) on a rotational basis may be worth serious thought. Representation from the junior cadres, if handled imaginatively, can prove to be the single most important factor in ensuring that employees feel commitment toward and alignment with the corporate goals.

How do I best utilize the project team?

In the beginning, projects tend to be a little overstaffed in terms of both skills and numbers. I think that is better and on the safer side, to counteract the potential for underperformers. As the project progresses and we get a more exact idea of work content, schedule, individual capabilities, and so on, we can transfer the jobs requiring less skill to the underachievers while still enabling the team as a whole to be well up the learning curve. Around the point where you have completed about 20 percent of the work, you can adjust the team size to an optimal level. Beware of overstaffing. For long-term and complex projects, I prefer not to load the team to 100 percent or beyond, but instead only up to, say, 85 to 90 percent. Many will object, but I find that doing so maintains the freshness and enthusiasm of employees until the very end. You can always add more people if there are any surprises in the last minute.

What is the #1 secret to project management?

People skills! Be very genuine with the team members and treat them as an extended family in a very true sense. They will come through for you and make you look like a champ.

What can you tell us about trends in risk management?

When we talk about risk management, we are dealing with both risk control and risk prevention. So, the natural trend will be toward refining the existing processes and bringing into practice more and more new methodologies in risk analysis and prevention. The increasing emphasis will be on incorporating new processes with adequate built-in risk control and containment measures from the start. Such processes will become an integral part of project management systems. These processes will be institutionalized, in the practice of project management, as dynamic, iterative, and responsive to change while taking into account human factors. Much of the current risk assessment at the grassroots level is qualitative in nature. Qualitative risk assessment, as we already know, is subjective and lacks consistency. The trend will be more and more toward quantitative risk assessment that deals with quantifying the identified project risks in terms of a dollar amount.

How do you define company culture, and why does understanding culture matter?

In my view, a company's culture is the way of life within the company. It is deemed acceptable to a majority of the company's workforce, including the senior management, for discharging the day-to-day work, internal and external communications, and interpersonal relationships. A positive culture adds value to the organizational objectives. A company's culture is, further, a generally accepted standard of doing business within the company. The stakeholders outside the organization also recognize, understand, and practice it while dealing with that company.

How does culture come about? When a company is founded, there is nothing called "company culture." As time passes, a dominating individual from senior management may bring along his own values and experiences. This can be one of the many ways a seed for the culture starts to develop. If a group of relatively junior employees are from same region or college, this can contribute to some extent in developing the work culture within the company. Market conditions and clients can also be contributing factors. These are just a few examples to start with. In fact, development of a company culture is a very complex phenomenon. It may take years and at least a thousand notable factors as contributors.

Over a period of time, the group settles into a certain way of functioning. It becomes the work culture of that company. It is likely to be unique to that group/company. This work culture may define the competitiveness, responsiveness, innovation levels, ethical standards, group dynamics, hire and fire policy, attrition, internal democracy, salary and benefits, and a million more things. The company work culture may be the single largest factor in building the brand value of the company. Even more, it can determine growth prospects and, to a large extent, whether and how long the company is likely to survive the competition. What level of talent a company can attract and retain is also determined by the company work culture. As you can see, it's important to understand the culture of your organization. Once you do, you can leverage its strengths to help you do your job more effectively.

What is the best teacher, experience or education?

Neither experience nor education alone is sufficient. Education gives you a chance to learn from the wisdom and knowledge accumulated over the centuries. Education may give you a thought process or, say, mind conditioning that enables you to deal with almost any situation in life.

Experience, on the other hand, takes a well educated mind to the next higher level in terms of learning and wisdom. It's said that experience is the best teacher in one's life, but if you learn from your own experiences only, the amount of learning and wisdom gained is likely to be smaller and the pace at which it is gained slower. While experience does teach, education helps you learn from the experiences of others. The learning curve in the latter case is considerably shorter. Education can be one of the wonderful mediums to learn from the experiences of others.

What are the top three lessons you've learned from your projects?

The top three lessons I've learned from most of my projects in the past revolve around the following three topics, listed in order of importance:

1. *Scope and client*: Controlling scope and managing client expectations are the most important parts of any project.

2. *Management*: Keep your boss and other managers apprised of the realities on the ground, both problems and successes. Managing expectations is critical here as well.

3. *The team*: Take great care while choosing your team members and leader. Thereafter, create a great working environment for the team. As a PM, be as ethical and transparent as possible.

What can you do to ensure the company culture doesn't dilute with growth? Can the PMO alone take on this challenge?

Unfortunately, not many employees appreciate or take this topic as seriously as required. The organizational culture flows from the top to the bottom. In my humble opinion, the PMO may not be at a sufficiently high level to have any influence on an organization's culture. It has to start right from the levels of CEOs and SVPs. Following is a short example from one of my previous employers.

Some time back I casually talked to some of the "oldies" in the company about this topic and they felt that, with company growth, the culture was going in a negative direction. I made the director aware of this by writing a short paper on my findings. The director agreed that action was needed and thus called a meeting of all the managers. Their suggestions were sought for how to maintain a healthy and open culture, which the company had when it was a small group as a start-up. One of the solutions was to train all newcomers in what company culture is, explain what levels of ethics and best practices they are expected to follow, and implement a host of other measures, all packed into a one-day training program. HR was asked to compile all the suggestions and give a more detailed, actionable report to the managing director. They were pretty serious about it.

Is project management an art or a science?

At root, project management is closer to an art. But the methodologies, tools, and formulas we use are attempts to make it more of a science. Still, in many situations, it's not possible to apply the scientific methodologies of project management, even though they are prescribed for that situation.

In many cases, the personality of the PM matters a lot, something to which tools and methods have little to contribute.

As a manager, how do you feel about working with experts or smart people who have little experience?

A team can't be made up of only smart people or only experienced people. It has to be a right mix. If the PM is confident in her capabilities, I would suggest that 80 percent of the team be made up of people who are above average in smarts and 20 percent be people with above-average experience. This way you have energy on the team, you have smartness and experience, and you also save on the cost of salaries. In such a case, the PM must be very well experienced in her job and have above-average smartness.

What CIOs Are Discussing

The policies of an IT organization or corporate IT department are governed by CIOs and IT directors. So it's important to understand what's important to them. I searched through some online CIO groups and their discussions. Listed here are some topics that appear frequently in their discussions. This is not an exhaustive list but fairly well represents what's on the mind of top management in IT organizations. I am listing only the topic names. A detailed discussion of these topics is beyond the scope of this book.

- Cloud computing and virtualization
    - Opportunities and threats with cloud computing
    - Cloud computing's impact on the IT operations staff's budget
    - Industry verticals that fit best with a cloud environment
    - Cloud computing security concerns
    - Data security in cloud environments
    - Cloud computing, SaaS, and the distributed workforce
    - Clouds and disaster-recovery and business-continuity planning

- Cloud computing and offshoring
- Enterprise-grade IT solutions
- Data centers
  - Efficient operations
  - Space challenges
  - Reducing energy consumption
- Green IT
- Managing quality of data
- IT operation models
- IT budgets for new system development
- Improving operational efficiencies
- Reducing IT support costs
- IT staff to business user ratio
- DBAs and their role in data centers and maintaining service levels in terms of database availability and security
- Aligning business with IT
- Business transformation
- IT consolidation for various business sectors
- Innovation and innovation management
- Scaling, developing, and supporting homegrown applications
- Migrating from mainframes to other technologies
- Enterprise architecture
- Enterprise application integration (EAI)
- ROI calculations for integration technologies
- Effectiveness of application testing
- Mergers and acquisitions and integrating heterogeneous systems and ERPs

- SAP operations
- BI and analytics
- Corporate governance and compliance
- Basic compliance practices
- Governance models
- IT trends, technology, and project priorities
- Middle management people issues
- Content management systems (CMS)
  - Commonly used CMS platforms
  - Criterion for selection
- Social media tools and the corporate world
- CITRIX upgrades
- Electronic signatures
- IT and customer service
- Third-party vendors and service providers
- IT security and asset management
- WikiLeaks and IT professionals
- Outsourcing
- Risk management while changing vendors
- Collaborative technologies

References and Suggested Readings

Chapter 1

[1] Amsden, Jim, Andrew Jensen, and Chris White, "Actionable Enterprise Architecture Management," ftp://ftp.software.ibm.com/software/emea/de/rational/neu/Actionable_Enterprise_Architecture_Management_EN_2009.pdf , June 2009.

[2] Adams, Jonathan, George Galambos, Srinivas Koushik, and Guru Vasudeva. *Patterns for e-business: A Strategy for Reuse.* Double Oak, TX: IBM Press, 2001.

[3] IBM, "Patterns for e-business for New IT Solutions," http://www.ibm.com/framework/patterns.

[4] Adams, Jonathan, George Galambos, Srinivas Koushik, and Guru Vasudeva, "Patterns for e-business: A Strategy for Reuse," http://www.ibm.com/developerworks/ibm/library/i-patterns/.

[5]   LinkedIn, Enterprise architecture groups, http://www.linkedin.com.

[6]   Daniel, Diann. "The Rising Importance of the Enterprise Architect,"
      http://www.cio.com/article/101401/The_Rising_Importance_of_the_
      Enterprise_Architect, March 31, 2007.

[7]   ORACLE, "API Specifications,"
      http://www.oracle.com/technetwork/java/api-141528.html.

Chapter 2

[1]   PMI. *A Guide to the Project Management Body of Knowledge*, 4th ed.
      Newtown Square, PA: Project Management Institute, 2010.

[2]   Cherniss, Cary, Michel Adler, Kim Cowan, Robert Emmerling, and
      Daniel Goleman. "Bringing Emotional Intelligence to the Workplace: A
      Technical Report Issued by the Consortium for Research on Emotional
      Intelligence in Organizations,"
      http://www.eiconsortium.org/reports/technical_report.html.

[3]   AllBusiness, Management articles, http://www.allbusiness.com.

[4]   Wikipedia, "Comparison of Project Management Software,"
      http://en.wikipedia.org/wiki/Comparison_of_project_
      management_software.

[5]   Garmahis, Michael, "Top 20 Project Management Tools,"
      http://garmahis.com/reviews/top-project-management-tools/, July 2,
      2009.

[6]   Serena Software Inc., "Openproj," http://openproj.org/openproj.

[7]   Wikipedia, "Comparison of Project Management Software,"
      http://en.wikipedia.org/wiki/List_of_project_management_software.

[8]   Wikipedia, "Redmine," http://en.wikipedia.org/wiki/Redmine.

[9]   Lijoi, Gina, "Effective Project Communications,"
      http://www.projectsmart.co.uk/effective-project-communications.html.

[10] Cusolito, Rick, "Common Challenges Project Managers Face and Tips
      for Solving Them," http://www.butrain.com/project-management-
      training-courses/project-manager.asp.

[11] Freedman, Joshua and Todd Everett, "EQ at the Heart of
      Performance," http://www.leabrovedani.com/wp-content/uploads/The-
      Business-Case-for-Emotional-Intelligence.pdf.

[12] Wikipedia, "Project Management Office,"
http://en.wikipedia.org/wiki/Project_management_office.

Chapter 3

[1] PMI. *The Standard for Program Management,* 2nd ed. Newton Square,
PA: Project Management Institute, 2010.

[2] Wikipedia, "Program Management,"
http://en.wikipedia.org/wiki/Program_management.

[3] Toolbox.com, Management Blogs, http://it.toolbox.com/blogs/it-blogs/.

[4] Unanet, Industry Solutions and White Papers, http://www.unanet.com.

Chapter 4

[1] Kotter, John. A Force for Change: How Leadership Differs From
Management. New York: Free Press, 1990.

[2] Hewlett-Packard, "HP Business Technology Optimization,"
https://h10078.www1.hp.com/cda/hpms/display/main/hpms_content.jsp?
zn=bto&cp=1-11%5E4864_4000_100_.

Chapter 5

[1] Kadre, Shailendra, Laxmi Narayan Sahu, and Radhika Unni. *Fusion of
Project and Portfolio Management Processes to Achieve Optimum Cost
Levels.* Bangalore, India: Project Management Practitioner's
Conference, 2006.

[2] Wyzocki, Robert K. and Rudd McGary. *Effective Project Management,*
3rd ed. New Delhi, India: Wiley Dreamtech India Pvt. Ltd., 2003.

[3] Proceedings of Satyam Project Managers Conference, Hyderabad, India:
Satyam Learning Center, 2004.

[4] Gartner, Research Papers on IT Portfolio Management,
http://www.gartner.com.

[5] CIO, IT portfolio management articles and white papers,
http://www.cio.com.

[6] Datz ,Todd, "Portfolio Management Done Right,"
http://corporateportfoliomanagement.org/article-29-Portfolio-
Management-Done-Right.

Chapter 7

[1] WhatsUpGold, "WhatsUp Gold Network Management Solutions," http://www.whatsupgold.com/solutions/.

Chapter 8

[1] Krill, Paul, "The Cloud-SOA Connection," http://www.infoworld.com/d/cloud-computing/cloud-soa-connection-724.

[2] The SOA Hot Place, "SOA-Cloud Combination Can Bring Benefits," http://thesoahotplace.blogspot.com/2010/10/soa-cloud-combination-can-bring.html, October 2010.

Chapter 9

[1] Wikipedia, "Finance," http://en.wikipedia.org/wiki/Finance.

[2] Investopedia, Richard Loth, "Financial Ratio Tutorial," http://www.investopedia.com/university/ratios/.

[3] Wikipedia, "Rate of Return," http://en.wikipedia.org/wiki/Return_on_Investment.

[4] Cost Leadership Strategy, "Cost Leadership Strategy," http://www.costleadershipstrategy.com/ February 26, 2011.

[5] PMI. *A Guide to the Project Management Body of Knowledge*, 4th ed. Newtown Square, PA: Project Management Institute, 2010.

Chapter 10

[1] Wikipedia, "Business Process," http://en.wikipedia.org/wiki/Business_process.

[2] Grover, Varun and William J. Kettinger. *Business Process Change: Reengineering Concepts, Methods, and Technologies*. Hershey, PA: Idea Group Publishing, 2010.

[3] Khosrow-Pour, Mehdi. *Cases on Information Technology and Business Process Re-engineering*. Hershey, PA: Idea Group Publishing, 2006.

[4] Weicher, Maureen, et al., "Business Process Reengineering Analysis and Recommendations," http://www.slideshare.net/Timothy212/business-process-reengineering-3917082.

[5] Nilakant, V., and S. Ramnarayan. *Managing Organisational Change*. Sage Publications, March 2001.

[6] Gartner, Gartner research data on Business Processes, http://www.gartner.com/technology/home.asp

Chapter 12

[1] Ganeshan, Ram and Terry P. Harrison, "An Introduction to Supply Chain Management," http://lcm.csa.iisc.ernet.in/scm/supply_chain_intro.html.

[2] Merino, "Products: Advanced Planning & Scheduling," http://merinoservices.com/apas.aspx.

[3] vsnew, "ERP vs. SCM: What's the Difference?" http://en.vsnew.com/erp-vs-scm-whats-the-difference.html.

[4] Hernandez, Jose A. *Roadmap to mySAP.com*. Premier Press, 2002.

[5] Gartner, Gartner research on ERP and SCM, http://www.gartner.com/technology/home.jsp.

[6] Cooper, Ellaran. *On Supply Chain Management*. SCM Research Literature, 1993.

[7] Gartner, Gartner research data on ERP and Supply Chain Management, http://www.gartner.com/technology/home.jsp.

Chapter 13

[1] OECD, "Risk Management & Corporate Governance," http://www.oecd.org/dataoecd/29/4/42670210.pdf.

[2] Investopedia, "Generally Accepted Accounting Principles—GAAP," http://www.investopedia.com/terms/g/gaap.asp.

[3] COSO, "About Us," http://www.coso.org/aboutus.htm.

Chapter 15

[1] Gartner, Gartner research on SOA, http://www.gartner.com/technology/home.jsp.

[2] Erl, Thomas. *Service-Oriented Architecture (SOA): Concepts, Technology, and Design*. Boston: Prentice Hall PTR, 2005.

[3] Erl, Thomas. *Service-Oriented Architecture: A Field Guide to Integrating XML and Web Services*. Boston: Prentice Hall PTR, 2004.

[4] Marks, Eric A. and Michael Bell. *Service-Oriented Architecture : A Planning and Implementation Guide for Business and Technology*. Hoboken, NJ: Wiley, 2006.

[5] McGovern, James, Oliver Sims, Ashish Jain, and Mark Little. *Enterprise Service Oriented Architectures: Concepts, Challenges, Recommendations*. New York: Springer, 2006.

[6] Barry, Douglas K. *Web Services and Service-Oriented Architectures: The Savvy Manager's Guide*. San Francisco: Morgan Kaufmann, 2003.

[7] Greer, Melvin B. Jr. *The Web Services and Service Oriented Architecture Revolution: Using Web Services to Deliver Business Value*. Lincoln, NE: iUniverse, Inc., 2006.

[8] Bieberstein, Norbert, Sanjay Bose, Marc Fiammante, Keith Jones, and Rawn Shah. *Service-Oriented Architecture (SOA) Compass : Business Value, Planning, and Enterprise Roadmap*. Double Oak, TX: IBM Press, 2005.

[9] Krafzig, Dirk, Karl Banke, and Dirk Slama. *Enterprise SOA: Service-Oriented Architecture Best Practices* (The Coad Series). Boston: Prentice Hall PTR, 2004.

[10] Gartner, Definitions on SOA, http://www.gartner.com/technology/home.jsp.

Chapter 16

[1] Porter, Michael E. "What is Strategy," *Harvard Business Review*, November–December 1996.

Index

Z

CPSIA information can be obtained at www.ICGtesting.com
Printed in the USA
236274LV00002B/1/P